CARLYLE AND MILL

CARLYLE AND MILL

AN INTRODUCTION TO VICTORIAN THOUGHT

BY *Edward*

EMERY NEFF

SECOND EDITION REVISED

New York

COLUMBIA UNIVERSITY PRESS

1926

Copyright, 1926
BY COLUMBIA UNIVERSITY PRESS

Printed from type.   Published June, 1926

THE PLIMPTON PRESS
NORWOOD MASS · U · S · A

To
WANDA

PREFACE

THE writer explains the quick exhaustion of the first edition of *Carlyle and Mill* by the greatly increased interest in Victorian England shown by the numerous significant monographs and general studies which have appeared since its publication in 1924. He welcomes the opportunity to make use of this material in a revised edition.

The passing of the fashion of belittling the Victorians makes it unnecessary to insist that they met courageously and resourcefully the first onslaught of problems which are still perplexing us, and proposed solutions upon which we have not notably improved. The purpose of this book is to make clearer and more vivid the relationship of the thought of the twentieth century to that of the nineteenth. A clue for guidance through the multitudinous and complex details involved in this undertaking has been found in a consideration of the relations of Thomas Carlyle and John Stuart Mill, whose representative character was abundantly recognized by their contemporaries. Explanation of the sympathies and antipathies of these leaders of thought necessitates consideration of the political, economic, religious, and literary background of the period. The addition of a classified and interpreted bibliography will, it is hoped, invite the reader of this introductory work to a more detailed study of British civilization since the French and the Industrial Revolutions. To the American reader such study should be especially interesting and fruitful, for under somewhat unfamiliar dress he will find reënacted the drama of the intellectual and social history of the United States which is passing before his eye in the twentieth century.

The writer wishes to express his especial obligation to Professor Ashley H. Thorndike, who suggested this study, and to Professors Graham Wallas and Louis Cazamian, who aided its progress with stimulating criticism. His debt is also great to Professor Wendell T. Bush, Dr. Roy F. Dibble, Mr. Henry K. Dick, Mr. Charles Everett, Professor Jefferson B. Fletcher, Professor Owen G. Groves, Mr. Roger Howson, Professor George B. Parks, Professor Rexford G. Tugwell, Mr. Gordon Wasson, Professor Raymond Weaver, and Professor Ernest Hunter Wright.

E. N.

March, 1926

CONTENTS

GIRAFFE AND OKAPI

CONTENTS

CARLYLE AND MILL

CHAPTER I

TWO REPRESENTATIVE MEN.

A NEW MYSTIC! " exclaimed Thomas Carlyle in
delighted surprise, as he read, in a lonely Scotch
farmhouse, a series of articles in the London *Examiner*
entitled *The Spirit of the Age*. At last, in the spring
of 1831, he had found in a newspaper the intimation
" that the age was not the best of all possible ages."
The anonymous writer was boldly prophesying that
" the nineteenth century will be known to posterity as
the era of one of the greatest revolutions of which
history has preserved the remembrance, in the human
mind, and in the whole constitution of society. . . .
Men are henceforward to be held together by new ties,
and separated by new barriers; for the ancient bonds
will no longer unite, nor the ancient boundaries con-
fine."

The cause of this impending revolution he found in
cheap printing and marvelously improved means of
communication, which had disseminated knowledge
and the spirit of discussion and criticism widely among
the people, and thereby made them aware that the
feudal system, which made inheritance the sole passport to political and economic power, failed lament-

ably to provide them with rulers who were wise and just. Weary of being governed by " fat, elderly gentlemen " who were opponents of all progress or change, the masses were now striving to become their own masters. Here was the danger point of the approaching social transformation. For the people, although intelligent enough to see the incompetence of the British aristocracy, were as yet too superficially educated to pilot the ship of state, and in blithe sciolism would run it upon the rocks. Government was an art which demanded the undivided attention of experts, not the scant leisure from the desk, the factory, and the plow. And it was furthermore the misfortune of the present period of transition that the elder statesmen, who were ripe in experience of men and affairs, were incapable of adapting the social structure to the revolutions in science, industry, and education which were bursting the feudal barriers; and that the young men of ability, who were desirous of building anew, were still too inexperienced to competently carry out this infinitely difficult undertaking. But he did not therefore advise a clinging to outworn feudalism for fear of a future thus beset with dangers. He unhesitatingly advised measures like the Reform Bill then before Parliament, calculated to transfer " worldly power . . . from the hands of the stationary part of mankind to those of the progressive part " and " leave no man one fraction of unearned distinction or unearned importance " ; for he was confident that steps toward democracy were not necessarily steps toward anarchy, but rather, after a few years of inevitable blundering and disorder, toward a stable government popularly chosen from the ablest among the younger generation, who would have become " wise by experience in addition to being wise by logic and imagination."

This trust in the future, resembling as it did his own belief in a beneficent Providence which sent men of unusual strength and wisdom to guide mankind through dangerous periods of transition, caused Carlyle to call the author of *The Spirit of the Age* a mystic. He was glad that another realized that the great majority of mankind were incapable of governing themselves, and that extension of suffrage by Reform Acts would lead to disaster unless the best and wisest could create for the popular guidance new social ideals to replace the old ideals of faith, divine right, and loyalty which had cemented feudal society. For the French Revolution had given impressive warning that failure to obey a new aristocracy of the fittest as implicitly as the old aristocracy of birth would render impossible the reconstruction of a stable and just social order.

The discovery of a sharer in his political beliefs encouraged Carlyle, who was just completing a book that endeavored to preach to the British nation the lessons of the French Revolution, an event which had profoundly influenced his life. He had been born a Scotch peasant's son at the time of the Terror, and had left Edinburgh University the year before Waterloo. The years of political reaction and high cost of living which followed the Napoleonic wars had aroused in the obscure and ambitious youth an inward revolt against the social system that permitted the landed aristocracy to live in luxury and waste its time shooting partridges, and forced the peasant and workingman to toil incessantly for what was often not even a bare existence. The subversive writings which had prepared the way to the Revolution across the Channel, the works of Voltaire and the Encyclopaedists, encouraged this revolt, and inspired " grave prohibitive doubts "[1] which cut short his preparation for the Calvinist ministry. French thought utterly destroyed his confidence in existing institutions, but could not show him, by precept or example, how to replace them with others. Carlyle had therefore passed through an uncomfortable period of fruitless search and questioning, without guidance or fixed occupation, which poverty, ill-health, and a temperament that craved faith and action aggravated to a veritable nightmare.

From this Gehenna of doubt, accidental contact with the contemporary German literature, then practically unknown in the British Isles, had rescued him. Fichte's Transcendental philosophy replaced the anthropomorphic Jehovah, worker of intermittent and capricious miracles, by an immanent God who made the universe an unceasing miracle. Herder and his school of philosophic historians showed that institutions corresponded to stages in the development of the human mind, and inevitably gave place to others as the race conceived new ideals. Goethe taught him the exalted rôle of men of letters, who were sent into the world to formulate these new ideals for each successive age.

Full of gratitude for his restoration to hope and certitude, Carlyle resolved to become one of the prophetic men of letters for his generation, and retired into the wilderness, like another John the Baptist, to mature his message. Since 1827 he had been living on the Scotch border at Craigenputtock farm, one of the most lonely and forbidding spots in the British Isles. There he had written for the *Edinburgh* and *Foreign* Reviews articles which took advantage of the opportunity afforded by an introduction of German literature to the British public to violently attack the negative French philosophy preached by the Utilitarians, and to warn the nation of the impending crisis. There, when a second Revolution in France and the introduction of a Reform Bill in the English Parliament brought the crisis he predicted, he had begun to write the ambitious book he was just completing; a strange, chaotic, brilliant work which he was to call *Sartor Resartus,* containing his matured views on contemporary religion, economics, and politics. The discovery of such encouraging " signs of the times " as the *Spirit of the Age* articles made more agreeable the prospect of marketing this book in London. For he might find among the famous writers gathered in the capital men like their author, with whom he could profitably discuss the problems of the time, which he considered one of the darkest in the world's history, overshadowed as it was by the French Revolution, and beset with portents of other revolutions.

On August 9, 1831, after five days' travel by steamship and stage-coach, Carlyle arrived in London with the completed manuscript. He was no literary tyro, going to the metropolis to seek his fortune, but a

mature thinker thirty-five years of age, the acknowl-
edged British authority on German literature, and the
author of a *Life of Schiller* whose translation into
German had been made under the eyes of the great
Goethe.   And he was introduced by none other than
Francis Jeffrey, Lord Advocate of Scotland and former
editor of the *Edinburgh Review,* to the equally famous
John Murray, Byron's publisher, as " a genius " who
" would likely became eminent." [2]

Nevertheless, his legitimate expectation of an immediate sale of the book was not fulfilled.   Murray
received him courteously, but procrastinated indefinitely in making an ultimately unfavorable decision.
Other booksellers, Fraser, Longmans, were meanwhile
sounded, with no better success.   The book trade was
stagnant.   The great Reform Bill was before Parliament, and all business held its breath while the middle
and upper classes fought for supremacy.

During his enforced sojourn, Carlyle turned to the
search of kindred spirits who might aid him in preaching the gospel of mysticism.   Gratified to find a British
Museum curator and some other young men already
converted by his Review articles, he decided that his
best work during the winter would be to investigate
the " quality, numbers, and aims " [3] of his London
disciples, for he realized that " men united are strong;
single, the strongest is weak." [4]   Of these prospective
associates he was most eager to meet the author of *The
Spirit of the Age.*   Empson, Jeffrey's son-in-law, was
able to identify the man he sought as John Mill, son of
the fanatical Utilitarian James Mill, whose inveterate

hatred of "German metaphysics" had cost Carlyle a chair at the recently established University of London. But Empson added reassuringly that the son was far different from the father, being "a converted Utilitarian who is studying German." [5]

On September third, Empson brought Mill and Carlyle together at the home of Mill's friend John Austin, whose wife was an admirer of Carlyle and of German literature. No two men could have been more unlike in appearance and manner than those who met that day. "He has the manners of the old school," [6] said Charles Kingsley of Mill in his later years. As a youth, he singularly combined dignity and grace. He was fastidiously dressed, composed and reserved but full of acuteness and sensibility, slight of figure and delicate of feature, with "rich auburn hair" [7] whose beauty Carlyle long remembered. Carlyle was serviceably and roughly clad by a provincial tailor. His tall, robust, large-boned frame, his shock of dark hair, his ruddy, wind-roughened skin, his firmly closed mouth and piercing blue eyes deep-set beneath shaggy brows, his quiet air of command, told of his humble origin and his achievement against great odds through sheer force of genius. Their manner of speech was equally diverse. Carlyle spoke as one having authority, and when excited launched into long monologues in a broad Scotch accent, punctuated by loud guffaws of mirth and scorn, and illuminated by flashes of unusual and picturesque imagery. Mill did not preach or lecture; he conversed. He spoke very slowly, with animation but almost without imagery, lucidly, per-

suasively.   " What he aimed to make you see you saw
as plainly as a conspicuous object set in the sunshine." [8]

Nevertheless, the meeting, strangely symbolic and
significant in the history of the period, resulted in
instant liking.   " This young Mill," Carlyle wrote
enthusiastically to his wife the day after, " this young
Mill, I fancy and hope, is ' a *baying* you can love ' ; a
slender, rather tall and elegant youth, with small clear
Roman-nosed face; modest, remarkably gifted with
precision of utterance, enthusiastic, yet lucid, calm; not
a great, yet a distinctly gifted and amiable youth. We
had almost four hours of the best talk I have mingled
in for long.   The youth walked home with me almost
to the door; seemed to profess, almost as plainly as
modesty would allow, that he had been converted by
the head of the mystic school, to whom personally he
professed very hearty-looking regard . . . these rudiments of a mystic school (better than I anticipated
here) are by far the most cheering phenomenon I see in
London.   Good will come of it." [9]

But the " willingness to learn from everybody " [10]
upon which Mill prided himself had misled Carlyle as
to the nature of their relation.   Actually he had met
his match in the youth of twenty-five.   Mill's ingenu-
ous manner screened a complete ability to think for
himself and an unwillingness to take any man's word
for gospel.   A forcing system of education had given
him an extraordinary mental maturity.   By independent thinking and eclectic reading he had approached
Carlyle's position from the opposite pole of opinion.

Mill had fallen heir to a ready-made set of opinions,

the negative philosophy of the French Revolution, which had driven Carlyle to despair. His father, James Mill, and Jeremy Bentham were the leaders of the sect of Philosophical Radicals which carried on in England the tradition of Voltaire and the Encyclopaedists. Believing with Helvetius that the brain of the babe is a plastic tablet upon which any pattern of thought may be impressed, they had determined to make John Stuart Mill a faithful mouthpiece for their doctrines. All that savored of mysticism was banished from his education, which began before the age of three. The curriculum centered in formal logic, which gave the pupil unusual understanding of the use of his mind as an instrument. He had no religious instruction; ethics was taught as a purely intellectual calculation of the comparative usefulness of courses of action. The result of the experiment justified Helvetius. At the age of sixteen, when he was declared independent of his schooling, John Mill was a reasoning machine, thoroughly indoctrinated in the tenets of the Benthamite school; empirical philosophy, Utilitarian ethics, Ricardian economics, and Radical politics which advocated representative government based on universal suffrage. He gathered about him a group of brilliant young men, and organized the Utilitarian Society, whose purpose was to emulate the destructive work of the French Encyclopaedists. For five years he was absorbed in propaganda for the Radical ideas, notably in the pages of the *Westminster Review*. From this intense and narrow partisanship he was rescued in 1826, when he was twenty years of age, by

an unexpected and obstinate fit of despondency which
made life seem stale and unprofitable. An accidental
reading of Wordsworth's poems at the end of a year
of despair revealed to him that the cause of his depression lay not in life itself, but in his education, which
had repressed emotion, and neglected the cultivation of
his feelings. Faith in the infallibility of his inherited
doctrines was shaken; he began to seek corrections
of them through a study of the opposed schools of
thought.

Coleridge and Carlyle's master Goethe taught Mill
catholicity of mind, whereby he came to see the necessity of opposed forms of thought, and the portion of
truth which lies in all outworn institutions and opinions; but they did not convert him from any of the
Benthamite doctrines. He read Carlyle's Review
articles, but they seemed only "insane rhapsody," [11]
and apparently reactionary in their denunciation of an
"age of unbelief." [a] Mill's inherited creed was vul-
nerable to attack only through the clear and logical
statement of the opposed opinions. The early *Traité
de Politique Positive* of Auguste Comte, speaking in the
name and the language of science, accomplished what
Carlyle and the Germans had failed to do. It convinced Mill of the merely negative character of the
revolutionary principles of Liberty and Equality, and
the necessity of new ideals for the reconstruction of
society. But these ideals were to be sought, not by

[a] But after Comte had won him to an understanding of their
background, he read them with "a very keen relish." Hence he
was predisposed to like Carlyle when they met.

intuition, as Carlyle and the Germans proclaimed, but through a careful study of scientific laws, which would result in a stable science of society. Comte and the Saint-Simonian school with which he had been associated gave also an aristocratic tinge to Mill's theories of democracy by showing the necessity of obedience to the expert, the *savant*, in the reconstituted society. It was Comte, and not Carlyle, who inspired the articles on the *Spirit of the Age*. The epithet "mystic," applied to Mill, was singularly inappropriate.

Mill's summary of his first impressions of Carlyle, written to their friend John Sterling, gave no hint of reverence or discipleship, but on the contrary denied to him originality of thought. From the German writers Carlyle's mind had derived "whatever breath of life there is in it." [12] Mill found in his writings "not philosophy to instruct, but poetry to animate." [13] The fire, the moral earnestness, the vivid verbal imagery of the Scotch mystic were grateful to one who had been, not long since, a "reasoning machine." [14]

On their second meeting, Carlyle had a hint of the limitations of Mill's mysticism. "Tuesday night," Carlyle wrote to his wife on September 14, "John Mill came in and sate talking with me until near eleven — a fine clear enthusiast, who will one day come to something; yet nothing poetical, I think; his fancy is not rich; furthermore he cannot laugh with any compass." [15] But he still retained the flattering belief that his writings had been the means of converting Mill from Utilitarianism. Mill did not disabuse him. He was eager to learn from Carlyle what he most lacked, the appreciation of poetry and *belles lettres*, the secret of an artistic and imaged literary style; and consequently 'he concealed his views in philosophy, theology, and ethics, which he knew would be extremely distasteful. Carlyle had from the first been outspoken on these subjects, and had shown, beneath his German Transcendentalism, a very substantial adherence to his inherited Calvinism. The existence of God was to him as clear as his own. Each man was sent by his Creator into the world with a special duty to perform. In the performance of this duty all claims for happiness should be renounced. Virtue was its own reward, and should be practiced unhesitatingly, in obedience to the voice of God. Thus interpreted, the universe was for Carlyle a place of wonder and mystery, pervaded by the Divine presence and sustained by the Divine laws. Mill, who had quite other views on these matters, did not protest while Carlyle poured vials of scorn on the atheists, the " logic-choppers," [16] and the Utilitarians who " would fain grind out virtue from the husks of pleasure." [17] He thought it sufficient that he agreed with Carlyle on political and social questions.

The common ground of the *Spirit of the Age* articles brought them closely together during an autumn and winter full of excitement and alarms. The House of Lords was refusing stubbornly to pass the Reform Bill, and the people were in an ugly mood toward their rulers. To London came the news of serious popular uprisings at Coventry, at Worcester, and at Bristol, where all the public buildings were burnt, and hundreds of lives were lost. In the industrial cities of the North the advocates of reform were organizing themselves into formidable " political unions," and there were threats that " Manchester would march on London." The alarmed Duke of Northumberland fortified his London house. And, like a visitation of God upon a rebellious people, the Asiatic cholera, which had been ravaging the Continent, announced its dread presence in the capital. Henry Drummond, Carlyle's old friend Edward Irving, and other London clergymen proclaimed the imminent end of the world. Carlyle was moved to exclaim: " A second edition of the French Revolution is distinctly within the range of chances; for there is nowhere any tie remaining among men. Everywhere, in court and cathedral, brazen falsehood now stands convicted of a lie, and famishing Ignorance cries, Away with her, away with her! God deliver us." [18] But he and Mill were willing to brave the peril of famishing Ignorance let loose, rather than bolster up a social system whereby idle and incompetent aristocrats, given the ownership of all the land of the kingdom, exploited the toiling multitude whom it was their duty to guide and instruct. " If there were but a few dozens of persons safe," declared Mill, " I should not care though a revolution were to exterminate every person in Great Britain and Ireland who has £500 a year. Very many amiable persons would perish, but what is the world better for such amiable persons? " [19] For it seemed possible to supplant feudalism with a new social order based on the Saint-Simonian formula, " to each according to his talent, and to

each talent according to its works " ; an order so just
and efficient that rebellion from it would be unthink-
able.

Carlyle and Mill discovered to their mutual surprise
and pleasure that both knew the doctrines of the Saint-
Simonian sect, which pointed the way to a new religion
of the brotherhood of man, and a new economic system which abolished inheritance and capitalism. Mill
brought the young Saint-Simonian apostle Gustave
d'Eichthal, with whom both had been in correspondence for more than a year, to Carlyle's lodgings, where
the little group discussed often and earnestly the means
whereby a liberated populace might be persuaded to
submit itself to the guidance of the wisest and the best.
Mill also introduced Carlyle to members of the British
Radical party, an outgrowth of the Utilitarian sect; to
Fonblanque, editor of the *Examiner*, whom Carlyle
adjudged " the best of the fourth estate now extant in
Britain " ; [20] and to Hyde Villiers, a Member of Parliament, and some young men of the diplomatic service.
It was even projected that Carlyle meet the aged
Jeremy Benthan, father of all Utilitarians. There
seemed an excellent possibility that a united group of
enlightened and capable young men might assume the
power which would soon be wrested from the hands of
their incompetent elders, and succeed where the Giron-
dins had failed in the France of 1790. Zeal for a
common cause at a moment of impending conflict deep-
ened the acquaintance of Carlyle and Mill into friendship. " Of male favorites, Mill stands at the top," [21]
Carlyle wrote in February, 1832, just before the

definite unsaleability of *Sartor Resartus* obliged his return to Scotland. " Carlyle passed the whole of a long winter in London " ; wrote Mill to Sterling three months later, " and rose in my opinion more than I know how to express, from a nearer acquaintance. I do not think you estimate him half highly enough; but neither did I when I last saw you." [22]

A two years' correspondence followed Carlyle's departure. On both sides the letters were written with great care and at great length. Mill gave Carlyle the news from the great world: of the immediate result of the passage of the Reform Bill, of the attitude of the new government toward the working classes, of the fortunes of the Saint-Simonians in France. It was, as they had foreseen, a time of hesitation and confusion. Election on the basis of an extended suffrage had not appreciably increased the quality of the House of Commons; a proof, Mill thought, that the country did not contain the men fit to lead into the new era, although the ability of some of the young men in the backgrounds of the Althorps and the Broughams promised better things for the immediate future. In France the Saint-Simonians had achieved no better results, and had themselves disintegrated under the joint influences of governmental prosecution and internal dissension. As the one encouraging sign of the times Mill sent Carlyle the Poor Law and Factory Commissioners' reports, which indicated that the government was at last becoming aware of the shocking human cost of refusing to control the tremendous new force of machine industry which was taking the place of feudal agrarianism.

From Mill also came frequent consignments of newly appearing books in the fields of Carlyle's interest. Carlyle reciprocated by praise of Mill's contributions to the periodical press and by interest in the fortunes of the Radical group. " I beg you will by no means let me lose sight of London; least of all, of your circle therein; many things of value for me, lie in it, which may yet become of more value. In London alone of all places I have found men (belonging to this century and not to a past one) who believed that Truth was Truth: of such men, how obstructed otherwise soever, all may be hoped, for they have attained the source of all. Considered as European Thinkers, our poor utilitarians make the mournfulest figure: yet in this one fact, that they were the re-originators of *any* Belief among us, they stand far above all other Sects. Young minds too will not end where they began; under this point of view, you and certain of yours are of great interest for me; indeed, I may say, form the chief *visible* encouragement I have to proceed in this rather hazardous course of mine." [23] Furthermore, Carlyle's letters, as well as his published writings, gave Mill a welcome contact with a new world of colorful imagery and intuitive insight. " You I look upon as an artist," Mill wrote admiringly, " perhaps the only genuine one now living in this country; the highest destiny of all lies in that direction; for it is the artist alone in whose hands Truth becomes impressive and a living principle of action. . . . My vocation, as far as I yet see it, lies in a humbler sphere; . . . to make those who are not poets understand that poetry is higher than logic, and that the union of the two is philosophy." [24]   In pursuance of this new vocation Mill tried to awaken in the Utilitarian coterie an appreciation of poetry by means of magazine articles entitled *What is Poetry* and *Two Kinds of Poetry*. These Mill recommended to Carlyle's attention along with others of his writings likely to be congenial, including an essay on the virtues and defects of Benthamism soon to be published; and an already published review which urged that some competent author should write a *Treatise on the Ambiguities of the Moral Sciences* which " would enable all kinds of thinkers, who now are daggers drawn, because they are speaking different dialects and know it not, to understand one another, and to perceive that, with the proper explanations, their doctrines are reconcilable " and thus " contribute a large part to what is probably destined to be the great philosophical achievement of the era, of which many signs already announce the commencement, viz., to unite all half truths, which have been fighting against one another since the creation, and blend them in one harmonious whole." [25]   These indications of apostasy from orthodox Utilitarianism, and Mill's outspoken personal admiration confirmed Carlyle in the belief that he was making a convert. " When you return to London," he instructed his brother John in February, 1833, " you must see Mill; he is growing quite a believer, *mystisch gesinnt*, yet with all his old utilitarian logic quite alive in him." [26]

The correspondence had continued for more than a year, before Mill realized the false impression his habit of avoiding collision and emphasizing points of agreement was creating in Carlyle's mind. The reading in May, 1833, of Carlyle's essay on *Diderot*, which declared that the atheism of the French *philosophes* would cause them finally to be forgotten, which sneered at those who could only believe in a " probable God " [27] discoverable through reasoning, and fiercely attacked the Utilitarian ethics, awoke Mill to the serious character of their disagreement. He was smitten with remorse at seeing " not honest," [28] and wrote at once: " I have found more to differ from in that article of yours than in anything in your writings. There has always been a considerable extent of undiscussed and unsifted difference of opinion . . . between us two; on some of which, too, I sometimes think the distance has widened rather than narrowed of late." [29] He promised thenceforward to be frank at all costs, but postponed a statement of precise differences until his visit to Craigenputtock in August. Carlyle accepted with good grace Mill's assertion of his " right to ME-hood." [30] " It was no secret to me that you and I differed over a whole half-universe of things, for indeed I think we stood at opposite sides of it; nevertheless " (he added tenaciously) " I will by no means fancy with you that we are moving *from* each other, but quite contrariwise. On the whole, however, when two men are agreed in recognizing one another's common recognition of the infinite nature of Truth, there is a beginning of all profitable communion between them, and nothing is more interesting thenceforth than the friendly conflict of their differences. Hesitate not, I pray you, neither in this August nor at any other time, to show me the whole breadth and figure of your dissent; God knows I need guidance." [31]

August found Mill unable to visit Craigenputtock, and thereafter he hesitated to confide to so clumsy a medium as the written word the communication of beliefs full of *nuances* and liable to misinterpretation. In the winter Carlyle precipitated his confession by challenging him to defend the Utilitarian zeal to promote the " good of the species " [32] (very like our contemporary concern for " service ") which he found somewhat ridiculous in its " universal Soup-Kitchen character," and less efficient in achieving good than the effort of the individual to realize what was best in himself; of which the good of others was a natural by-product. " If you still differ from me," Carlyle wrote encouragingly, " even with vehemence, I will not take it ill; in the calmest manner . . . I will appeal to the future John Mill, and he shall decide between us." [33]

Thus urged, Mill replied with a candid confession, not only upon this point, but upon all others of probable disagreement. This he prefaced with an explanation of his having represented himself in too favorable a light. When a " schoolboy fresh from the logic school " who " had never conversed with a reality," [34] he had outdone his older and wiser associates in radicalism, and had stated the Utilitarian doctrines in their most paradoxical and offensive form. At the time when Carlyle met him, he had fallen, in reaction from this narrow and tactless partisanship, into the opposite error of too great catholicity. His desire to learn from everybody had led him insensibly into the seeming

insincerity of which he had but lately become conscious.
" This (is) my intellectual history," Mill concluded,
" in relating which I have faith that I have not pre-
sumed too much upon your interest in me." [35]   His
frankness was equal to his modesty.   He adopted the
offensive phrase, " a probable God," to explain his
theistic position; God's existence was not immediately
present to his consciousness by faith or intuition, and its
rational proof, as well as that of personal immortality,
was inconclusive, as Carlyle himself admitted.   He
was therefore incapable of believing that each man
came into the world with a task Providentially assigned
him, and thus in all moral problems had to fall back
for guidance upon Utilitarianism of an unorthodox sort
peculiar to himself, which was difficult to describe in a
letter.   In ethics, however, where Carlyle feared they
were apart, they were really close to agreement.   For,
while believing the " good of the species . . . to be
the ultimate end " [36] of action, he was ready to agree
with Carlyle that individual self-development was the
best means of achieving that end; and Carlyle could
find out his appointed task only " by discovering in
what manner such faculties as he possesses or can ac-
quire may produce most good in the world." [37]   With
a touch of humor he pointed out that there Carlyle
outdid him in his efforts to address himself " through
the press, to the ' species ' at large." [38]

    With much solemnity Carlyle enjoined " silence on
that highest discrepancy of ours," [39] believing that Mill
would some day, on the humble path of well-doing and
renunciation, find God in a sudden and unmistakable

intuition. For the rest, he insisted, "The creed you write down is singularly like my own in most points — with this single difference, that you are yet consciously nothing of a Mystic; your very Mysticism (for there is enough of it in you) you have to translate into Logic before you give it place." [40]

Mill replied by agreeing that his mysticism, if he had any, was to be gauged by its translatability into logic; and asked Carlyle whether that translatability were not the means of distinction between "the mysticism which is of Truth, and mere dreamery, or the institution of imaginations for realities." [41] He also asked the meaning of the "humility" (*Entsagen*) to which Carlyle gave prime importance in the moral life, perhaps implying an inconsistency with the individualism on which he had just been insisting. Whereupon Carlyle, who by this time had also found difficulty in expressing himself satisfactorily on paper, postponed reply until they should meet in London a few weeks later. How the oral discussion then proceeded we do not know, but we may guess its upshot from the fact that eight months after this meeting Carlyle was privately complaining that Mill was "negative" and "narrow." [42] The hope of making a proselyte died hard.

But metaphysical differences were being pushed aside by a practical enterprise of great mutual interest; a history of the French Revolution, which was to be an object lesson to contemporary England. Mill was to have written it, and had collected many books and pamphlets on the subject; but he had recently abandoned the enterprise because it necessitated the impolitic avowal of his conviction that Christianity was obsolete. It then devolved on Carlyle, whose attitude toward Christianity, although far from orthodox, was much more sympathetic. Made desperate by consistent inability to gain a tolerable livelihood by his pen, he decided to write the history as a last bid for recognition before emigrating to America.

The decision obliged him to remove to London, where he could have access to the requisite books and pamphlets, and where Mill's expert advice could be near. He welcomed the change, for he had been tiring of solitude. Ralph Waldo Emerson, who had visited him in the summer of 1833, had found him " turning his eyes towards London with a scholar's appreciation." [43] To maintain himself there he had 200 pounds, the meager savings of six years of solitude, and certain hopes. These hopes concerned a new Radical quarterly of which Mill had written him a month before the letter of confession. The Radicals had not had the influence they expected upon the legislation of the Reformed Parliament, and much of the blame for their failure had been laid upon the party organ, the *Westminster Review*, whose editor-owner, Colonel Thompson, had not maintained it in the vigor of its early years. As a means of restoring the unity and courage of the little Radical group in Parliament, the best minds of the party had decided to launch the *London Review*. John Mill, as their leader, had been the logical choice for its editor, but his employment at the India House had made acceptance impossible. He wrote, however, that he considered Dr. William Fox, a Unitarian clergyman, " quite as fit " [44] for the position as himself. Mill invited Carlyle to write " *for* the review, or at least *in* it," [45] but, having a distinct remembrance of his own initial difficulties in comprehending *Sartor Resartus,* warned him of the necessity of adapting the style of his articles to the taste of his readers. " The prejudices of our Utilitarians are at least as strong against some of your writings as those of any other person whatever. . . . What revolts them is the combination of opinions new and often strange to them, with a manner to them equally new and still more strange, which prevents them not only from understanding your meaning but from desiring to understand it." [46] But it was the dress of the opinions, more than the opinions themselves, which offended. If Carlyle would free his style from its most exaggerated mannerisms, and refrain from attacking the Utilitarians directly, his contributions would be welcome. His contemplated essay on John Knox would be suitable for the Review. Knowing that the editorship was Mill's to give, Carlyle, despite the mention of Fox, hoped secretly it might be his, and afford him what he most desired, steady literary employment at a fixed salary.

Mill's cordial reception of the news of his decision to remove to London strengthened his hope. He quitted Craigenputtock in late April, 1834. Mill visited him in what was to be his lifelong home in Cheyne Row soon after his arrival. The projected Review was discussed. Carlyle hinted his desire as

plainly as pride would permit him.   He was ready to
make what he considered great concessions to the Radical party.   A few weeks later, Mill informed Carlyle
that Fox had been definitely chosen as editor.   To Carlyle, he seemed " rather ashamed " [47] of this announcement, and betrayed by his manner that he had been
conscious of his friend's unspoken wish.   It hurt sorely
to be thus passed over by the man he loved, who still
seemed " almost fonder than ever " [48] of him.   Some
strong pressure must have been exerted upon Mill in
Fox's favor.   Carlyle suspected a Mrs. Taylor, whom
Mill had introduced to him as his " dearest friend," [49]
a married woman with whom, gossip said, Mill was in
love.   She was a close friend of Dr. Fox, and must
have urged his candidacy.

But cooler reflection told Carlyle that there were
many logical reasons for passing him by.   The chorus
of indignant protest that had gone up against *Sartor
Resartus*, whose publication in *Fraser's Magazine* had
just been completed, as unintelligible mysticism expressed in a barbarous half-German jargon, had made
Carlyle's a dangerous name to put at the head of a
Review.   Furthermore, he would be hardly the man
to ensure in the articles " a general tendency not in
contradiction with the object of the publication," [50] one
of the duties Mill demanded of the editor.   Carlyle
admitted that he would have endeavored to throw
over the Benthamic formulae, and make the publication
radical according to his own conceptions of radicalism.
Undoubtedly Dr. Fox was the " safer man." [a]

[a] It was finally arranged that Mill should have general supervision over certain sub-editors.

In the mature retrospect of his *Reminiscences* Carlyle realized that " Mill and Co." gave little thought to his pretensions, and congratulated himself on escaping the post, which might have tarred him with the brush of Utilitarianism.   At the moment bitterness was great.   The divinely appointed prophet to his age had been at the point of making friends with the forces of unbelief, and his utmost concessions had been disregarded.   " *Ebbene*," he reflected, " I can already picture the Radical Periodical and even prophesy its destiny; with myself it had not been so; the only thing certain would have been difficulty, pain, and contradiction." [51]

Mill divined the disappointment, and held out an olive branch by proposing to publish at his own expense Carlyle's essay on the *Diamond Necklace*, that he might have the pleasure of reviewing it.   He sent him " barrowfuls " of books on the French Revolution, his own collection, which he had made when intending to write on the subject.   Carlyle was touched by the genuineness of this regard.   " Nothing can exceed the obligingness of Mill," he wrote . . . " Mill, I think, alone of them, would make any great effort to help me." [52]   A threatened rift in the friendship had been safely avoided.

" Sabbath bells were not more regular than Mill's friendly visit to Cheyne Row," [53] said Carlyle in reminiscences of these years.   Mill was adopted as a part of the Carlyle clan.   " Mill is a Presbyterian's grandson — Glory to John Knox: our Isle never saw his fellow! " [54]   In their regular Sunday walks the two men talked chiefly of politics.   Mill was Fabian in

his political theories, seeing in education the only means
of political progress. Carlyle was of much the same
opinion. " If I stir in any public matter, it must be
this of national education. Radicalism goes on as fast
as any sane man could wish it, without help of mine.
Conservatism I cannot attempt to conserve, believing
it to be a portentous embodied sham, accursed of God
and doomed to destruction, as all lies are; but woe the
while if the people are not taught, if not their reason,
then their brutish folly will incarnate itself in the
frightfulest reality." [55] His history of the French
Revolution would impressively preach this sermon.

However, Carlyle kept an eye on practical politics.
He attended a meeting of the unenfranchised workingmen organized by the Radical party. The reaction
after the Reform Bill had swung to the extreme. The
Tories were in office, the first Peel ministry. Two
thousand of " the better kind of operatives " [56] were
met in a hall, and Carlyle got a thrill from their collective " bark " at the mention of the " insults " of the
Tories. Carlyle thought that the Duke of Wellington had descended to the devices of a " drill sergeant "
in his effort to maintain the existing order, but pitied
him personally. Radical Carlyle was, with the condition of the working class occupying more and more
of his thought.

But his radicalism had nothing in common with
another variety with which Mill was intimately associated. Carlyle dined with Fox and Mrs. Taylor, and
became thus acquainted with a group of what he called
" friends of the species," [57] the early feminists. The

facility of divorce which they advocated, their individualistic conception of the marriage relation, shocked
Carlyle's Calvinistic morality, his belief in the proper
subordination of the wife to the husband and the permanence of contract. He feared for Mill, though he
conceived him " far above all that." [58]

That Carlyle and his wife were no doubt gossiping
about Mill's relations with Mrs. Taylor, a tragic inci-
dent on March 6, 1835, brings to light. Carlyle thus
wrote, three weeks after the event, when the first poignant bitterness was over: " Mill had borrowed that
first Volume of my poor French Revolution (pieces of
it more than once) that he might have it all before him,
and write down some observations upon it, which perhaps I might print as Notes. I was busy meanwhile
with Volume Second; toiling along like a *Nigger*, but
with the heart of a free Roman; indeed I know not
how it was, I had not felt so clear and independent,
sure of myself and of my task for many long years.
Well, one night about three weeks ago, we sat at tea,
and Mill's short rap was heard at the door. Jane rose
to welcome him, but he stood there unresponsive, pale,
the very picture of despair; said, half-articulately gasping, that she must go down and speak to ' Mrs. Taylor.' " [59] Mrs. Carlyle went down at once, sure that
the expected elopement was taking place and Mill was
to be exiled from England. Carlyle's narrative con-
tinues: " After some considerable additional gasping, I
learned from Mill this fact; that my poor Manuscript,
all except some four tattered leaves, was *annihilated!*
He had left it out (too carelessly); it had been taken

for waste paper, and five months of as tough labor as I could remember of, were as good as vanished, gone like a whiff of smoke. There never in my life had come upon me any other *accident* of such moment; but this I could but feel was a sore one. The thing was *lost,* and perhaps worse; for I had not only forgotten all the structure of it, but the spirit it was written with was past; only the general impression seemed to remain, and the recollection that I was on the whole well satisfied with that, and could now hardly hope to equal it." Mrs. Carlyle now returned with Mrs. Taylor, having been able to get nothing from her except that it was not an elopement, and was curiously relieved to learn just what had happened. Mrs. Taylor soon departed, but " Mill whom I had to comfort and speak peace to remained injudiciously enough till almost midnight, and my poor Dame and I had to sit talking of indifferent matters; and could not until then get our lament freely uttered. *She* was very good to me; and the thing did not beat us. I felt in general that I was a little Schoolboy, who had laboriously written out his *Copy* as he could, and showing it not without satisfaction to the Master; but lo! the Master had suddenly torn it, saying: No! boy, thou must go and write it *better*."

Mill made " a passionate entreaty " to do what money could do to repair the irreparable. Carlyle finally consented to receive as a maximum the amount of his household expenses during the five months he had spent in writing the volume, but was unwilling to be paid for his time and labor. Mill sent 200 pounds, which Carlyle cut down to 100, the budget of his extremely economical wife. Mill continued his loan and gift of books. Carlyle read novels for a fortnight; then set courageously to work again. Mill helped him indirectly by buying for the *London Review* a paper on *Mirabeau,* and often walked with him in the afternoons when he took a short respite from his labors.

A year after the burning of the manuscript, when the rapprochement seemed as great as ever, Carlyle went down to visit Mill and his sisters in their country house. It was July, 1836; their father, James Mill, had been but a month dead. Carlyle, who had written them a generous letter of condolence, praising his old enemy as one who had " left a brave man's life behind him," wrote thus to his wife concerning his visit: " They were as hospitable as they could be. I was led about, made attentive to innumerable picturesquenesses, etc., etc., all that evening and next day. . . . There was little sorrow visible in their house, or rather none, nor any human feeling at all: but the strangest *unheimlich* kind of composure and acquiescence, as if all human spontaneity had taken refuge in invisible corners. Mill himself talked much, and not stupidly — far from that — but without emotion of any discernible kind. He seemed to be withering or withered into the miserablest metaphysical *scrae,*[a] body and mind, that I almost ever met with in the world. His eyes go winking and jerking with wild lights and twitches; his head is bald, his face brown and dry — poor fellow after all. It seemed to me the strangest thing what this man could

[a] Dialect for " old shoe."

want with me, or I with such a man so *unheimlich* to me. What will become of it? Nothing evil; for there is and there was nothing dishonest in it. But I think I shall see less and less of him. Alas, poor fellow! It seems possible, too, that he may not be very long seeable; that is one way of its ending, to say nothing of my own chances." [60]

Carlyle's nerves, irritated by constant work on his history, and by the uncertainty of his prospects, were sensitive to the slightest discord. The warmth of affection among the Carlyle clan prevented him from suspecting that James Mill had demanded respect, but discouraged the expression of love, from his children. A letter of John Mill's to Gustave d'Eichthal expressed a sense of loss which contradicts Carlyle's impression, but Mill's habitual disinclination to talk about himself wholly concealed this. Mill's capacity for emotion had furthermore been depleted by the exhaustion of his nervous energy in a "brain fever," the result of over-work, from which he had suffered during the previous summer. Nevertheless, the abnormal physiological condition of both men only set in clearer light what was an essential incompatibility of temperament. Mill was strangely like a medieval schoolman, subtle, analytic, abstract, mortifying the body for the sake of the intellectual life. Carlyle was emotional, synthetic, insistent on health and vigor. Mill was preparing a treatise on logic; Carlyle, in the mood of a creative artist, was describing a "smoke- and flame-conflagration in the distance." [61]

This instinctive recoil of Carlyle was the beginning

of the end of the intimacy. The next week Carlyle made a special call at the India House to bid Mill Godspeed on a trip to the Continent for his health, and greeted him at Nice with a letter recommending the " curative virtue of idleness," but the exact state of his feelings came out in a letter to their friend Sterling: " His (Mill's) health is a little, and but a little improved. Mrs. Taylor, it is whispered, is with him, or near him. Is it not very strange, this pining away into desiccation and nonentity, of our poor Mill, if it be so, as his friends all say, that this charmer is the cause of it? They are innocent, says Charity; they are guilty, says scandal: then why in the name of wonder are they dying broken hearted? One thing only, is plainly clear to me, that poor Mill is in a bad way. Alas, tho' he speaks not, perhaps his tragedy is more tragical than that of any of us: this item that he does not speak, that he never could speak, but was to sit imprisoned as in thick ribbed ice, voiceless, uncommunicating, is it not the most tragical circumstance of all? " [62] Even in 1833 he had complained to Mill of his lack of " heartiness," of confidingness; now a trace of jealousy was mingled with his pity.

Mill was still to do him a signal service as partial amends for the destruction of the manuscript. His *History of the French Revolution,* a book come " direct and flamingly from the heart of a living man," [63] was to appear in mid-summer, 1837. Mill determined to forestall unfavorable criticism by a prompt review from the proof sheets which should set the tone of comment. His critique in the July number of the

London and Westminster Review was passionate in
praise: " No work of greater genius, either historical or
poetical, has been produced in this country for many
years." [64]   He anticipated objections to Carlyle's style
by pointing out the epic character of the work, which
should be read like poetry.   Other reviewers took the
cue, and a chorus of plaudits followed.   It had the
unique quality of pleasing both Radical and Tory.
Mill gleefully quoted Carlyle's sympathetic description
of the sack of a château, and emphasized his conclusion
that the Revolution was necessary for the overthrow of
a great imposture.   But the condemnation of the negative character of the Revolution, its lack of constructive
power, appealed to the conservative instincts of the
nation.   Carlyle did much to encourage the Victorian
scorn of " the red fool-fury of the Seine." [65]

The completion of the *History* left Mill and Carlyle
with much less in common.   Carlyle had no great
sympathy with Mill's work on logic, being, as Mill
noticed, " intolerant to no class but metaphysicians." [66]
" If John Mill were to get up to heaven," he complained humorously, " he would hardly be content
until he had made out how it all was." [67]   Mill's efforts to influence practical politics by his Radical publication seemed likewise misdirected.   " Mill I saw last
night," he wrote in July, 1838, " borrowing some
Books from him.   Friendly as ever when we meet,
but that is now rarely; our paths diverge more and
more; to me he is now nearly altogether barren; to him
I am perhaps oppressive in the self-subsistence which
he (tho' only in Benthamic speculation of Radicalism)

very properly aims at." [68] Carlyle was also becoming
more and more piqued by Mill's preference of Mrs.
Taylor's company to his own. This was the more
irritating because he suspected that it was her careless-
ness which had brought destruction on his manuscript.
After the accident Mill had told him that " It had not
only the *one* reader you mentioned but a second as
good " : and Carlyle thought it had perished at the
hands of the housemaid at her home in Kingston,
where she was living apart from her husband. Furthermore he thoroughly despised the clique to which
Mrs. Taylor attached Mill. Believing that Mill had
made his choice, Carlyle wrote to Sterling in 1837 with
annoyance and pathetic regret: " Mill is in better
health, still not in good. The set of people he is in
is one that I have to keep out of. No class of mortals
ever profited me less. There is a vociferous platitude
in them, a mangy hungry discontent; their very joy is
like that of a thing scratching itself under disease of
the itch. Mill was infinitely too good for them; but
he would have it, and his fate would. I love him
much as a friend frozen in ice for me." [69]

Their contact was chiefly kept up through Mill's
Radical *Review*. Mill needed the aid of Carlyle's
pen, and the *French Revolution* had brought Carlyle
much less money than fame. In 1838, Carlyle offered
to sell his services for the following year exclusively to
the *London and Westminster* for two hundred pounds.
But Mill was obliged to reply that the coming withdrawal of a large part of the financial support of the
Review would make such an arrangement impossible,

since most of its contents must thenceforward be contributed gratis. He added, however, that there was still money enough to purchase occasional articles, and requested that Carlyle prepare a study of Cromwell. Carlyle had got well under way with research in the Protector's life, when Robertson, a young sub-editor, took advantage of an absence of Mill on the Continent to make the astonishing request that Carlyle cease work, as he " meant to do the Cromwell himself." His pride hurt to the quick, Carlyle determined to complete the study and publish elsewhere. His anger was roused against the entire Radical party. " To be edited by him and Mill and the Benthamic formula! " he exclaimed, realizing his anomalous and humiliating position. Mill, on his return, made amends by publishing in September, 1839, a laudatory summary of Carlyle's whole literary achievement, written by their mutual friend Sterling.

Vengeance upon the Radicals for Robertson's slight came quickly. In the summer of 1838, Carlyle had put in Mill's hands an article entitled *Chartism*. The demand of the English workingmen for the adoption of the famous Five Point Charter, whose chief demand was universal suffrage, had just been met by military repression. Carlyle, with the French Revolution vivid in his imagination, was sure that persistence in this course would mean revolution. Universal suffrage was unwise, but the lower classes would force it upon the nation if justice were not done them. The government must ensure a living wage and better hours and conditions of work, or the masses would arise and overthrow it. Mill felt Carlyle was right, but dared not publish the article. Its plain speaking concerning the attitude of the middle class toward factory operatives would offend the subscribers to the *Review*, the most influential of whom were industrials. Carlyle, out of patience with the Radicals, determined to throw a bomb-shell in their midst by offering it to the Tories. Lockhart, editor of the *Quarterly*, gave the idea encouragement, but when the completed article came to his hands in the autumn of 1839, " he sent it back, seemingly not without reluctance, saying ' we dare not.' " Carlyle turned again to Mill as a last resort, and found him unexpectedly enthusiastic about it. In the year that had passed since Mill first saw the manuscript, the *Westminster* had become an admitted failure. It was soon to be discontinued. Mill had no one to placate, and hoped to make a great sensation with his article in his last number, as " the last dying speech of a Radical Review." Carlyle was at first inclined to please Mill, but his wife and his brother John felt that he should not endanger his reputation by identifying himself with an admittedly lost cause. He saw the soundness of this advice, and was inwardly glad of the opportunity of revenge it afforded. " I offered them this very thing two years ago, the blockheads, and they dared not let me write it then. If they had taken more of my counsel, they need not perhaps have been in a sinking state at present. But they went their own way, and now their Review is to cease, and their whole beggarly unbelieving Radicalism may cease too, if it likes, and let us see if there be not a believing Radicalism possible." [70] *Chartism* was published as a pamphlet, at the author's expense, before the end of the year, to the indignation of all parties. But Carlyle was satisfied, having had his say. "This thing has been in my head and heart these ten, some of it these twenty, years. One is right glad to be delivered of such a thing on any terms. No sect in our day has made a wretcheder figure than the Bentham-Radical sect. Nature abhors a *vacuum*: worthy old girl, she will not make a wretched, unsympathetic, scraggy Atheism and Egoism fruitful in her world; but answers to it: Enough, thou scraggy Atheism; go thy ways, wilt thou! " [71]

When Mill proposed a study of Cromwell, he had no premonition that it would nourish in Carlyle opinions diametrically opposed to his own. Carlyle began the study with the then common preconception of Cromwell as an unscrupulous usurper; he completed it in 1845 convinced of his sincerity and ready to justify all his acts. The undemocratic turning out of the Long Parliament was the just domination of a wise minority over a foolish majority. The Drogheda massacre was necessary "surgery." [72] Right and might were in the end identical. "As to Cromwell," wrote their mutual acquaintance Caroline Fox, in her *Journal* of May 29, 1846, "Mill does not always agree with Carlyle, who tries to make him out ever in the right. He could not justify the Irish massacres, though he fully believes Cromwell thought it was right, as a matter of discipline, or he would not have done it." A significant difference of opinion, later to manifest itself dramatically in the famous Governor Eyre controversy. Carlyle's *Past and Present* (1843), proclaiming his discovery of the advantages of the feudal system, had already marked a turning toward the Conservatives. Mill, under the influence of Mrs. Taylor and the Saint-Simonians, was moving in the opposite direction of industrial democracy. He was undertaking a revision of the orthodox political economy of Smith and Ricardo in the light of new discoveries in the science, and was cautiously feeling his way in the direction of collectivism. Collisions of opinion were being added to incompatibility of temperament, and the friendship of Mill and Carlyle was practically at an end. They met for the last time in October, 1846. Margaret Fuller was in London with a letter of introduction from Emerson, and Carlyle thought of Mill as one she would like to meet at a dinner he was giving in her honor. " I went one day to the India House to invite him," said Carlyle in his old age, " and before I got there I met him coming along the street, and he received me like the very incarnation o' the East Wind, and refused my invitation peremptorily." [73] Carlyle was at a loss to recall what he had done to offend Mill, unless some one had indiscreetly, carried to Mill an amusing story which he had related concerning the *naïveté* of Mill's affection; a story of the most harmless sort which Mill might have misconstrued as a jest at what was to him sacred. It may be that he had given no particular cause for offense, and that Mill's action was only part of the general policy of withdrawal from society which he was then instituting, partly as a means of protecting Mrs. Taylor from embarrassing contacts.[a]   Carlyle often thought of writing a request for an explanation, but did not.   After her husband's death had left Mrs. Taylor free to marry Mill in 1851, Carlyle ventured to write Mill business notes, which received courteous replies.   But the promise of a visit conveyed in the second (1858) was not fulfilled, and the hint conveyed in the third (1866) that a call would be welcome, was not accepted.   In 1869, a final and pathetic note from Carlyle, aged seventy-four and recently bereaved, to Mill, himself ten years a widower, accompanying two books which had belonged to Mill's father, and suggesting that Mill might also be interested in receiving a memento of Mrs. Carlyle, thawed Mill perceptibly. " Your kind note would have revived, even if they had ever been dormant, many old memories and feelings. . . . Any communication from you — not to mention your bodily presence — would be most welcome." [74] But though Mill lived four years longer, they never met.[b]

It was a strong emotional attachment that could thus survive thirty-seven years of misunderstanding and separation.   And its strength was the more remarkable in that those were also years of increasing intellectual divergence, which at times involved Mill and Carlyle

[a] For the rest of his life Mill was observed to grow " suddenly aged " whenever Carlyle was mentioned. *Thomas Carlyle*, by Moncure D. Conway, p. 90.

[b] For interesting conjectures as to the cause of their separation see *Carlyle on Cromwell and Others*, by D. A. Dawson, p. 171 ff.

in spectacular public conflict. The first and most violent of these collisions took place three years after they had parted in the street.

When the long-expected revolutions broke out on the Continent in 1848, Carlyle was disappointed by their leveling and Jacobin character. The policies of the French provisional government, the most successful of these revolutionary groups, aroused him to vigorous protest. He rejoiced in the overthrow of the " old scoundrel " Louis Philippe, but was alarmed " that all the world, in its protest against False Government, should find no remedy but that of rushing into No Government or Anarchy (kinglessness), which I take this republican universal suffragism to inevitably be." The proposed " organisation of labor " was " precisely the question of questions for all governments whatsoever," but communistic equality would not solve it. Its solution demanded " true *government* by the wise, true and noble-minded of the foolish, perverse, and dark, with or *against* their consent." [75]

Where such an ideal government was most needed was in the British West Indies, where the liberated slave, gaining his sustenance by half an hour's labor a day, was refusing to work and letting the sugar and spice plantations go to ruin. It maddened Carlyle to think of " Black Quashee " lolling in the shade " up to the ears in pumpkin," while the Irishman, famine-driven, could find no work wherewith to earn his bread. Carlyle was glad of the opportunity to shock England into a realization of the dangers of equality and individualism by presenting his opinions in their most offen-

sive form.   The article on *The Nigger Question* which
he contributed to *Fraser's* of December, 1849, advocated a resumption of Negro slavery.

To Carlyle the idleness of the Jamaica Negro seemed
a defiance of fundamental laws, human and divine.
The man-discovered law of aristocracy demanded that
the Englishman, being born " wiser," should rule the
negro.   In Jamaica at the moment there already
existed a worse slavery than Negro bondage, " the
slavery of the Wise to the Foolish " — for were not
equality and supply and demand bringing the white
planter to financial ruin?   Calvinism had taught Carlyle that every man was sent into the world to labor, to
do the work " his Maker of him intended."   The
English held Jamaica as a fief from God.   They deserved it because they had made best use of it, reclaimed
it from jungle by the expenditure of blood and treas-
ure.   But their continued tenure was dependent on
their making the island productive.   They must set
aside economic liberalism and force the Negro to fulfill
the God-given mandate to labor.   Otherwise, " Brother
Jonathan," who still knew the necessity of slavery,
becoming the stronger, would take the colony away
from England.

This article struck against all that Mill held most
sacred.   His sectarian training of freedom and individualism, his historical knowledge of the moral degeneration of slave and master inevitable under the
" peculiar institution," his humanitarianism, which
made tyranny intolerable to him; all made him see in
slavery, as he later expressed it, " the summing up and

concentration of social evil, the stronghold in which the principle of tyrannical power, elsewhere only militant, reigns triumphant." He wrote a fierce letter in reply, which was published under the title *The Negro Question* in the very next number of *Fraser's*.

The opening paragraph of this letter was one of the most indignant Mill ever wrote. " Your last Number," he began, " contains a speech against the ' Rights of Negroes,' the doctrines and spirit of which ought not to pass without remonstrance. The author issues his opinions, or rather ordinances, under imposing auspices; no less than these — ' the Immortal Gods,' ' the Powers,' the ' Destinies ' announce through him, not only what will be, but what *shall* be done; what they ' have decided upon; passed their eternal Act of Parliament for.' This is speaking as one having authority, but authority from whom? If by the quality of the message we may judge of those who sent it, not from any powers to whom just or good men acknowledge obedience. The so-called ' eternal Act of Parliament ' is no new law, but the old law of the strongest, a law against which the great teachers of mankind have in all ages protested. . . . If ' the gods ' will this, it is the first duty of human beings to resist such gods. Omnipotent those gods are not, for powers which demand human tyranny and injustice cannot accomplish their purpose unless human beings coöperate."

Mill turned to the attack of Negro slavery the very argument Carlyle had used in *Past and Present* in his protest against the spiritual starvation of the overworked English factory laborer. " In opposition to the 'gospel of work,'" Mill wrote, "I would assert the gospel of leisure, and maintain that human beings *cannot* rise to the finer attributes of their nature compatibly with a life filled with labor . . . the real labor, the exhausting, stiffening, stupefying toil of many kinds of agricultural and manufacturing laborers." Work in itself was not good, but only work for some worthy object. If the Negro was to be forced to labor more than was necessary for the satisfaction of his physical wants, it should surely not be for spices and sugar, the luxuries of material civilization, but rather only for his intellectual and moral development, which would make him really a civilized being.

Mill likewise denied that the law of aristocracy demanded that the Negro be the slave of the white. Slavery, on the contrary, nullified the true aims of aristocracy. True aristocracy was government for the sake of the governed; slavery, the exploitation of the many for the sake of the few. True aristocracy aimed to raise the level of intelligence of the community; slavery, to lower it. Moreover, that the White had the right to rule the Negro because born " wiser " was a gratuitous assumption. Mill strenuously denied its biological validity because, like all theories asserting the mental inequality of individuals at birth, it threatened the most chershed of his beliefs, the belief in the essential equality of the sexes. Negro inferiority was the result of environment only; the Egyptian civilization had been a Negro civilization. The flattering theory of Anglo-Saxon divine right had yet to be proved. Mill closed the letter by denouncing Carlyle's article as "a true work of the devil," in that it would encourage the supporters of slavery in the United States.

Mill's attack piqued and hurt Carlyle, for he had loved him. In his *Journal* under the date of February 7, 1850, is the melancholy obituary of the friendship. "Nigger article has roused the ire of all philanthropists to quite an unexpected pitch. Among other very poor attacks upon it was one in *Fraser;* most shrill, poor, and insignificant, which I was surprised to learn proceeded from John Mill. . . . He has neither told me nor reminded me of anything I did not very well know beforehand. No use of writing that kind of criticism. For some years back Mill, who once volunteered a close constant intimacy for a long time, has volunteered a complete withdrawal of himself; and now, instead of reverent discipleship, which he aspired to, seems to have taken the function of getting up to contradict whatever I say. Curious enough. But poor Mill's fate in various ways has been very tragic. His misery, when I chance to see him in the street or otherwise (for we never had a word of quarrel), appeals to my pity if my anger was rising."

In the years that followed, the differences separating the two former friends became steadily greater. The *Nigger Question* was the first of a series of *Latter Day Pamphlets,* in which Carlyle repudiated representative government and advocated in its stead an efficient despotism, centralized in a hero or fittest man, with an organized foreign policy of imperialistic aggression. He supported his political theories with a

monumental history of the reign of Frederick the
Great, completed in 1864, which showed their success
in building up the flourishing kingdom of Prussia.
Mill supported the opposite extreme of individualism
in his *On Liberty* (1859), and advocated a modified
democracy in his *Representative Government* (1862).
In the sixties, Carlyle was the intellectual leader of the
conservatives, Mill of the advanced liberals. Civil
War in America, reopening the Negro question, awakened in them conspicuously opposite sympathies. A
second Reform Bill, which gave the vote to the working class, found them no longer united as they were in
support of its predecessor of 1832. Mill, a member
of Parliament, cast his vote for the Bill, which to Carlyle was a dangerous leap in the dark, and would end
in anarchy before fifty years had passed. In a pamphlet entitled *Shooting Niagara* Carlyle advised the
members of the aristocracy who had opposed Disraeli's
yielding to popular clamor, to retire to their estates,
and train private armies for a *coup d'état* when the
inevitable anarchy should arrive.

This increasing belief in the use of military force for
the preservation of order brought Carlyle into sharp
conflict with Mill in 1866. For a second time events
in Jamaica were the direct occasion of their clash.

On October 11, 1865, disputes at Morant Bay between the whites and blacks over possession of land
broke out into rioting, during which Negroes armed
with sticks and knives attacked and burned the court
house. The rioters were quickly dispersed by the arrival of soldiers. The governor of the island, Eyre, a

distinguished Australian explorer, considered the rioting the result of an organized rebellion, and immediately declared a state of martial law for all the county
in which Morant Bay was located, with the exception
of Kingston, the capital.

Near Kingston lived George William Gordon, a
fanatical Baptist minister, whom Governor Eyre had
come to regard as the leader of the blacks in all disputes
with the whites. A warrant was sent out for Gordon's
arrest for high treason. On learning this, Gordon
went to Kingston, his place of business, and gave himself up at military headquarters. Governor Eyre put
him on a ship of war and sent him to Morant Bay,
intentionally to deprive him of trial in a civil court.
There he was tried before a court martial composed of
two young naval officers and a subaltern in the army, a
court illegal because constituted by representatives of
two different services. Gordon was hanged on October
23, protesting his innocence.

Meanwhile the soldiers had been gleefully pursuing
the rioters. The *Kingston Morning Journal* of October 30 published a letter from a Captain Ford: " This
is a picture of martial law. The soldiers enjoy it: the
inhabitants dread it. If they run away at our approach,
they are shot for running away." Before the soldiers
were tired of their sport, 439 Negroes had been put to
death by courts-martial, over 6,600, including many
women, severely flogged, and over a thousand dwellings had been burned.

The news of these events aroused great indignation
among English liberals. The Jamaica courts-martial

seemed a menace to the hard-won right of every British subject to a trial by due process of law. If, as the Tories maintained in Governor Eyre's defense, martial law were the negation of all law, and a governor responsible only to his executive superiors, the fundamental rules of justice and humanity could be entirely abrogated on the plea of danger and necessity. The liberal leaders formed an association called the Jamaica Committee, to investigate the outrages. Mill was the most active member of this Committee, and hotly urged that Eyre be brought to trial before a civil court for misdemeanors committed during his term of office. When the majority decided upon this course, Mill was elected chairman of the Committee. In a speech of unusual fire, he supported on the floor of the House of Commons the motion for Eyre's criminal prosecution. The plea of Eyre's sincerity he brushed aside as he had Carlyle's defense of Cromwell's sincerity. Robespierre, Fouquier Tinville, and the organizers of the massacres of St. Bartholomew were likewise sincere. If the punishment of Eyre for his excessive zeal should not be made an object lesson for colonial governors, British subjects would be always at the mercy of irresponsible executive power. "You approve of my speech," Mill wrote to one of his supporters, " because you see that I am not on this occasion standing up for the Negroes, or for liberty, deeply as both are interested in the subject — but for the first necessity of human society, law. One would have thought that when this was the matter in question, all political parties might be expected to be unanimous. But my eyes were first

opened to the moral condition of the English nation
(I except in these matters the working classes) by the
atrocities perpetrated in the Indian Mutiny, and the
feelings which supported them at home. Then came
the sympathy with lawless rebellion of the Southern
Americans in defense of an institution which is the sum
of all lawlessness, as Wesley said it was of all villainy
— and finally came this Jamaica business, the authors
of which, from the first day I knew it, I determined I
would do all in my power to bring to justice, if there
was not another man in Parliament to stand by me." [76]

Public opinion was preponderantly against Mill.
The upper and middle classes supported Eyre. The
military caste, the Pan-Saxon imperialists, and those
Tories who still sympathized with slavery, were as
heartily in his defense as Mill was against him. To
Carlyle, the prosecution was much ado about nothing.
He summarized the case in a simile: " a ship had been
on fire: the captain, by immediate and bold exertion,
had put the fire out, and had been called to account
for having flung a bucket or two in the hold beyond
what was necessary. He had damaged some of the
cargo, perhaps, but had saved the ship." [77] When
Eyre's personal danger became very great, Carlyle
went up to a meeting of the newly formed Eyre Defense Committee, which was as yet very weak in numbers and influence, and let himself " be voted into the
chair, such being the post of danger on the occasion." [78]
His enormous influence among literary men soon infinitely improved the quality of the Committee. Ruskin, ever-faithful, Tennyson, Charles Kingsley,

Tyndall, Murchison, and James Froude gave their sympathy and support. Carlyle and Ruskin carried the war into the newspapers.

The trial dragged out over two years. England, like France during the Dreyfus case, was divided into well-defined warring camps. With Mill were the evolutionary scientists and the Positivists, tribes accursed to Carlyle; Darwin, Wallace, Huxley, Spencer, Frederic Harrison, Leslie Stephen, John Morley; with Carlyle were men of letters of Tory or Anglican breeding, with the notable exceptions of Tyndall and Dickens, who were bound to Carlyle by personal loyalty. A Tory county refused to give a bill of indictment, and one had to be secured through Bow Street. The report of an investigating commission caused the Government to remove Eyre, and withhold his pension. Froude records that he never knew Carlyle " more anxious about anything." Carlyle drew up a petition to the government for the restoration of the pension, but it was too vigorously worded to be to the Defense Committee's liking. He met Eyre and was well impressed: " Eyre's self down here, visibly a brave, gentle, chivalrous, and clear man, whom I would make dictator of Jamaica for the next twenty-five years were I now king of it." [79]

Mill's party finally won on principle; the Lord Chief Justice, in his charge to the jury, maintaining the final authority of civil procedure thoughout the Empire. But the jury, failed to convict. " It was clear," commented Mill on the result of the trial, " that to bring English functionaries to the bar of a criminal court for abuses of power committed against negroes and mulattoes was not a popular proceeding with the English Middle Classes." [80] Popular resentment against Mill manifested itself in anonymous letters, grading in violence from vulgar caricatures to threats of assassination.

The contrasted interests of the two men were further shown in their addresses on similar occasions. In 1866, Carlyle was chosen Rector of Edinburgh University, his alma mater. In 1868, Mill was chosen Rector of St. Andrew's University, Glasgow. Mill's address of acceptance was a careful study of the curriculum, a plea for the balance and mutual tolerance of classical and scientific studies. Carlyle ignored the curriculum. Health and sanity were to him more important than book learning; character-building, with emphasis on religious belief and respect for superiors, the true function of the teaching body. Because he felt that British Universities stood for these things, he closed on a note of hope unusual for him: " Wir heissen Euch hoffen."

This address, stripped of the eccentricities of Carlyle's usual style and echoing the deepest-seated of British opinions, was universally understood and approved. Carlyle was recognized as a great man. Poor neglected *Sartor Resartus,* in its new appearance in a shilling edition, sold rapidly to the extent of 20,000 copies. Among the letters of congratulation on the success of his speech which poured in to Carlyle, came one from John Stuart Mill as a courtesy due an old friend. Mrs. Carlyle sent his letter to her husband, who was revisiting his paternal farm in Scotland, ex-

pecting him to " scream at such a frosty nothingness."
He did not scream, he answered, for he had ceased to
care what Mill might do or forbear to do. Mill was
essentially made of sawdust, he and his " great thinking of the Age " and was to be left lying, " with good-
bye and peace to him for evermore." [81]

But the news of Mill's death in 1873 came none the
less as a shock to Carlyle, who was then seventy-eight
years of age, and beginning to be aweary of the sun.
" What! John Mill dead! " he exclaimed to his in-
formant, Charles Eliot Norton.   " Dear me, Dear me,
John Mill! how did he die and where?   And it's so
long since I've seen him, and he was the friendliest of
men to me when I was in need of friends. Dear me,
it's all over now.   I never knew a finer, tenderer, more
sensitive or modest soul among the sons of men.
There never was a more generous creature than he, nor
a more modest. He and I were great friends, and
when I was beginnin' work on my *French Revolution*
there was no man from whom I got such help. . . .
And he was always forward with the most generous
encouragement, and as the book went on he began to
think there never had been such a book written in the
world, — a verra foolish piece o' friendliness, — and
when the first volume was finished nothing would serve
him but that he should have it, and needs must take it
to that woman, Mrs. Taylor, in whom he'd discovered
so much that no one else could find. . . . She was the
daughter of a flourishing London Unitarian tradesman,
and her husband was the son of another, and the two
families made the match. Taylor was a verra respect-

able man, but his wife found him dull; she had dark, black, hard eyes, and an inquisitive nature, and was ponderin' on many questions that worried her, and could get no answers to them, and that Unitarian clergyman that you've heard of, William Fox by name, told her at last that there was a young philosopher of very remarkable quality, whom he thought just the man to deal with her case. And so Mill with great difficulty was brought to see her, and that man, who, up to that time, had never so much as looked at a female creature, not even a cow, in the face, found himself opposite those great dark eyes, which were flashing unutterable things while he was discoursin' the unutterable concernin' all sorts o' high topics." [82]

Carlyle went on to tell how their intimacy grew, how officious friends of Mr. Taylor, misinterpreting it, had brought about a separation of husband and wife, and how he had been friendly with them in spite of scandal, but how a remark of his own concerning what he was convinced was an innocent affection might have been the cause of Mill's sudden break with him. " Dear me! " he said. " And many a night I have laid awake thinkin' what it might be that had come between us, and never could I think o' the least thing, for I'd never said a word nor harboured a thought about that man but of affection and kindliness. And many's the time I've thought o' writin' to him and sayin' ' John Mill, what is it that parts you and me? ' But that's all over now. . . . And after a time, when Taylor died, he married the widow, and then he gave up all society, and refused all invitations, for he knew that hard things

had been said about his wife and about himself, and he
would see no one who was not ready to do her absolute
honor. And they were always said to be very happy
together, till she died, and now he's gone after her
whom he loved."

Mill's *Autobiography*, which came to his hands in
the autumn, brought back the mood of bitter dissent.
No piece of writing could have been more different
from his own emotional and spiritual autobiography
related in such apocalyptic colors in certain chapters of
the *Sartor Resartus*. Its lack of color, its avoidance of
anecdote, its severe concentration on the history of the
development of Mill's intellect and opinions, greatly
disappointed Carlyle, who yearned, as old men will, for
a revival of acts and faces from the dead past of his endeavor. He thus voiced his spleen to his brother John:
" You have lost nothing by missing the autobiography
of Mill. I have never read a more uninteresting book,
nor should I say a sillier, by a man of sense, integrity,
and seriousness of mind. . . . It is wholly the life of a
logic-chopping engine, little more of human in it than
if it had been done by a thing of mechanized iron.
Autobiography of a steam-engine, you may sometimes
read it. As a mournful psychical curiosity, but in no
other point of view, can it interest anybody. I suppose
it will deliver us henceforth from the cock-a-leerie
crow about ' the Great Thinker of his Age.' Welcome, though inconsiderable! The thought of poor
Mill altogether, and of his life and history in this poor
muddy world, gives me real pain and sorrow." [83] The
pæan of triumph over his foe in controversy abruptly

changed to tenderness toward the man he had loved, as a flood of memories flowed in upon him. With pity and regret the lonely old man bade farewell to the closest friend of his young manhood, a friend whom he had never understood.

Chapter II

A CHANGING ENGLAND.

THE lives of Carlyle and Mill are largely typical of the intellectual and spiritual history of the age of transition into our twentieth century world. Their problems, furthermore, remain our problems, and we have not notably improved upon the solutions which they offered for them. A more detailed study of the genesis and development of these solutions therefore promises to reward us with illuminating pictures of one of the most interesting crises in the history of human thought, and with assistance in meeting the problems of our own day. The agencies of transition were industrialism, democracy, and pure science, which effected an economic, a political, and an intellectual revolution. In England the impacts of these forces upon a feudal civilization were most nearly simultaneous. England was also the birthplace of industrialism, whose immediate influence was the most powerful. It is therefore in England that we find the most violent psychological reaction to a transformation at once unforeseen, rapid, and irresistible.

The man of to-day, especially the American, must exert no small effort of the imagination to appreciate the extreme novelty of the material civilization with which he has always been familiar. It was practically

non-existent a century and a half ago; it had its beginning in England about 1760, the year George III
came to the throne. Before that date the returned
spirit of William the Conqueror would have found
Britain much the same as he left it; more cultivation,
more towns, bigger sail boats, but little qualitatively
changed. The Renaissance, the only period in English history of comparable transforming power, had
left the outward aspect of the Isles practically untouched. The discovery of the Americas gave a few
luxuries, but its chief value was spiritual, inciting to
new voyages of the soul. Humanism and the printing
press had inaugurated a mental, not a material revolution. Gunpowder, which had begun to upset the
balance of military and political power, was economically useful only for blasting, and, indirectly, by freeing for agricultural implements much of the iron which
had been used for weapons and armor. George II
enjoyed practically the same comforts as Henry II,
Chaucer as Addison. Their clothing was made in the
same manner, their houses lighted by the same means.

The great qualitative change in material civilization
which began in the middle of the eighteenth century
was a result of the application of machinery to manufacture. Until that time cloth had been spun and
woven by wheel and handloom as Penelope had spun
and woven it, iron mined as by the Athenian slaves,
and forged as by Weland Smith. In farm cottages all
over England could be heard the hum of the spinning
wheels plied in spare moments by wives and daughters
to provide the family clothing or to add to the income

from agriculture. The surplus yarn thus produced just sufficed to keep in moderate activity the hand looms in the weavers' cottages scattered about the countryside or clustered in some village of artisans. In 1770 there were in the Lancashire village of Mellor fifty or sixty farmers, of whom not more than six or seven drew their subsistence entirely from the land. The rest had additional income, according to a contemporary account, " from some branch of trade, such as spinning or weaving woolen, linen, or cotton. The father of a family would earn from eight shillings to half a guinea at his loom, and his son, if he had one, two, or three alongside him, six or eight shillings each per week. But the great sheet anchor of all cottages and small farms was the labor attached to the hand wheel; and when it is considered that it required six or eight hands to prepare and spin yarn sufficient for the consumption of one weaver, this shows clearly the inexhaustible source there was for labor for every person from the age of seven to eighty years (who retained their sight and could move their hands), to earn their bread, say one to three shillings a week, without going to the parish." [1] " The small farmer, spinner, or handloom weaver," wrote Dr. Gaskell retrospectively in 1836, " presented an orderly and respectable appearance. It is true that the amount of labor gone through was but small, — that the quantity of cloth or yarn produced was but limited, — for he worked by the rule of his strength and his convenience. They were, however, sufficient to clothe and feed himself and family decently, and according to their station; to lay by a

penny for an evil day, and to enjoy those amusements
and bodily recreations then in being. . . . The domestic artisan possessed a very limited degree of information; his amusements were exclusively sought in bodily
exercise, quoits, cricket, the dance, the chase, and
numerous seasonal celebrations; he lived in utter
ignorance of printed books, beyond the thumbed Bible
and a few theological tracts; he sought his stimulus in
home-brewed ale; he had for his support animal food
occasionally, but subsisted generally upon farm produce, meal or rye bread, eggs, cheese, milk, butter,
etc., the use of tea being quite unknown, or only just
beginning to make its appearance; he had a sluggish
mind in an active body; his labor was carried on under
his own roof, or, if exchanged at intervals for farming
occupation, this was going on under the eye, and with
the assistance of his family; his children grew up under
his immediate inspection and control; no lengthened
separation taking place till they got married, and became themselves heads of families engaged in pursuits
similar to his own, and in a subordinate capacity.
Lastly, the same generation lived age after age on the
same spot, and under the same thatched roof, which
thus became a sort of heirloom, endeared to its occupier
by a long series of happy memories and home delights
— being in fact loked on as an old and familiar friend;
and in the end they crowded the same narrow tenement
in the quiet and sequestered church-yard." [2]   An exceptionally prosperous weaver might own several
looms, at which he employed apprentices, while,
mounted on a pack horse, for the roads were often too

bad for wheeled traffic, he collected yarn from the farmhouses or carried manufactured goods to a cloth market; but there was as yet very little division of labor or capitalistic control. The same primitive and piece-meal methods of production were employed in potteries, in coal- and iron-mining, in every form of manufacture.

The textile industries first felt the stir of change. The nice equilibrium which had been established between spinning and weaving was upset by a series of inventions of machinery. First Kay's flying shuttle (1733) tripled the output of the weavers, and put the spinners correspondingly behind. Then Hargreaves' spinning jenny (1764), Arkwright's water-frame (1769), and Crompton's "mule" (1779), the latter two propelled by water instead of hand, more than overcame this lead. The loom retaliated by receiving in 1785 the still more powerful aid of steam, which had just been efficiently controlled by Watt and Boulton. In 1791 a Manchester firm ordered 400 of Cartwright's power-looms, and the fate of the handloom weaver was sealed; first in the new cotton industry, then in the linen, and by 1815 even in the conservative woolen manufacture, which had long been the pride of England. Steam replaced hand and water power in every branch and process of manufacture, taking it from cottages and lonely stream sides and concentrating it in factories situated in cities close to coal and iron deposits, and with easy access to the sea. The steam engine also ran mine pumps, and thereby facilitated enormously the production of iron and coal. Abundant coal smelted abundant iron, which steam-driven trip hammers helped convert into more engines and more machinery. In 1831 machinery achieved the logical goal of its development in the perfection of the automatic mule by Richard Roberts. An abundant supply of cheap labor was ready at hand in the domestic manufacturers whose skill the machines replaced, and in the small farmers ruined by a similar and simultaneous revolution in agriculture.

Stimulated by this happy combination of favorable influences, production increased by leaps and bounds. In 1833 a girl at a steam-loom could produce over nine times as much cloth as the best adult handloom weaver.[3] In 1835, one man could spin as much yarn as two hundred and fifty or three hundred men in 1760;[4] a man and a boy print a hundred times as much cotton cloth.[5] The estimated number of power-looms in England and Scotland rose from 2,400 in 1813, to 14,500 in 1820, to over 116,000 in 1835.[6] In 1787 there were forty-one cotton mills in Lancashire; half a century later, there were 157. To meet the demand for raw materials, imports mounted to dizzy heights. From 1815 to 1835, the supply of silk was quadrupled.[7] In 1834 six times as much foreign wool came into the United Kingdom as in 1801.[8] The consumption of raw cotton rose from 54,203,433 pounds in 1801 to 775,469,008 in 1849.[9] Manufactured articles left British ports to invade foreign markets at a correspondingly accelerated speed; the official value of exported cotton goods grew from 7,050,809 in 1801 to 102,416,264 in 1851.[10] The increasing competitive

power of these machine-made products may be gauged
by the fall in the cost of production of a certain piece
of cotton goods from 32s. 3d. in 1795, to 25s. in 1800,
to 5s. 6d. in 1834.[11]

This unprecedented productiveness required outlet
into new markets, and by quicker communications. The
markets were supplied by the Napoleonic Wars, which
discouraged the Continental nations from making immediate use of the new methods of production, and
gave England control of the seas. Interior communications were cheapened by the numerous canals which
followed the Duke of Bridgewater's in 1757, and made
more rapid by toll pikes and macadamized roads suited
to wheeled traffic, that replaced boggy paths fit only
for packhorses, or the ill-defined trails over open country which had spread travelers sometimes " a mile
abreast in pursuit of the best track." [12] Still easier
access to markets at home and abroad was provided in
the second half of the nineteenth century by the steamboat and the locomotive, new kinds of machinery came
to the aid of the factory shuttle. In 1812 the first
British steamboat cut the waters of the Clyde. In
1838 there were three Atlantic crossings and returns
without the aid of sails. With 1840 the Cunard Line
began a regular trans-Atlantic service which has continued uninterruptedly to this day. In 1823 came the
first English railroad. In 1829 George Stephenson's
" Rocket " attained the remarkable speed of twenty-
nine miles an hour. In the late eighteen-thirties began
the great railway boom; though in 1835 there was only
one passenger line in England, in 1845, 2,264 miles [13]

of railroad were in operation, and in 1850, 6,621
miles.[14]   Furthermore, England found herself ideally
equipped by nature for commerce and manufacture.
Her numerous broad and gently flowing rivers serve as
natural canals; no point in her borders is more than
seventy miles from the sea, and good harbors are
abundant; her coal and iron deposits lie close together
in the North and West; her damp climate is entirely
suited for cotton manufacture.   Through extraordinary good fortune she found herself " the world's factory, the world's money market, and the world's
carrier "; [15] and she took advantage of this fortune
with feverish activity.   By 1840 she was fast losing
her mediaeval aspect and becoming very like the England of to-day.

This change in physical aspect was more radical than
one can well imagine.   To Daniel Defoe, who wrote
an account of a *Tour Thro' Great Britain* in 1727, five
thousand inhabitants constituted a considerable city.
His England was agricultural and pastoral, ruled by
country squires.   The statistician Gregory King [16] estimated that three-quarters of the approximately 5,500,-
000 English and Welsh subjects of William and Mary
in 1696 were engaged in farming.   London, the seat
of the court, alone fulfilled our present conception of a
great city.   Its population of a half-million, chiefly
engaged in handicrafts and commerce, was unrivalled;
the populations of the port of Bristol and the woolen
centre Norwich, the second and third cities of the
realm, being only about thirty thousand.   Outside of
London, the entire urban population, including even

small market towns supported by agriculture, was scarcely eight hundred thousand. The countryside of that day did not present the neat appearance which it has now; the rectangular hedge-bordered fields presided over by scattered cottages, interrupted here and there by the carefully gardened parks of great landowners. Gregory King estimated that over a quarter of the area of England and Wales was wild moor, heath, and fen. Hedged fields were largely confined to pastoral counties. In about three-fifths of the English parishes, lying for the most part in a broad strip stretching from the Wash to the coast opposite the Isle of Wight, the arable fields were unfenced, and cultivated by a population collected in villages. These so-called "open field" territories were tilled according to a system transitional from a primitive communism to the private enterprise prevalent to-day.[17] Communal plowing, though long discontinued, had left its mark in the division of the typical "open field" parish into three great fields of some five hundred acres. Two of these fields were planted with cereal crops, usually wheat and barley, and a third left fallow each year, according to a plan of rotation concerted between the Lord of the Manor, who owned about three-quarters of the land, and the peasant proprietors or "yeomen" who owned the rest. The twenty-acre holding of the average yeoman lay in unfenced acre or half-acre strips in the three arable fields and in the meadow land, scattered among similar strips leased by the tenants of the Lord of the Manor. The rest of the parish consisted in undeveloped land called the "common," technically

the property of the Lord, but subject to customary
rights of tillage and fuel, held by the yeomen in proportion to their holdings in landed property, by the
Lord's tenants, and even to a certain extent by squatters. As it was easy to rent land in small patches down
to a half-acre, it was rare that an inhabitant of the
village, even the blacksmith or the domestic manufacturer, was without access to the land.[18]

Within the village, there was no sharp division of
classes; the freeholder and the copy-holder (semi-
independent tenant) had an important voice in the
Jury of the Manor, which decided the agricultural
policy of the parish. In these rural communities,
isolated and self-sufficing, there was seldom any change.
One-fifth of the villagers were generally paupers, forbidden by the Law of Settlement to leave the parish,
and the rest rarely dreamed of doing so. The population remained practically stationary, for new cottages
were rarely built by the Lord for his tenants. In peace
and stillness, the ignorant rustics lived like true children of earth, employing implements and methods of
cultivation handed down unaltered from time immemorial, and classing indifferently as " foreigners " the
French and the inhabitants of the next parish.

Such was England before the advent of machine
industry and scientific agriculture. The latter had
come simultaneously with the first machines. In 1733,
the year of the invention of the spinning jenny, Jethro
Tull had published his *Horse-Hoeing Husbandry*,
which described new methods of sowing and of preparing the soil, that were of particular value in increas-

ing the turnip crop. Viscount Townshend soon demonstrated the advantage of Tull's methods by employing on his Norfolk estate a four-crop rotation of wheat, turnips, barley, and clover, which did away with the necessity of leaving the ground fallow after two successive cereal crops. Turnips also became an important winter food for cattle, which had never been even moderately fat until midsummer. Sheep were gaunt and long-legged, fit only for wool, until about 1745, when Bakewell produced by selective breeding the short-legged and compact "New Leicesters," that proved of great service in supplying the increasing demand for meat in the new factory towns. After 1765 the demand for cereals exceeded the domestic supply; never thereafter has England been completely self-sustaining. The large landholders saw the advantage of scientific methods which promised production adequate to these new markets; but here their interest conflicted with that of the yeomen and small tenants, who preferred the traditional policy of farming for subsistence rather than for profit, or else shrank from the expense involved in the proposed changes.

The landlords found easy means of overriding this opposition in the Manor Courts by application to the Central Government, wherein their class was supreme. By a series of private Acts of Parliament they were empowered to put an end to coöperation with their humble neighbors. About a third of these Acts provided for the extension of cultivation through reclamation of commons or wastes; the rest gave the large landowner the right to collect his piecemeal strips of already arable land into hedge-bordered fields which he could farm independently. These latter Professor Slater has called " Acts for extinguishing village communities," [19] for they made it convenient to lodge the tenant close to the field he tilled. Convinced of the greater efficiency of farming on a large scale, the landlord generally refused to let his land in small amounts. Consequently the small tenant, deprived of his grazing privileges on the common, and (through the rise of the factory system) of his income from spinning, sank to the state of a mere laborer, entirely dependent, like the factory hand, upon money wages. His immediate employer was no longer the Lord of the Manor, but an efficient steward, or an enterprising capitalist farmer who leased large quantities of land for definite periods at a money rent; an arrangement that persists to this day.

The landlords were repaid for the expense of enclosure, reclamation, and selective stock-breeding. Arthur Young, the celebrated advocate of scientific agriculture, reported increases in wheat yield from the traditional seventeen or eighteen to twenty-six bushels per acre, and in fleeces from three and a half to nine pounds. Between 1710 and 1795, the average weight of sheep and cattle sold at Smithfield market rose as follows: beeves from 370 pounds to 800 pounds, calves from 50 to 148 pounds, sheep from 28 to 80 pounds, and lambs from 18 to 50 pounds. [20] " On Townshend's Norfolk estates, light, sandy soil where hitherto ' two rabbits fought for every blade of grass,' a new prosperity set in. One farm for which the rent was

£180, thirty years later brought in £8,000, another rose from £18 to £240." [21]   As a result of improved methods, starvation wages for the farm laborer, the Napoleonic Wars, and after the Peace, from 1815 to 1846, high tariff on foreign grain, rents almost everywhere rose rapidly for over a century. But what brought prosperity to the landlords and to the large farmers who became the new middle class of the agricultural districts, ruined the old middle class of peasant proprietors. The yeomen were generally unable to produce the written titles to their lands which the Enclosure Commissioners were authorized to demand. [22] And even if they were so lucky as to establish their titles, their financial inability to meet the obligation to enclose or drain usually forced them to sell out at low prices. By 1790 the yeoman class, which had formed the most important part of Cromwell's armies, had become almost extinct; and with it went the squatters and many small squires unable to meet the competition of large-scale farming. The 4,503 Acts which between 1761 and 1844 enclosed 5,740,226 acres left little trace of the common lands, the wastes, the open fields and the small farms of Old England. [23]

The small squires and the yeomen possessed of sufficient capital often became tenant farmers in the system of large-scale cultivation. But most of the dispossessed agriculturists flocked to the factories; those fortunately retaining some money as employers, the rest as operatives. The quick expansion of machine industries, with their especial demand for child labor, an administration of poor-relief which put a premium on large families and bastardy, and a lowered standard of living in both town and country, combined to stimulate an unprecedented. growth of population. The first national census in 1801 gave England and Wales a population of 8,892,356; in the next fifty years their population more than doubled, reaching 17,927,609 in 1851.[24] Equally remarkable was the change in the national occupation from agriculture to manufactures and commerce. The proportion of the population engaged in agriculture dwindled from about 75% in 1698 to 35.2% in 1811, and to 25.93% in 1841, when it was only about half that engaged in commerce and manufacturing.[25] Between 1811 and 1821, while the entire population of England and Wales increased 18.06% (the greatest proportional increase ever known in British history), Wiltshire, a typical agricultural county, increased but 14%, and Lancashire, the seat of the cotton industry, 27%.[26] The inhabitants of Lancashire were estimated in 1750 as 297,400; the 1831 census numbered them as 1,336,854.[27] The West Riding of Yorkshire, where woolen manufacture was concentrating, had a 73% growth between 1801 and 1831.[28] The advantage of locating factories in centers of rail and water communication close to iron and coal mines rapidly shifted population to the North-West. The center of population in Defoe's day was the Central Midlands. Outside of London fertile and quiet Wiltshire was most thickly settled; much of Lancashire and the West Riding was wild moorland, the haunt of highwaymen, poachers, and smugglers. By 1800, the change in the national occupation had rearranged popu-

lation along a belt following the west coast from Bristol
to Glasgow.　To-day the heart of England is west of
the Wash and north of the Severn.　The Kingdom
faces the Irish Channel and the Isle of Man.

This redistributed population congregated in large
cities, another peculiarly modern phenomenon.　Defoe's "great towns" [29] soon lost their importance.
Although London doubled its size in the first half of
the nineteenth century, it did not hold its own relatively to the entire urban population; for between 1770
and 1831 Liverpool probably quintupled, and Glasgow
grew seven-fold.　Manchester, center of the cotton
industry, may be taken as typical of the new manufacturing cities.　Magnificently situated with respect
to mines and communication, it grew like an American
boom town.　Its population in 1774 was estimated as
41,032; the 1801 census gave it 95,000 inhabitants, the
1831 census, 270,961. [30]　At the very beginning of the
nineteenth century, it had assumed most of the characteristics of a modern industrial center.　In the oldest
part of the city, great chimneys made darker the
gloomy Northern sky.　In the canal was incessant shipping; to the banks of the Irwell, " the hardest worked
river in the universe," [31] crowded lines of tall, severe
buildings, from which came a ceaseless rattle of bobbins.
About the factories clustered workers' slums, including
a special quarter for Irish cheap labor, colonized from
across the Channel.　In distant suburbs lay the clean
and pretentious villas of the " cotton kings."　Three
decades later, puffing and screaming locomotives disturbed rural solitudes in bringing to Manchester food,

coal, and manufacturing supplies. A new and Gargan-
tuan England had arisen in the North-West, with its
activity, roar, and gloom.

These changes in the occupation and geographical
distribution of the British population brought a corresponding change in the political organization of the
nation that was all the more striking because it was
long delayed. At the close of the Napoleonic Wars,
the state of the franchise and of representation in the
House of Commons was most anomalous. Almost
five-sixths of the English members were elected from
boroughs designated by the Crown, but no new borough
had been created since the time of Charles Second.
Great industrial centers like Manchester, Birmingham,
Leeds, and Sheffield elected no members; but decayed
towns like Old Sarum, then entirely without inhabitants, Gatton, with only six houses, and Dunwich, almost
completely sunk beneath the encroaching North Sea,
each returned two members. In boroughs which had
kept up with the growth of the country, eligibility to
vote was often confined to the inhabitants within cor-
porate limits fixed centuries before; Westminster and
the old City of London were boroughs, but the inhabitants of the rich residential section that had grown
up north of Oxford Street and about Regent's Park
could vote only in the county of Middlesex. Boroughs
were so confined to the formerly populous South of
England that in 1815 ten Southern counties, with a
population of about 2,900,000, returned 237 members,
while the remaining thirty English counties, with about
8,350,000 population, returned only 252.[32] Thus it

came about that most of the boroughs were dominated
by great landowners, usually members of the aristocracy. In 1817 it was estimated that 197 members
returned from English boroughs were the arbitrary
choice of local patrons, and that 238 other seats were
subject to their predominating influence.[33]   Gatton had
only one elector, Sir Mark Wood, who owned all six
houses in the village; the Duke of Bedford owned
every house in Camelford, which had nine electors.[34]
Although the electors returning the twenty-four representatives of Wales were honest and independent, the
ninety Irish and the forty-five Scotch representatives
were even more dominated by the nobility than the
English; in fact, the Scotch nobles shamelessly sold
the representation of the ancient kingdom for titles and
places to whatever Government, Whig or Tory, happened to be in office.   The franchise in the forty English counties was held only by those who had land with
an annual rent of £50 or more.   There was no uniform qualification for the English borough franchise.
In fifty-three boroughs the franchise was extremely
wide, belonging in most cases to those who paid local
taxes, frequently to those not paupers, and in one case
to all adult male inhabitants without exception.   In
thirty-seven it depended upon the ownership of land
formerly held upon feudal tenure; in thirty-six it
belonged to members of the municipal corporation;
and in seventy-seven it was the monopoly of freemen
as defined by ancient municipal constitutions.   This
extremely complex and anachronistic system sometimes gave the suffrage to the poor to the exclusion of

the rich; notably in the freeman boroughs of Liverpool and the City of London, and in the manufacturing
town of Preston. But in the usual small borough
a humble elector had no other choice than that involved in selling his vote to the local patron or to
the wealthy merchant or manufacturer who tried to
outbid him. The elections, in which the voters, unpro-
tected by the secret ballot, were swayed by bribery,
threats, violence, or intoxication, had become a national
scandal.

In 1785 the Prime Minister, William Pitt the
Younger, had made a cautious proposal of a more
equable representation. But the outbreak of the
French Revolution soon thereafter inspired in him, as
in most of his generation, " a panic dread of change."
He used the bogey of Sanscullotism to defeat decisively
a motion introduced in 1793 by Charles Grey, and
supported by a group of young Whigs, which merely
suggested a Parliamentary investigation into bribery
and the monopoly of boroughs by patrons. Thereafter, until the close of the wars with France, to advocate reform of Parliament was to court the charge of
treason. When peace came, agitation for reform was
resumed, not by the demoralized Whigs, but by shop-
keepers and laborers, who hoped thereby to secure a
government more sympathetic with their economic distress. In 1819 a peaceful assemblage of about sixty
thousand men and women in St. Peter's Field, near
Manchester, for the purpose of electing a " Legisla-
torial Attorney " who would press the demand for
reform, was dispersed by mounted troops, who killed

eleven and wounded several hundred.[35]   The Tory
Government, who regarded any attempt to change the
Constitution as treasonous, responded to such demonstrations by the repressive Six Acts, which made popular assemblies in unincorporated cities like Manchester
and Birmingham impossible.   The blood and iron
policy of the " Savage Parliament " of 1819 failed,
however, in its object, for it roused many upper- and
middle-class Whigs to the jeopardy of the traditional
rights of the subject.   The divorce proceedings against
Queen Caroline in the following year, another evidence
of the despotic attitude of the Crown and its Ministers,
cemented the union of Whig moderates with working-
class and middle-class Radicals.   In 1821 their united
influence was sufficient to procure the disfranchisement
of the corrupt borough of Grampound.   This broke
the charm of the Constitutional fetish, but serious
changes did not become imminent until 1830, when
successful rebellions of the French and the Belgians
against their autocratic kings set the British people an
encouraging example.   Then the impetus toward drastic change began in Birmingham, the center of the iron
industry, where an important " Political Union " of
industrial workers and their employers, who had become increasingly aware that the capitalist class was the
rival of the landowning aristocracy in wealth and influence, became allied with the Benthamite Radicals of
London in agitation for manhood suffrage.

Before the end of that year, the Whigs came into
power after having been out of office, save for one
year, since 1783, and introduced a measure for whole-

sale Parliamentary reform according to a few simple
principles. On July 5, 1831, the brilliant young
orator Macaulay presented the Whig case in a vivid
contrast of the new industrial civilization with the old
governmental machinery which pretended to control
it: " Our fields are cultivated with a skill unknown
elsewhere, with a skill that has extorted rich harvests
from moors and morasses. Our houses are filled with
conveniences which the kings of former times might
have envied. Our bridges, our canals, our roads, our
modes of communication, fill every stranger with wonder. Nowhere are manufactures carried to such perfection. Nowhere is so vast a mass of mechanical
power collected. Nowhere does man exercise such a
dominion over matter. These are the works of the
nation. Compare them with the works of the rulers
of the nation. . . . Can there be a stronger contrast
than that which exists between the beauty, the com-
pleteness, the speed, the precision with which every
process is performed in our factories, and the awkwardness, the rudeness, the slowness, the uncertainty of
the apparatus by which offences are punished and rights
vindicated? . . . Surely we see the barbarism of the
thirteenth century and the highest civilization of
the nineteenth century side by side; and we see that the
barbarism belongs to the government and the civilization to the people." [36] Opposed tooth and nail by the
Duke of Wellington and the House of Lords, Reform
was not carried until May, 1832, when a threat of
armed rebellion from the Political Unions which had
sprung up in numerous cities in imitation of that at

Birmingham, and of a run on the banks from the London Radicals, made the Tories surrender at discretion.

The famous Reform Act transferred the center of political power from the landed aristocracy to the commercial and manufacturing middle class. It abolished or reduced the representation of eighty-nine of the insignificant boroughs, gave representation to sixty-three important cities and towns, chiefly in the manufacturing regions, and created sixty-two additional seats for the more populous counties. It made uniform the borough franchise, conferring it upon occupants of houses renting at ten pounds annually, and extended the county franchise to tenants paying fifty pounds annual rent, thus making political rights depend on monied capital rather than land. Not only was the agricultural interest weakened, but also the workingmen, many of whom had at least the empty honor of the vote under the old Constitution, and some of whom exercised real power in large democratic boroughs like Westminster, Southwark, and Preston, were almost wholly disfranchised.

The triumph of machinery and cash in the political and economic realms excited sober middle-class Englishmen to dithyrambs of praise and thanksgiving. Porter introduced his statistical account of *The Progress of the Nation* (1836) with a proud reference to " this country and the present generation, by which have been made the greatest advances in civilization that can be found recorded in the annals of mankind." [37] Dr. Ure, in expounding *The Philosophy of Manufactures* (1835), extolled " the benignant power of steam,"

under whose " auspices, and in obedience to Arkwright's polity, magnificent edifices, surpassing far in
number, value, usefulness, and ingenuity of construction, the boasted monuments of Asiatic, Egyptian, and
Roman despotism, have, within the short period of
fifty years, risen up in this Kingdom, to show to what
extent capital, industry, and science may augment the
resources of the state, while they meliorate the condition of its citizens.   Such is the factory system, re-
plete with prodigies in mechanics and political economy,
which promises in its future growth to become the great
minister of civilization to the terraqueous globe, enabling this country, as its heart, to diffuse along with
its commerce the life-blood of science and religion to
myriads of people still lying ' in the region and shadow
of death.' " [38]   This happy union of imperialism and
piety which was to be the peculiar note of British
foreign policy was echoed by Baines in his *History of
the Cotton Manufacture* (1835): " The civilization of
England flies abroad on the wings of its commerce.
Philanthropy could not desire a more powerful agent
for diffusing light and liberty through the world." [39]

CHAPTER III

THE new science, which had indirectly brought about so many social changes by changing man's material environment, had also a direct influence on social ideals and mechanisms which amounted to an intellectual revolution. This influence had been cumulative ever since Copernicus, in the sixteenth century, had wounded man's pride by demonstrating that he did not dwell at the immovable center of the universe, circled about by the sacred spheres of heaven itself. In the following century the astounding discoveries of Harvey, Galileo, Descartes, Leibnitz and Newton had conversely restored his self-esteem by enormously increasing the scope and promise of his knowledge and power. He predicted the courses of the stars, and rapidly made the powers of nature his servants. The science that had removed heaven to an infinite distance seemed about to build a new heaven upon earth. It was therefore not surprising that the consciousness of their enlightenment concerning the external world caused men to reflect upon their ignorance of the functioning of their own bodies and of the social organizations into which they had been born. The utility, the fertility, and the seeming infallibilty of the results of mathematical, astronomical, and

physical investigation put sharply in relief the incon-
clusiveness of political, ethical, and religious controversies. " I was especially delighted with the mathematics," wrote Descartes in the introductory chapter of
his *Discourse on Method*, " on account of the certitude
and evidence of their reasonings; but I had not as yet
a precise knowledge of their true use; and thinking
that they but contributed to the advancement of the
mechanical arts, I was astonished that foundations, so
solid and strong, should have had no loftier super-
structure reared on them. On the other hand, I compared the disquisitions of the ancient moralists to very
towering and magnificent palaces with no better foundation than sand and mud. . . . Of philosophy I will
say nothing, except that . . . I saw that it had been
cultivated for many ages by the most distinguished
men, and that yet there is not a single matter in its
sphere which is not still in dispute." [1] Many other
advanced thinkers in the seventeenth and eighteenth
centuries followed Descartes' example in applying the
scientific methods to the study of human institutions
with the enthusiasm of a new hope. The founders of
the new science of man, Descartes, Hobbes, Spinoza,
Leibnitz, employed exclusively the methods of mathematics, the mother of the sciences. The inductive or experimental method of the newer sciences, the Novum
Organum or New Instrument eloquently championed
by Lord Bacon, had slowly to win its way to recognition. Certain book titles are significant: *Novum
Organum* (Bacon); *Discours de la méthode* (Descartes); *Ethica ordine geometrica demonstrata* (Spi-

noza); *A Treatise of Human Nature, being an attempt
to Introduce the Experimental Method of Reasoning
into Moral Subjects* (Hume). Its eventual use by
Locke and Hume greatly quickened the development
of the social sciences and inspired Voltaire, Diderot,
D'Alembert, Condorcet, Helvétius, and other French
philosophers to daringly concrete criticism of the established social organization. This criticism did much
to precipitate the French Revolution, which enthroned
the Goddess of Reason, and popularized the notion of
the self-directed progress of humanity which has since
dominated the thinking of Western civilization. England, although the cradle of social science, felt its
practical application a generation later than France.

English thinkers were generally unmolested in the
mere expression of heterodox opinions, and were not
goaded into carrying them into action by interference
and persecution from a despotic church and king.
Their heritage of the Magna Charta, the Habeas
Corpus Act, and the Principles of 1688 gave them
confidence in reform through slow constitutional
change. Furthermore, Locke's doctrine that the
human brain was a blank tablet at birth, and gained its
content only through the impact of stimuli from without, encouraged them to believe that they could completely change human opinions through the medium
of education. They enjoyed the patronage of the
more liberal-minded of the aristocracy, and expected
them to institute a scientific reorganization of the
national life. The outbreak of revolution in France
blasted these hopes. The English aristocracy, fright-

ened at the overthrow of what was traditional,
orderly, and sacred, and accustomed to high-handed-
ness through the conduct of the subsequent fifteen
years' war against innovating France, became the determined foe of reform. Many of the partisans of
scientific reorganization, aghast at the seemingly inevitable consequences of their opinions exemplified in
events in Paris, or perhaps intimidated by the power of
the reactionary forces, recanted. Those who remained
steadfast in their faith and purpose were obliged to
break their aristocratic connections, and appeal to the
unprivileged populace for support of a radical reform
of the Constitution, of which the Reform Bill of 1832
was only a partial realization.

The chief of these persistent reformers was Jeremy
Bentham. The son of a respectable and wealthy London lawyer, Bentham had every prospect of a brilliant
legal career when he enrolled at Lincoln's Inn in 1763,
at the early age of fifteen. But his severely logical
mind and kindly heart alike revolted from what was
then the law of the land. The Common Law of England, which Bentham's teacher Blackstone was then
extolling as " the perfection of reason," consisted of an
unorganized mass of ancient feudal customs arbitrarily
twisted by judges' interpretations to some semblance of
applicability to changing social conditions. It was
therefore impossible for a layman to understand the
law, and judicial decisions were in effect *ex post facto*.
When social changes made some offense alarmingly
prevalent, it was only too often that some judge decided to stamp it out by making it a felony " without

benefit of clergy " (a technical distinction surviving from the struggles of Thomas à Becket with Henry II), and consequently punishable by death. So frequently had such rash precedents been made, that Blackstone enumerated 160 felonies thus punishable.[2] Pocket-picking for a shilling or more, forgery, coining sixpence, and robbing hens from an enclosed yard were dealt with as severely as treason or matricide. The Acts of Parliament which supplemented this unwritten law had been enacted to meet special emergencies, and were therefore unsystematic and incomprehensive. There was no one act forbidding the reception of stolen goods. Separate acts provided against receiving stolen gold or pewter pans, but there was no provision against receiving horses or banknotes. The technicality and the ferocity of the penal law combined to make it largely inoperative; the guilty notoriously escaped through some loophole in the law, or through the unwillingness of witnesses to testify, or juries to convict, when conviction involved such disproportionate penalties. Although only about one-fifth of these convicted finally suffered death, ninety-six were nevertheless hanged in a space of ten months at the Old Bailey Gaol alone. The state of the Civil law was almost as bad. The operation of conveying title to land so bristled with technicalities as to call forth from Blackstone a eulogy of the mental powers of the lawyers who performed it. The legal profession had not failed to take advantage of conditions which made its services indispensable to extort enormous fees from bewildered clients. " The elaborate processes which had to be gone through before a hearing could be obtained; the distance of the courts from the litigants; the bandying of cases from court to court; the chicaneries about giving notice; the frequent nullification of all that had been done on account of some technical flaw; the unintelligible jargon of Latin and Law French which veiled the proceedings from the public; the elaborate mysteries of 'special pleading,' the conflict of jurisdictions, and the manufacture of new pleas and new technical rules; the 'entanglement of jurisdictions'; (and especially) the distinction between law and equity, which made confusion doubly confounded " ; [3] all made for fat fees and the frequent ruin of the litigants. The central government aggravated these evils by levying taxes on all law suits, which even in the most trifling suits amounted to " no less than £24 on the plaintiff's side alone."

Bentham refused to become an accomplice in these iniquities. He promptly " put to death " several cases which his father had " at nurse " for him, advising the plaintiff in an equity suit for about £50 that the suit " had better be put an end to, and the money which would be wasted in the contest saved." [4] After a long struggle with his devoted and ambitious father, he succeeded (1773) in abandoning what had promised to be a distinguished career at the bar, in order that he might retire to his study and construct " the law as it ought to be." [5] Regarding the law " as no peculiar mystery, but a simple piece of practical business, wherein means were to be adapted to ends, as in any of the other arts of life," [6] he attempted to replace

" judge-made law " with a comprehensive and orderly
code deduced from a few simple ethical principles and
written in the plainest English, so as to be comprehensible to any one who could read. He believed,
being then twenty-five years of age, that such a code
would instantly recommend itself to the good sense of
the Bar and Parliament, and be soon adopted as the
law of the land.

Secured in philosophic detachment by bachelorhood,
a substantial independent income, and the patronage of
Lord Shelburne, he was not hurried in the execution
of the encyclopædic undertaking. It was not until 1789,
when he was forty-one years old, that its ground plan
appeared under the title, *An Introduction to the Principles of Morals and Legislation.* Execution of its
details proceeded even more slowly, for Bentham's
head was buzzing with a multitude of minor projects
for benefiting the lot of mankind, including reforms of
the currency and banking legislation, a treatise on
Political Economy, a Frigidarium, or device for preserving food, and a Panopticon or model prison. In
1802 his principles of civil and penal law were published in Switzerland in a French translation and digest
by his pupil Dumont, entitled *Traités de législation,*
but they did not begin to appear in their original English until after 1815. Bentham had meanwhile devoted his best energies to an attempt to induce the
British government to make a trial of the Panopticon,
which applied practically his theories of criminal law.
Bentham's attention had been drawn to the shocking
state of British prisons by the exposures of the philan-

thropist John Howard, who, after a personal investigation of most of the prisons in Europe, pronounced those in England the worst of all, breeding places of disease and vice through their utter lack of sanitation, and their herding of minor offenders, women, and children with the most hardened criminals. Bentham proposed to better these conditions by allowing the keepers gratuities for the continued health of their charges, and by treating punishment as a means of reform, not of revenge. His model prison received its name from a device whereby the keeper could see from a single point what was going on in every cell, and thus exercise the reforming influence of " an invisible omniscience." In 1794 Parliament voted the trial of this project, directing Bentham to purchase a site for the prison; but it neglected to appropriate any money to reimburse him. Bentham eagerly invested the greater part of his own fortune in the necessary terrain, only to find the expected appropriation vexatiously withheld. It became increasingly clear, especially after Bentham's indiscreet publication in 1803 of *The Constitution Defended*, an exposure of the high-handed acts of authorities in the penal colonies, colonies for which the Panopticon was to be a substitute, that the government had little or no intention of keeping its promise. But it was not until 1811 that the plan received its deathblow at the hands of George III, who refused to authorize the transfer of land which Parliament had finally voted. " Never was anyone worse used than Bentham," wrote the Tory philanthropist Wilberforce; " I have seen the tears run down the cheeks of that strong-minded man through vexation at the pressing importunity of creditors and the insolence of office underlings, when, day after day he was begging at the Treasury for what was, indeed, a mere matter of right. How indignant did I often feel when I saw him thus treated by men infinitely his inferiors. I could have extinguished them." [7] Bentham gave vent to his anger by composing a private *History of the War between Jeremy Bentham and George Third, By one of the Belligerents.* This heartbreaking failure completed his disillusionment concerning the willingness of the ruling class to welcome everything clearly to the benefit of the people. He had found " Judge and Co." opposed to every measure of legal reform which he had suggested, and, in attempting to go over their heads, he had found Judge and Co. solidly intrenched behind the King and the greater part of the aristocracy, whether Whig or Tory. " I was . . . a great reformist," Bentham remarked in a later review of his career, " but never suspected that the people in power were against reform. I supposed that they only wanted to know what was good in order to embrace it." [8] He now thought that reforms were impossible without a change in the Constitution, but both education and temperament made him shrink from political agitation. Brought up in a Tory family, accustomed to expect reforms to come from an enlightened despot, and contemptuous of what he styled the " anarchic fallacies " of the French Revolutionists, he hesitated to take their logical recourse of arousing the populace against their rulers. He was furthermore a shy scholar, well past the prime of life, with no fitness

for practical politics. Nevertheless, to resign himself to things as they were was to confess his life a
failure. He had sacrificed a brilliant career at the
bar, in order to find himself at sixty almost a bankrupt,
and generally laughed at as a " projector," a crank who
pestered sensible people with visionary schemes. On
the Continent, thanks to Dumont, he was taken seriously; but in his own country, for whose benefits he
had intended his labors, he was wholly without honor.

From this predicament he was rescued by the unexpected acquisition of a young, enthusiastic, and emi-
nently able disciple, who was destined to make the
name of Bentham respected or feared throughout every
class of British society. In 1809 a handsome Scot of
some five and thirty years of age made a pilgrimage to
Queen's Square, London, to pay his respects to the
man who, he believed, had made the " greatest progress
. . . of all men, in all ages, who made the philosophy
of law their study." [9] James Mill, for this was the
visitor's name, inflamed Bentham's resentment against
the government by bringing to his attention a flagrant
example of the close alliance between the cabinet and
Judge and Co. As a journalist associated with the
Whig Opposition, Mill was in grave danger of prosecution for libel under conditions which made his conviction almost inevitable. In its determination to
silence criticism of its conduct of the war with France,
the government, aided by compliant judges, was boldly
overriding the constitutional rights of its opponents.
The law left the decision as to the fact of libel entirely
in the hands of a jury of the accused's peers; but Lord

Ellenborough, the Chief Justice, was making use of all
the influence of his office and his eloquence in openly
instructing juries to convict. And to make assurance
doubly sure, the prosecution kept in readiness special
juries " packed " with volunteers whose loyalty could
be relied upon.[a] Mill's representations resulted in
Bentham's preparing in 1809 a treatise entitled *The
Art of Packing as applied to Special Juries; Particularly in Cases of Libel Law,* which so violently assailed
the governmental policy that Sir Samuel Romilly, his
co-worker in legal reforms, was moved by fears for his
safety to persuade him to withhold it from publication.

But Romilly's cautious counsels did not long counteract Mill's influence. By 1818 Bentham had been so
completely won over to Mill's opinions that he published a pre-election proclamation urging the defeat
of Romilly for Parliament, and the return of his
Radical opponent, Byron's friend John Cam Hobhouse.
Mill had not found it difficult to persuade Bentham, in
the resentful mood in which the Panopticon failure had
thrown him, that the source of all abuses of power was
the mode by which the legislators were chosen. He
had also easily convinced him that the advocacy of an
extension of suffrage did not necessarily involve subscription to the " anarchistic fallacy " of the rights of
man, but was a moral obligation springing from the
necessity of making the interests of the rulers coincide
with the interests of the ruled. As early as 1809 Bentham was at work on a *Catechism of Parliamentary*

---

[a] For considerations possibly modifying this view see Halévy,
A History of the English People in 1815, p. 141.

Reform. Mill did not rest satisfied in having acquired Bentham's pen for the Reform movement; he also brought him into contact with the active politicians identified with it. It so happened that the center of Reform agitation was the very Borough of Westminster in which Bentham and Mill resided. The terms of the borough franchise were unusually liberal. All were voters who rated to the poor rates for separate houses, about ten thousand out of a total population of one hundred and fifty-three thousand. Small tradesmen were in a majority among these voters, but until 1807 they had docilely elected to Parliament one Whig and one Tory representative of the resident great families. But in that year, on the vacating of one of these seats by the death of the great Whig leader, Charles Fox, William Cobbett, a sensational popular journalist, and Francis Place, a Charing Cross tailor, succeeded in arousing the class consciousness of the shop-keeping majority and electing Sir Francis Burdett, who advocated an extension of the suffrage to all throughout the kingdom who paid direct taxes. Bentham had been quite oblivious to the electioneering and the fifteen days' animated polling which had then taken place in his neighborhood, but in 1810 he was moved to resentment at Burdett's imprisonment on the charge of having supported a certain Jones in his criticism of Parliament for going into secret session during the airing of the Walcheren expedition scandal. In 1809 he had corresponded with Cobbett, who was then serving a sentence for libel; in 1811 he met Major Cartwright, who had been agitating the question of universal suf-

frage since 1776; [10] in 1812 Mill introduced him to
Place. Under the influence of these new associates,
Bentham went with astonishing rapidity to the opposite
pole from his inherited Toryism, and became an advocate of the bestowal of the suffrage on all adults who
could read. When the close of the Napoleonic wars
turned the nation's attention back to domestic affairs,
and bad harvests and the burden of the war debt made
the masses acutely conscious of the special privileges of
the aristocracy, Bentham became prominently identified
with the growing forces of discontent. In 1818 his
Plan of Parliamentary Reform, prefaced by a long
disquisition on the *Necessity of Radical, and the Inadequacy of Moderate, Parliamentary Reform*, which had
already appeared in pamphlet form the preceding year,
was brought directly to the lower classes through the
columns of a Republican newspaper, *The Black Dwarf*.
In the same year Bentham furnished the content for
twenty-six resolutions, including demands for universal
suffrage, the creation of electoral districts equal in
population, and annual elections to Parliament, presented before the House of Commons by Sir Francis
Burdett. The stern repressive measures taken by the
government after the widespread popular demonstrations in the North during the following year gave
Bentham a bad quarter of an hour. " Cartwright,
Burdett, are under prosecution," he wrote in 1820,
" Hobhouse has already endured, manfully endured,
his punishment.[a] As to *me*, who, I hear it said con-

[a] For the publication of an anonymous pamphlet attacking Parliament, Hobhouse was imprisoned in Newgate from December 14,

tinually, am more criminal than any of them . . . it belongs not to me to say what hitherto has saved me. But my hour cannot be far distant. Already for what *I* have written others have been punished. Not in the hermitage from which I write, but in some prison shall I die." [11] Yet in the midst of these alarms the indomitable old man began to construct a voluminous "Constitutional Code," "having for its object," he remarked quaintly, "the bettering of this wicked world, by covering it over with Republics." [12]

This Constitutional Code was the final item of Bentham's program of scientific social reform, which had spread from his original domain, the law, into the broad fields of ethics, education, logic, economics, and politics. As elaborated by James Mill, and by other collaborators whom Mill brought to Bentham's aid, it represented the most unflinching and comprehensive attempt to apply the methods and categories of the new natural science to the field of mental phenomena that had ever been made. The storehouse of science from which Bentham and his associates drew their tools was, however, very much less stocked than it is to-day. At the beginning of the nineteenth century, physics and chemistry, then just differentiating themselves from the blanket classification of "natural philosophy," and biology, botany, and geology, likewise just emerging from "natural history," were too little developed to

1819, to February 29, 1820. Burdett was fined £2000 and sentenced to three months' imprisonment for criticizing the attitude of the ministry toward the Peterloo affair. For seditious utterances concerning this same affair Cartwright paid a fine of £100.

exert great influence on their thought. Bentham had studied chemistry under Fordyce,[a] but his social philosophy shows no trace of the conception of a compound totally unlike its ingredients. " The community is a fictitious body, composed of the individual persons who are considered as constituting as it were its members," he wrote in his *Introduction to Principles of Morals and Legislation*. " The interest of the community then, is what? — the sum of the interests of the several members who compose it." [13] He was an enthusiastic botanist, and his mania for classifying and codifying may owe something to the Linnean Classification which then constituted that science, but he was untouched by the evolutionary speculations of Erasmus Darwin. James Mill was a close friend of the chemist Thomas Thomson,[b] and knew something of botany, but he performed no experiments, and retained a predominantly deductive method of thought. Of physiological psychology he made a thorough study at second hand in the writings of the physicians Hartley, Cabanis, and Erasmus Darwin, but that science was still in its infancy, and borrowed its technic from mechanics. The only sciences which had developed sufficiently to seem to offer sure guidance in the exploration of the

[a] George Fordyce (1736–1802) F. R. S. confirmed in an indirect manner the Priestly-Lavoisier demolition of the phlogiston theory. Cf. Transactions of the Royal Society, Vol. LXXXII.

[b] Thomas Thomson (1773–1852), Professor of Chemistry at the University of Glasgow, was the first to give Dalton's rehabilitation of the atomic theory to the world (1807). He also made an interesting attempt to demonstrate that the atomic weights of all the elements were multiples of that of hydrogen.

largely uncharted field of human nature were the mathematics, and the mathematical sciences of mechanics and astronomy. These, therefore, Bentham and his co-workers took for guides.

From Galileo and Newton they accepted certain fundamental assumptions. They believed that their senses gave them a substantially correct and full report of the nature of external reality; in technical language, they were empiricists. Bentham went so far as to style all concepts which were not represented directly by sense objects, benevolence, for instance, as "fictitious entities." They believed that all the relations existing between entities in the outer world were intelligible to the human mind; technically, they were rationalists. They furthermore believed that these relations were generally of the simplest kind, and might all be ultimately reduced to a few formulae, or even a single formula. All differences of quality, for instance, were reducible to differences of quantity, which could be measured mathematically. Finally, they chose to define cause as invariable succession, and were thus able to banish from their consideration all metaphysical questions of supernatural source or agency. Astronomy demonstrated that the material universe was a vast machine which ran of itself; Bentham and his group were ready to concur in the inference of Harvey and the microscopists that the microcosm of man was also a marvelous mechanism.

To these five assumptions, empiricism, rationalism, simplicity of relations, deductibility of quality, and the non-metaphysical nature of causation, they added two

others which they believed firmly established by the
previous investigations of Locke, Hume, Helvetius,
and others as applicable to the special field of the
science of man. The first of these was that no ideas,
whether of God, morality, or space and time, were
innate: the brain of the new-born babe was a blank
tablet, ready to receive all its inscriptions from sense
impressions from the outer world. The whole complex system of ideas and feelings which formed the
content of the mature brain were the product of certain
mechanical laws of association, perhaps of the single
law of contiguity, as James Mill was inclined to think;
the mind added nothing to the " gifts " of sense.
Since all differences in mental content were thus trace-
able to differences of environment, it was an important
corollary that all men were born substantially equal in
mental capacity. The second assumption peculiar to
the science of human nature was that pleasure and pain
were the mainsprings of the man-mechanism. " Nature has placed mankind under the governance of two
sovereign masters, *pain and pleasure,*" began Bentham's
*Introduction to the Principles of Morals and Legis-
lation.* " It is for them alone to point out what we
ought to do, as well as to determine what we shall do.
On the one hand the standard of right and wrong, on
the other the chain of causes and effects, are fastened
to their throne." [14] From the absolute character of
their domination, it followed that man was necessarily
egoistic. Bentham's associates were practical men of
the world, who prided themselves on their disillusionment. They did not deny that there were sometimes

cases of genuine altruism, although Bentham rivaled Rochefoucauld in revealing the springs of selfishness behind most seeming-generous acts, but they unhesitatingly declared that the average man, the representative of the majority, almost invariably obeyed what Bentham styled the " self-preference principle." From another point of view, the average man, who must thus ruthlessly push aside all obstacles to his pleasures, was the helpless tool of those pleasures and their corresponding pains. " There is, or rather ought to be, a *logic*, of the will, as well as of the *understanding*," [15] wrote Bentham; threats of pain and promises of pleasure could be as well calculated to control acts, as could arguments to compel assent to propositions.

The average man, whose psychology was explained by these two simple principles, was the key to Bentham's interpretation of society. Society was nothing more than the average man writ large. If the mental furniture and moral character of the human unit were at the mercy of his environment, it followed that, by controlling education, and contriving penal laws, a legislator could make of an agglomeration of these units whatsoever he would. Such a condition was unlimited in its possibilities of good and of evil. Bentham saw only the possibilities of good, for he happened to be a philanthropist, bent on using the gifts of science to improve the state of his fellows. He seized upon the doctrine of the infinite malleability of human nature as a revelation of the means whereby the criminal laws could be made reformative, not merely retributive. In the terms in which he conceived it, his problem was paradoxical. Having to deal with a race of egoists, he must effect an artificial identification of their individual selfish interests with the interest of the race as a whole by attaching to each anti-social act a penalty sufficient to overbalance the pleasure of its commission. Since all punishment was painful, and therefore an evil, it must furthermore be employed only in order to prevent a greater evil. Bentham therefore was obliged to find a means whereby he could make a nice calculation of the amounts of pain which would just counterbalance given amounts of pleasure. For this purpose he invented his celebrated " moral arithmetic," which permitted the comparison of the pain resultant upon an act with the concomitant pleasure in regard to six criteria: intensity, duration, certainty, propinquity, fecundity, and the number of persons affected. The motives which led to anti-social acts were left out of consideration in the determination of appropriate penalties for their commission; not only were motives hard to discover, but the same motive often led to results which were good, bad or indifferent. Bentham's general science of the law concerned itself solely with consequences, save for its provision that judges have discretionary, power to consider motives when they were indubitable. Thus Bentham believed he had constructed a workable " mill for grinding rogues into honest men."

The test of the value of a law or an action by computing the quotient of the quantity of pleasure or of pain it had caused or would cause multiplied by the number of persons it affected, or, in other words, by ascertaining whether it conduced, according to his famous phrase, to "the greatest happiness of the greatest number," Bentham extended just as confidently to civil and constitutional law and to private ethics. From this greatest happiness formula he deduced in minute details the best possible form of government and code of laws, and recommended their use, with the qualification of changes to fit the climate and the race, to England, Russia, France, and the South American republics alike. To oblige the rulers to promote the happiness of the majority of their subjects, he provided that they be chosen annually by the vote of all adult males, whom the device of the secret ballot would protect from intimidation. Among existing constitutions that of the United States of America was his favorite, but he wished to go beyond it in the direction of pure democracy by eliminating checks and balances. Neither in his political nor in his legislative theory did he consider the possibility that the happiness of a cultured and intelligent aristocracy might be preferable to that of a mediocre majority, for the scientific method did not permit him to recognize qualitative differences in pleasures. " Pushpin is as good as poetry if it gives the same pleasure " was the foundation of the political and ethical maxim, " everyone to count as one and no more than one."

The greatest happiness principle was also made the standard of private ethics; but in this domain, which Bentham restricted to those acts upon which the influence of legislation was largely or wholly inefficacious, the method of artificial identification of interests was by definition inapplicable. Here Bentham set out to prove that honesty was the best policy, that an enlightened egoist should perceive that regard for the happiness of others would, in the long run, be more conducive to his own interests than the direct path of selfishness. Indeed, he advocated the voluntary practice of benevolent acts when those involved no self-sacrifice; for by it there would be " so much added to the capital of good will, and this addition has cost nothing." [16] His system left no room for the conscience, and reduced moral choice to a calculus of the probable painful and pleasurable results of a contemplated action. It was directly opposed to the Christian doctrine of abnegation, which Bentham considered a mere aristocratic device to keep the masses in subjection. The democratic virtue of prudence was lauded as the chief of the virtues. " It is no more fitting," wrote Bentham, " to make disinterestedness a virtue, than to make spending a merit in political economy." [17] " The ethics of the Benthamites," M. Halévy has summarized finely, " is their economic psychology put in the imperative mood." [18] Human relations were to be kept up by a barter of good offices.

The political economy which so greatly influenced the Benthamic ethics was more closely identified with James Mill than with Bentham. It was Mill who perceived that the urgent problems of post-war reconstruction, the incidence of the heavy taxation demanded by the huge national debt, the protection of British agriculture from foreign competition, and the care of the unemployed, whose numbers had been swelled alarm-

ingly by the disbanding of the armies and the loss of
the monopoly of European manufacture, called for a
scientific study of the distribution of wealth among the
different social classes. It was Mill who, realizing
what political capital could be made of the results of
such a study, persuaded his friend David Ricardo to
undertake it.

Ricardo was not a pioneer in economic science. He
inherited from his most important predecessors, Adam
Smith and Thomas Malthus, a vast collection of economic facts, and some very suggestive theories. He
consequently made little effort to seek out new material, and limited himself to criticizing previous
theories and arranging them and their corollaries in a
logically consistent system. His *Principles of Political
Economy* (1817) were presented in the form of a
deduction from two theories of Malthus, the theory
of rent, and the theory of population.

Malthus' *Essay on the Principle of Population* had
startled the world on its publication in 1798. Its
famous thesis that population, which increases in geometrical progression, always tends to exceed the means
of subsistence, which can only increase in arithmetical
progression, was so irrefragible in its premises, and so
plausibly confirmed by the high food prices and manifest rapidity of population increase in England during
the period in which it was written, as to challenge dis-
proof. Yet its acceptance involved conclusions in the
highest degree pessimistic and unpalatable. Malthus'
answer to what was superficially a serious objection
gave his theory a particularly sinister character. If the

rate of unrestrained human increase could legitimately be assumed to equal or exceed that then taking place in the United States of America, whose population was doubling every twenty-five years, why did European nations grow so slowly? Fundamentally, Malthus replied, because they had comparatively so little arable land to support them. Whole nations were not already on the verge of starvation only because various secondary checks to multiplication were especially operative in highly civilized communities. Great cities increased the death rate by pestilential slums, luxury, and vice; the new manufactures, by hard labor and disregard of sanitation. The institution of marriage prevented promiscuous breeding. The glaringly unequal distribution of wealth brought the lower classes to an artificial starvation limit while there was still sufficient food for everybody and arable land left fallow for deer parks. And with the advance of civilization war had not appreciably relinquished its toll of human life. The so-called major evils therefore existed in order to save a fortunate few from the greatest of evils. Most benevolence was short-sighted; feeding paupers increased their numbers, and reduced their standard of living. Equality was incompatible with progress.

Malthus drew an inexorably frank picture of the appalling condition of the exploited lower classes, only to remark that it was better that their sacrifice present to their superiors leisure to enjoy the good things of life, than that equality should plunge all into a common misery. But, like Bentham, Malthus combined with a tough-minded recognition of harsh realities a benevolent interest in the happiness of mankind.[a] He therefore urged the repeal of the existing poor laws, whose indiscriminate doles encouraged reckless propagation and discouraged the self-supporting laborer, and the substitution of a workhouse system which would guarantee food to all those willing to work. " It may," he wrote, " appear to the interest of the rulers, and the rich of the state, to force population, and thereby lower the price of labor, and consequently the expense of fleets and armies, and the cost of manufactures for foreign sale; but every attempt of the kind should be carefully watched, and strenuously resisted by the friends of the poor, particularly when it comes under the deceitful garb of benevolence, and is likely, on that account, to be cheerfully and cordially received by the common people." [19] In the second edition of the *Essay* (1803), which supported his position by an imposing array of statistics gathered in his travels on the Continent, Malthus urged upon the poor the moral duty of delaying marriage until they were certain of being able to support a family. Being an orthodox clergyman, he condemned artificial birth control. God was not to blame for creating the harsh conditions of human existence, he insisted, for did not the Bible prescribe chastity?

Malthus held stanchly to his theory in the face of a storm of protests from the supporters of the contrary Biblical injunction to increase and multiply, and to the

[a] The title of his second edition is significant: *An Essay on the Principle of Population; or, A view of its past and present effect on human happiness.*

controversy over a proposed import duty on agricultural product which raged in 1815, contributed an important corollary drawn from it, the theory of differential rent. Increasing population, Malthus reasoned,
caused increasing demand for the products of the soil.
Consequently, since the law of diminishing returns
operated to prevent improved methods of tilling the
land already in use from meeting this demand indefinitely, new and generally worse lands thereby tended
to be forced into cultivation. The market price of
foodstuffs rose with the increasing difficulty of their
production, and was always above the cost of their
production on the worst land forced into use. The
owners of the better lands, which yielded foodstuffs
more easily, consequently benefited by excess profits of
varying proportions. Their excess of the profits from
the better lands over those from the worst Malthus
called "differential rent." The son of a country
gentleman, he saw no injustice in the pocketing of this
rent gained without expenditure of labor; for had not
the original occupiers of the better lands won them by
a struggle? He furthermore believed that his discovery of differential rent lent an argument to the
supporters of a tariff wall against the products of
fertile foreign lands, whose inflow might drive the
worse English lands out of cultivation and seriously
reduce the profits from the better lands.

Malthus' *Inquiry into the Nature and Progress of
Rent* (1815) drew an immediate and significant reply
from David Ricardo. Ricardo welcomed the theory
of rent as an important truth, but emphatically dis-

sented from the conclusions which Malthus had drawn from it. A wealthy Jewish banker, with no interested or sentimental attachment to the land, he was free to point out the evil consequences of a food tariff, which would force more of the worst land into cultivation, and thereby contribute to the farther gratuitous enrichment of the owners of the better lands at the expense of the consumer. From Malthus' own premises, he drew the conclusion that " the interest of the landlord is necessarily opposed to the interest of every other class in the community." [20] Ricardo's logic carried little weight with Parliament, which, before the year was out, enacted the famous Corn Laws, which prohibited the importation of foreign grain before the domestic price had reached the famine height of 80 shillings per quarter.[a]

To secure the repeal of these Corn Laws was one of the most important immediate aims of Ricardo's comprehensive *Principles of Political Economy and Taxation*, which appeared two years after their enactment. In order to appreciate the political import of Ricardo's reasoning, one must have in mind the peculiar status of the British agricultural lands. No revolution had, as in France, broken up the great feudal estates; almost all the surface of the British Isles belonged to the aristocracy. The class-conscious landlord seldom assumed personal direction of his patrimony, but usually leased

[a] Corn from the British Colonies was admitted when the domestic price was 57 shillings or more per quarter. Corn in these instances must be taken to mean wheat; but the restrictions on the importation of the other grains were proportional.

his land, whether for agricultural or mining purposes, or for factory sites, to a capitalist who paid him cash rent, and hired the necessary laborers. Ricardo therefore assumed a rough division of his countrymen into landlords, capitalists, and laborers, and used Malthus' theories as clues to the discovery of the distribution of the national production between these classes. He thus concluded that, with the growth of population, the landlord's rent tended to increase at the expense of the capitalists' profits, while the laborers' wages remained practically stationary at or near the lowest level which would permit them to subsist and to rear children. Taxes meanwhile fell most heavily upon the capitalist's incomes and on the necessities of life consumed by the laborers.

This analysis of the existing economic order completed the strictly scientific portion of Ricardo's work, but Ricardo went on to pronounce moral judgment. That the lion's share of worldly goods should go to those who had done little or nothing to produce it, and that taxes should bear most heavily upon those who worked most and received least, seemed to him palpably unjust. In his opinion, the capitalist was most deserving, for he supplied the brains of nearly every economic enterprise. The laborer was also deserving, for he contributed physical force. But the landlord could seldom claim more than the merit of getting himself well born. Ricardo therefore proposed legislation which would stimulate production by making remuneration more nearly proportionate to labor. He would shift the tax burden to the shoulders of the rich, and repeal all restrictions on trade. Free trade, he argued, would bring a host of benefits; it would reduce rent, increase the profits of the capitalist, insure the employment of labor where it would produce most, and give the manufacturer cheaper raw materials and the laborer cheaper food.

Free trade had been previously advocated by arguments of another sort, that had been advanced in Adam Smith's *Wealth of Nations*, which had convinced Ricardo as early as 1799. Smith had written in 1776, when the industrial revolution was hardly on its way, in behalf of business enterprises hampered by guild monopolies and unintelligent government regulation. The medieval trade guilds had been invaluable as protectors of nascent industry in the midst of a military society, but, as close corporations are wont, they had aged into blind conservatism. They did not adopt new methods of manufacture or trade, and attempted to prevent outsiders from experimenting. Each town guild was furthermore independent, and usually hostile to the immigration of guild members from other towns. It was only after a sharp contest that Glasgow University was able to thwart the effort of the local guild of mathematical instrument makers to prevent James Watt, the inventor of the steam engine, from making such instruments in that city. The church-inspired laws against usury were still on the statute books, and made it extremely difficult to borrow money for ventures in any wise hazardous. The government, misled by a theory of national prosperity based upon a crude analogy drawn from the fact that a man receiving money for his goods always seemed to gain by the exchange, was endeavoring to secure a cash balance of trade in England's favor by placing a high import duty on all goods except raw materials for manufacture, by encouraging foreign at the expense of domestic trade, and by fixing the quality and price of manufactured goods, and even the wages of labor, so as to insure victory in foreign markets. To disprove this theory Smith brought forward a mass of economic facts, patiently collected during ten years, to support his contention that exchange benefited both parties concerned, and that consumable goods were more valuable than money. He showed by striking examples the benefits of the division of labor, which ran counter to the guild rules, and urged from analogy the advantages of a territorial division of labor, which would disregard national boundaries, and permit each variety of goods to be produced at the portion of the earth's surface most suited to its production. He therefore repudiated the entire system of artificial encouragement of manufactures, and advocated the limitation of the functions of the central government to the maintenance of justice, the national defense, and public institutions which private philanthropy would not supply. In his disgust with stupid interferences with economic enterprise he went to the opposite extreme, and declared that "all systems, either of preference or restraint, being . . . completely taken away, the obvious and simple system of natural liberty establishes itself of its own accord. Every man, as long as he does not violate the laws of justice, (should be) left perfectly free to pursue his own interest in his own way, and to bring both his industry and capital into competition with those of any other man or order of men." [21] The conflict of the interests of wholly selfish men, intent on their own profit, tended to a result which they did not foresee; the provision of society with the best and cheapest product. Production adjusted itself to the needs of society according to the law of supply and demand. Demand created supply; if supply exceeded demand, something was withdrawn, labor, land, or capital, and the balance was readjusted.

Smith's theories tallied so completely with the experience of the leaders of the rapidly expanding British commerce and industry, and appealed so well to their vanity, that they had strong support from the moment of their publication. Nor was this support limited to those thus immediately concerned. Jeremy Bentham made a bold application of Smith's point of view in his *Defense of Usury* (1787), which was an important contribution to the quick downfall of the usury laws. The young Premier, William Pitt, was an early convert, and made the first step toward international free trade by arranging a reciprocity treaty with France in 1786. In 1813, with the repeal of the Statute of Apprentices (enacted in 1563), which had given to Justices of the Peace, who were usually country gentlemen, the power to fix wages, the last restriction on freedom of contract between employer and laborer was removed. Foreign trade alone felt restraint; domestic trade and manufactures had been entirely wrested from governmental control. In post-war England the régime of absolutely free competition, usually known by its French name, *laissez-faire*, was practically supreme.

Ricardo accepted this competitive system; but without Smith's optimism. To him it was not the best of all conceivable systems; it was the inevitable result of the situation of a greedy and multiplying race upon a planet limited in physical resources. The law of rent disclosed, furthermore, a fatal disharmony among the three great economic classes. Even if all tariff walls could be broken down, the law of diminishing returns would still limit the gains of the capitalists, and incite them to attempts to pare down the laborers' wages. The capitalists might protect themselves by throwing taxes back upon the landlords; the laborers might secure higher wages by limiting their numbers; but these palliations of the effect of inevitable natural laws could be obtained only at the cost of struggle and privation. "The niggardliness of nature and the greed of man " [22] made economics a melancholy science.

Ricardian economics put much content into the abstract and somewhat vague "greatest happiness principle." It gave what purported to be scientific proof that the aristocracy, because of its monopolies and its special privileges of tariffs and taxes, was inimical to the material well-being of the rest of the population. It placed especial blame for the misery of the lower classes on the pauperizing Poor Laws, and the Churches, both Established and Dissenting, which proscribed birth control, and by their mutual jealousies stood in the way of national education. It showed that government was necessary for the protection of property, but revealed the danger of government by a single class. *Laissez-faire* translated into political terms was *la carrière ouverte aux talens*. Thus reinforced by economic arguments, the Benthamic popular party became, in the third decade of the century, a force to be reckoned with in national politics.

The leaders of the movement for the reorganization of society upon the bases of scientific knowledge and personal merit were a strongly contrasted pair. Bentham greatly resembled the popular caricature of the philosopher. He was one of those grown-up boys who never achieve dignity, " a comical old fellow," [23] as he well described himself. Bashful and ill at ease in society, he buried himself in his " hermitage " to divide his day between writing and conversing with his few intimates while " trotting " about his garden, pecking with his cane at objects near his path. He was methodical in his habits, rose and retired early, dressed with Quakerish simplicity, ate sparingly, and was practically a vegetarian and teetotaler. But the champion of the greatest happiness principle was no ascetic; he enjoyed jokes and hilarity, music, and country scenery. At meals he ate his fruit first in order not to lose a whit of its delicate flavor. His conversation and writings curiously combined the cynicism of the man of the world with a naïve confidence in the influence of reason on the acts and opinions of mankind. Even in 1812 he tried to persuade that hide-bound Tory, Lord Sidmouth, to reform the penal code, and in 1828 scolded the " Iron Duke " of Wellington for having fought a duel. His early writings were lucid and vivacious; he hit off Doctor Samuel Johnson as " the pompous vamper of commonplace morality — of phrases often trite without being true." [24] But in his later works he almost lost the art of communication through being enamored with a theory of precision which substituted arithmetical signs for verbs and built sentences of a maze of parentheses. His face, which strikingly resembled Benjamin Franklin's, wore an habitual smile of benevolence, but over trifles he was often childishly petty. His affections, which were broad enough to embrace the whole sentient creation, and inspire a plea for kindness to animals, were not deep. He was a bachelor, and had had only one, and that a slight, attack of the grand passion; in his " Table of the Springs of Action " he made no mention of conscience, honor, or duty. But it was from this very limitation that his influence sprang; no man acquainted with the subtleties and complexities of the human heart could have so confidently employed the simple scientific categories known to his time for the description of society.

James Mill's character was complementary to Bentham's; therein lay the peculiar strength of their alliance. Bentham, secure in his independent income, could afford to shun society; Mill, whose only capital was his talents, had been obliged to attract the attention of his superiors by address and display of talent. His education and his start in journalism he had owed to a patron, Sir John Stuart, who had sent the talented village boy to Edinburgh University, and, on his fail-

ure as a Presbyterian minister, brought him to London.[a]
Self-confidence and a pleasing manner had won him
almost immediate employment by the famous *Anti-
Jacobin Review*, and the friendship of the rising politician Henry Broughan, who gave him an entree into
the *Edinburgh Review* in 1807. His unfortunate mis-
calculation of the time necessary for the writing of a
History of British India, which, begun in 1806, took
twelve instead of four years to complete, only served
to sharpen his faculties by interposing another obstacle
to his getting on. Handsome, well-dressed, tactful,
and dignified, Mill moved easily in any society. The
charm of his conversation was notable, even in an age
of great talkers. His voice was clear and resonant,
his expression animated. He had but little command
of imagery, but the brilliance and cogency of his thinking, and the ripeness of his wisdom, fascinated his
hearers. Although not a very original thinker, he had
an unusual faculty for assimilating and organizing the
ideas of others. At a time when high-class journalism
was just becoming a power, few equaled him in the
ability to present new and difficult ideas in the clear
and simple form suited to the comprehension of an
enlarging reading public. A stern sense of civic duty
which he had caught from Plato drove him into active
politics, although he could ill spare the time, and
although his social and economic status was endangered
by the unpopularity of his opinions. His determination to impose his exacting standards of conduct upon
others exposed the less pleasing side of his character.

[a] On coming to take his seat in Parliament in 1802.

He unduly exalted public at the expense of private virtue, the intellect and the will at the expense of the feelings. He was blind to the beauties of nature and art, and unappreciative of the value of leisurely contemplation. "For passionate emotions of all sorts, and for everything which has been said or written in exaltation of them, he expressed the greatest contempt." [25] "He thought human life a poor thing at best, after the freshness of youth and of unsatisfied curiosity had gone by. . . . He would sometimes say, that if life were made what it might be, by good government and good education, it would be worth having: but he never spoke with anything like enthusiasm even of that possibility." [26] Yet his private expressions of contempt for those who were indifferent to what he considered "good government and good education," [27] that is, for the vast majority of the human race, were intense enough. Regarding with severity the shortcomings of even the most able men, he did not disguise his disdain of his wife's intellectual powers, and subjected his children to an education of more than Spartan rigor. Nevertheless, in spite of his loyalty to ideas and ideals rather than to men, his devotion to those men whom he considered valuable exponents of the right opinions, to a Bentham, a Ricardo, was conspicuous. Nothing could exceed the patience with which he humored Bentham's moods of boyish petulance and pique.

Bentham quickly perceived the value of such a lieutenant. He insisted upon so close an intimacy that Mill was his constant summer guest in the country from 1809 on, and from 1814 to 1830 was his neighbor in

Queen's Square itself, where Bentham paid half his
rent during the period of his worst financial difficulties.
Mill amply repaid these favors by rapidly carrying
Bentham's doctrines from the study to the market
place. He pushed many of Bentham's accumulated
writings into print, personally editing the *Table of the
Springs of Action* (1815–17), got others translated
from Dumont, and inspired his political writings.
During the decade 1808–18, in spite of the handicaps of his *History of India*, and the maintenance and
education of a large family, Mill himself wrote much
in the *Edinburgh Review*, and in the *Philanthropist*,
a Quaker publication, in favor of the liberty of the
press and law reform. Through friendship with its
proprietor, John Black, he enlisted an influential London newspaper, the *Morning Chronicle*, in the cause of
law reform. A joint campaign for the establishment
of non-sectarian public schools especially equipped for
teaching the sciences brought Mill and Bentham into
collision with the ecclesiastical monopolists of education. Bentham, a confirmed Voltairian, attacked these
new enemies in a series of boldly skeptical works:
Church of Englandism: its Catechism Examined
(1817–18), the anonymous *Examination of the Influence of Natural Religion on the Temporal Happiness
of Mankind* (1822), and *Not Paul but Jesus* (1823).
Thenceforth organized religion, which they privately
denominated " Jug " (Juggernaut),[28] became an object
of equal detestation with " Judge and Co." Ricardo,
on the floor of the House of Commons, and James
Mill's oldest son, John, in the *Morning Chronicle* and

the *Westminster Review* defended the bookseller John Carlile, who was sentenced to prison for publishing atheistical tracts.

After the publication of his *History of British India* in 1818 had freed his hands and secured him well-remunerated employment with the India Company, James Mill greatly quickened the popularization of Bentham's ideas. He took full advantage of the strategic opportunity afforded by employment in the preparation of the supplement to the fifth edition of the *Encyclopaedia Britannica* to give wide publicity to his advanced opinions. To this supplement he contributed articles on the vital topics of education, government, liberty of the press, and law of nations, some gaining an even wider circulation by being reprinted in pamphlet form. He followed up the success of Ricardo's writings by inspiring J. R. McCulloch to trumpet the claims of political economy in his journal, *The Scotsman*, which began to appear in 1819. Mill presented Ricardo's ideas in a simpler and more readable form in his own *Elements of Political Economy* (1821), which he intended for use as a textbook, and saw with pleasure the appearance of another treatise on the new science by McCulloch in 1825.[a]

By the early eighteen twenties, Mill had presented Bentham with the " school " which the aged philosopher had hoped for since 1790. This school consisted of two groups: an elder, contemporary with Mill, which included Ricardo, Hume, Place, McCulloch,

---

[a] Malthus also had published *Principles of Political Economy* in 1820, but these contained many heterodoxies.

Tooke the economist, and (to some extent) Brougham;
and a younger, dominated by Mill's personality,
which included John Grote and his business partner
Prescott, Eyton Tooke, George Graham, William
Ellis, John Roebuck and Mill's precocious son, John.
To these Bentham's personal influence added John
Bowring, curiously enough a Dissenting clergyman and
author of the hymn, *In the Cross of Christ I Glory*.

With the exception of Bowring, these adherents to
Bentham's ideas took their color from Mill rather than
Bentham. Their ideal was the dispassionate scientific
observer who could also be a citizen and a man of
affairs. In their desire to purify the reason by freeing
it from disturbing influences, they distrusted the emotions, were indifferent or hostile to poetry and religion.
They were devotees of logic, even to the verge of
intellectual pharisaism. Ridiculing the cloud castles
of metaphysics, they riveted their gaze on hard facts,
on the immediate, the practicable, the useful. Economics and politics were their major interests. The
younger group called itself Utilitarian, thus emphasizing the practical aspect of Bentham's greatest happiness principle.

But generalizations concerning the Benthamic school
must contain a large amount of paradox. These cold
rationalists were zealous for the welfare of humanity;
these cautious skeptics were advocates of universal
peace; these contemners of religion had fanatic faith
in the power of reason to perfect mankind. Individualists, they devoted themselves to the service of
society; hedonistic moralists, they led lives of notable

austerity; skilled detectors of inconsistencies, they
failed to notice the conflict of the principle of the artificial identification of interests, which underlay their
theory of legislation, with the principle of the natural
identification of interests, which reigned in their economics. "The way to be comfortable," wrote Bentham, "is to make others comfortable; the way to
make others comfortable is to appear to love them; the
way to appear to love them is to love them in
reality." [29] James Mill, in the opinion of his son, had
"scarcely any belief in pleasure." [30] Eyton Tooke
committed suicide at twenty-six; Bowring was a clergyman. James Mill and Francis Place, zealous logicians
and Malthusians, were fathers of nine and seventeen
children, respectively.

In 1824 the Benthamites proclaimed themselves a
third national political party. Financed by Bentham,
the *Westminster Review* entered the comparatively
new field of dignified political journalism as an opponent of the *Edinburgh* and *Quarterly* reviews, which
had been founded in 1802 and 1809 respectively. It
called itself the champion of the common people, but
recently made politically conscious by means of cheap
printing, and boldly avowed its general adhesion to
"French principles," and to the natural sciences, upon
which the Church was already beginning to look with
suspicion. In its very first number appeared James
Mill's celebrated exposé of the *Edinburgh's* policy of
"see-saw", or writing on both sides of every question
so as to bid for popular support while maintaining its
original aristocratic backing. With this pussyfooting

the *Westminster* proudly contrasted its straightforward advocacy of radical reform of the constitution. Indeed, it attacked the aristocracy chiefly on moral grounds. The six hundred aristocratic families, together with their dependents of the Church, the Bench, the Army and Navy, set, the *Westminster* asserted, a bad example for their inferiors; for they were supported parasitically by the labor of others, through land rents, tax exemption, and tariffs. Their monopoly of politics, education, and commissions in the army and navy discouraged ambition among the unprivileged and thus deprived the nation of the benefit of the exercise of its best talents. Against land monopoly and tax immunity the Benthamites used the language of the modern socialistic opponent of vested interests, but they were friends of the institution of private property itself. Bentham had taken pains to write *Radicalism not Dangerous* (1820) to separate his cause from that of the communists. Encouraged by the diffusion of property which had already taken place since the heyday of feudalism, he was confident that more liberal land laws, limitation of inheritance, and absolutely free competition would put property in the reach of all who were industrious. If once the menace of a few great fortunes were removed, he believed that the poor, provided with the suffrage and given access to impartial courts of justice, could protect themselves against oppression by the rich. Although thus an essentially middle class movement, Benthamite Radicalism made a strong bid for the support of the working classes, whose hardships it laid at the door of the landed interests, who made food dear, imposed taxes on the necessities of life, and stifled protests by violence, as in the late memorable " Manchester Massacre." It pointed out to the poor the road to self-help and self-respect through Poor Law reform, national education, and universal suffrage. So convinced were Place, Hume, and Ricardo, through the results of the Westminster elections, of the political support of the lower classes, that they secured in 1824 the repeal of the Combination Acts, which had outlawed labor unions. Not only did Mill believe that the poor would choose the rich, who had the leisure to study the governmental problems, as their representatives, but he even relied on their ability to decide rightly upon public questions, if once uncensored information could be given access to them, through the abrogation of the Six Acts of Castlereagh.[a]   Mill believed that " when various conclusions are, with their evidence, presented with equal care and with equal skill, there is a moral certainty, though some few may be misguided, that the greater number will judge right, and that the greatest force of evidence, wherever it is, will produce the greatest impression." [31] The Benthamites were sincere in their declaration that there was no conflict between capital and labor which was not forced upon them both by the landlord's tariff-

[a] One of these Acts (1819), most of which were never enforced, made it practically impossible to call a public meeting without the consent of a governmental agent; another made banishment the penalty for a second conviction of blasphemous or seditious libel; and another subjected the popular newspapers, which had previously sold as low as twopence, to the newspaper tax of 4d. a sheet.

supported rent, or which the laborers did not ignorantly bring upon themselves through inability to limit their numbers to correspond to the demand for labor. They hinted at the coming of coöperative industry, after the era of universal education and equality of opportunity would have come.

The pens of the young Utilitarians, who did the bulk of the writing, gave the *Review* an unusual liveliness and effrontery. Political economy, the reader was informed, should be read like Euclid; the greatest happiness principle solved political problems " with arithmetical precision." [32] These new truths were being rejected by those who had " inherited the ignorance of their ancestors along with their estates," [33] and by clever, but malevolent rulers, who perceived that " war . . . is self-defense against reform," [34] and that in political economy the people had found " the art of preventing (themselves) from being robbed by (their) betters." [35] To the tender-minded objectors to Benthamic ethics it was replied: " The ascendency of personal interest has been stigmatized by superficial men as a degrading doctrine. What we are most concerned in knowing is, not how far it is degrading, but how far is it true? " [36] " Mr. More is a poet," wrote Bingham in the first number, " and is therefore not a reasoner." [37] " Encourage poetry," was the ironic answer to protests against such remarks, " because poetry is fiction, and fiction is what is not true. Besides, the things most dangerous to you, are said in prose. Make a great outcry about elegant literature; for distress is an inelegant thing, and elegant literature

will never touch it." [38]   " Wars," went another re-
sounding generalization, " have always been hoaxes on
one side, and generally upon two." [39]

In spite of such reckless sowing of the wind, the
Review attained an importance quite disproportionate
to the number and reputation of its contributors.   For
it proposed a program of reconstruction greatly superior
in reasonableness and comprehensiveness to any which
the nation was then being offered.   Such works as Bentham's *Book of Fallacies, Rationale of Evidence,* and
Constitutional Code, James Mill's *Analysis of the
Phenomena of the Human Mind,* which proposed to
make the functioning of the mind " as plain as the road
from Charing Cross to St. Paul's," [40] and the economic
treatises of Mill, McCulloch, and Nassau Senior, gave
material for reviews even more influential, substantial,
and penetrating than James Mill's sagacious analyses
of the political situation.   Furthermore, " it was a time
. . . of rapidly rising Liberalism. . . .   The renewed
oppression of the continent by the old reigning families,
the countenance apparently given by the English Government to the conspiracy against liberty called the
Holy Alliance, and the enormous weight of the
national debt and taxation occasioned by so long and
costly a war, rendered the government and parliament
very unpopular.   Radicalism, under the leadership of
the Burdetts and the Cobbetts, had assumed a character
and importance which seriously, alarmed the Administration; and their alarm had scarcely been temporarily
assuaged by the celebrated Six Acts, when the trial of
Queen Caroline roused a still wider and deeper feeling

of hatred.   Though the outward signs of this hatred
passed away with its exciting cause, there arose on all
sides a spirit which had never shown itself before,
of opposition to abuses in detail." [41]   Supported by this
new spirit, Radicalism made advances on all sides.

Although Ricardo died in 1823, Ricardian political
economy, popularized by Mill, McCulloch, and Nassau
Senior, and supported by a petition of the London
Merchants for Free Trade drawn up in 1820, began to
make an impression on the cabinet itself.   Huskisson
withdrew practically all import duties except those on
agricultural products.   In 1825 a parliamentary committee reported favorably upon a proposition to reform
the Court of Chancery, whose scandalous delays had
been an especial object of Bentham's attacks, and the
Home Secretary, Robert Peel, had tentatively begun
law reform.   Of sixty legal abuses denounced by
Brougham in a brilliant speech in 1828, only five
remained a decade later.   The founding of the Benthamite University of London (1828) broke the
Church monopoly of higher education.   Nor could the
older universities escape the contagion of Radical ideas.
In 1825 Nassau Senior was called to the newly established chair of Political Economy at Oxford.   In
Cambridge, where Paley, whose ethical system was
very like Bentham's, had long been the official moralist,
the younger generation of Benthamites were making
the Union a hotbed of what was coming to be known as
Philosophic Radicalism.   There Carlyle's pupil,
Charles Bulwer, was made a convert, and Macaulay
and Maurice received a strong impress from the doc-

trines they combated.   The same sort of influence was brought to bear on the younger graduates of the Universities through *The London Debating Society,* founded by John Stuart Mill and his fellow Utilitarians in 1825.   Radicals were also prominently identified with attempts to broaden the educational field; with *The Society for the Diffusion of Useful Knowledge* (established 1827), and the Mechanics' Institute (established 1823), which inaugurated the strictly scientific curriculum.   As Brougham said in the Commons, the schoolmaster was abroad in the land, inciting the people to criticize the traditional and the established.

Although the *Westminster* never had a circulation larger than 5000, as compared with the 13,000 attained by both the *Edinburgh* and the *Quarterly,* its body of readers was greater than these figures would indicate, for many of them were so poor as to be obliged to buy it in clubs.   Its chief influence, nevertheless, was upon the fairly-well-off middle class population, whose aspirations it encouraged.   Factory owners, shopkeepers, wholesale merchants, and bankers translated the gospel of utility into " efficiency," and the creed of progress into " push."   Empiricism encouraged their insistence on " hard facts."   The economic man, selfishly intent on material gain, was the object of their emulation.   For the most part Dissenters, they favored the limitation of the power of the Established Church. Self-made men, jealous of aristocratic special privilege, they were the backbone of the movement for Parliamentary Reform.

The ever-increasing power of this industrial and

commercial class obliged the Whigs to cease their see-sawing, and declare for a moderate reform of the Constitution before the movement for Radical reform had got beyond control. From Bentham's *Book of Fallacies*, which he reviewed for the *Edinburgh* in 1825, Sydney Smith took the material for his famous *Noodle's Oration*, ridiculing the prejudices of the hide-bound Tory. Espousing a cause at last become respectable, and reaping where the Radicals had sown, the Whigs made Parliamentary reform a reality in 1832.

At the passage of the first Reform Bill, the prestige of Philosophic Radicalism was at its height. Conservative England was in a panic as institutions and beliefs which had been unquestioned for centuries were suddenly being called upon to give reasons for their existence. Reasons were slow in forthcoming, for they had long been thought unnecessary. Such as were given in the stupefaction of the moment were weak and untenable enough. Men of a logical turn were quick to see this, and radicalism spread rapidly among the intellectuals. The even more unexpected and bewildering industrial revolution was Radicalism's powerful ally, disturbing as it did the balance of political power, making the externals of feudal civilization rapidly obsolete, and creating for the English population a new environment which fostered a psychology receptive of materialistic and mechanical theories of human nature. " Utilitarianism," wrote the apprehensive Carlyle in 1831, " spreads like a dog-madness: till the whole World-kennel will be rabid." [42]

Chapter IV

ANTI-BENTHAM.

BUT the success of Utilitarianism was deceptive. It had seized strategic positions in its sudden onslaught, but it had not permeated the great mass of the nation; neither the aristocracy, nor the professions, nor the working classes.

Loss of political monopoly through the Reform Act had by no means made the aristocracy impotent. It retained ownership of by far the greater part of the land; it officered the Army and Navy, held the important livings in the Established Church, controlled education and the administration of justice; it was the arbiter of taste and the glass of fashion. The upper house of Parliament, impressive with the pomp and dignity of peer and bishop, represented the aristocratic interest exclusively. The Crown looked to the great families as bulwarks against levellers and republicans. The protected shipping and lumber trades and the West Indian planters sought their aid against the common enemy, the Free-Trader. The legal and medical professions were largely supported by their patronage. The freedom with which the British aristocracy renewed itself with fresh blood saved it from the isolation that had been fatal to the French nobility. The wealthy banker, merchant, and even manufacturer turned Tory in the hope of buying a title and founding a family. Sir Robert Peel, Tory leader in the Commons, was the son of a cotton manufacturer and the grandson of a yeoman. Furthermore, it was difficult for Englishmen of any station of life above the poverty level not to show deference to the wealth and respectability of the great Whig and Tory families, and not to aspire secretly to admission to the charmed circle of their society. " Our middle class," wrote John Mill in 1829, " has but one object in life: to ape its superiors; " [1] an observation abundantly confirmed by Thackeray's novels. Radical opinions kept a young man from " getting on." They were " bad form," an offense against respectability, which Bulwer, in his *England and the English*, pointed out as the cardinal British virtue four years before Victoria ascended the throne.[a] It was thus not altogether idly that many die-hard Tories dreamed of a counter-revolution that would wipe the Reform Act from the statute books.

That the possibility of such a reaction was recognized by the Whig leaders who passed the Reform Bill and by the Radicals in the first Reformed Parliament, is manifest in their attitude toward the revolt of agricultural laborers in the Southern counties which began in 1830. In the South no factory smoke on the horizon reminded the landlord that the power of his class was being challenged; and the enclosure movement, in ruining the yeomen, had left him without an agricultural competitor. He received high rents from his

[a] For an amusing illustrative anecdote see Bulwer's *England and the English*, Book II, ch. I, pp. 82–83.

tenant farmers, whom he ensured a monopoly market for produce through his maintenance of the Corn Laws and an abundant supply of cheap labor through his local administration of the Poor Laws. For the Speenhamland Decision of 1795 provided that wages insufficient to give subsistence to the laborer and his family should be supplemented from the poor rates levied on the property in the parish.[a] His will was supreme in the village, whose inhabitants worked in his fields or supplied the miscellaneous needs of his manor house, and paid him rent for their cottages. One of his younger brothers, the "squarson," Sydney Smith aptly called him, probably preached at the local Anglican church, and was supported by tithes levied on all the propertied inhabitants of the parish, regardless of their church affiliation. Another might command a man-of-war that patrolled the coast, or the red-coats who could be called from the nearest garrison to protect him from the insurrection of peasants which the great French Revolution and the recent French Revolution of 1830 taught him to fear.

In 1795 incipient revolt of agricultural laborers starving on wages that had not kept up with the rapid war-time rise of prices had been checked by the Speenhamland policy, which guaranteed them subsistence at the cost of the last vestige of their independence. The consequent rise in the poor rates, which in the years of agricultural distress immediately following the Napoleonic Wars frequently absorbed as much as eighty or

[a] Halévy shows that these taxes fell chiefly on the tenant farmers, *History of the English People in 1815*, p. 331.

ninety percent of the entire cost of local administration,[2] weighed so heavily on the tenant farmers that there was great pressure upon the Poor Overseers to reduce the doles. In 1830 the official standard of subsistence for the laborer had dropped a third below that calculated thirty-five years before at Speenhamland as just sufficient to support life.[3] Wages remained so low that a Member of Parliament could write: " An English agricultural laborer and an English pauper, these words are synonymous." [4] In the early part of that year William Cobbett, the great popular journalist, on a tour through the agricultural counties, found wretches cutting hedges in Sussex and working in gangs on the Norfolk roads for 1s. 6d. a day, less than half the pay of the common soldier and even less than the value of the food allowance of the criminal. Yet the current rates for labor in other counties were even less; in Wiltshire, 7s. weekly, in Hampshire, 8s., and in Berkshire, 7s. to 9s.[5] In Leicestershire Cobbett described the laborers' cottages as "hovels made of mud and straw, bits of glass or of old cast-off windows, without frames or hinges frequently, and merely stuck in the mud wall. Enter them and look at the bits of chairs or stools, the wretched boards tacked together to serve for a table, the floor of pebble broken or of the bare ground; look at the thing called a bed, and survey the rags on the backs of the inhabitants." [6] The peasant was lucky if meat was added to his meagre bread and potatoes once a fortnight; but about him the woods and hedges swarmed with fat pheasants which the Game Laws forbade him to kill on penalties which rose to transportation for seven years at the third offense.

In late August, 1830, the news of another French Revolution, in which peasants were burning the ricks of their restored landlords, came across Channel to the farm hands of Kent, who were being deprived of work by threshing machines and imported Irish labor, and thrown upon the mercies of parsimonious Overseers. The Kentishmen took the signal to rise as they had risen with Jack Cade four centuries before. They smashed the offending machinery, escorted unpopular Overseers out of their parishes, frightened off the Irish, and forced the farmers to raise their wages to two shillings a day. Some farmers bargained with them to raise their wages in return for their assistance in obliging the clergy to resign part of their tithes. The revolt spread rapidly through fifteen other agricultural counties. Obdurate farmers and landlords found their ricks in flames, and received threatening letters signed " Swing," a name that bore all the terror " Ludd " had inspired during the riots against factory machinery in 1812. But the violence fell on property alone; the starving and desperate men took no human life.

The centering of these disturbances about London gave the Government and the propertied citizens of the capital the impression that the entire Island was the prey of anarchy. Toward the end of November, when the revolt was at its height, there came into power under Lord Grey the first Whig ministry since 1807. Grey was a liberal and a humanitarian, but his primary interest was in Parliamentary reform. And the only way to protect a reform measure from the " anti-property " cry which the Tories had successfully raised against it since the first French Revolution seemed to lie in demonstrating that the Whigs were as severe against destroyers of property as any Tory could be. So while the Tories looked on with a certain irony, the new Home Secretary Lord Melbourne took no account of the economic grievances of the laborers, and crushed their unarmed and usually unresisting bands with soldiery. The judicial vengeance that followed was terrible. The savage laws of the time permitted the punishment of offences against property by the execution of three men and the transportation of four hundred and fifty-seven others for periods ranging from seven years to a lifetime.[7] The behavior of the unhappy, exiles on their arrival at the penal colony of Van Diemen's Land was such as to cause its governor to exult over the efficacy of the mode of punishment with which he was associated. " If, my Lord," he wrote to the Whig Minister Lord Goderich in 1834, " the evidence, or conduct, of particular individuals, can be relied on as proof of the efficiency or non-efficiency of transportation, I am sure a strong case indeed could be made out in its favour. I might instance the rioters who arrived by the *Eliza,* several of whom died almost immediately from disease, induced apparently by despair. A great many of them went about dejected and stupefied with care and grief, and their situation after assignment was not for a long time much less unhappy."[8] Cowed by the loss of its leaders, the agri-

cultural proletariat attempted no other revolt. But
sporadic firings of ricks continued to express its sufferings, which Disraeli's *Sibyl* (1845) and Kingsley's
Yeast (1848) showed unchanged.

The Radicals Burdett and Hobhouse raised no protest in Parliament against this ruthless maintenance of
" law and order " ; Brougham, as Lord Chancellor,
actually took part in the repressive measures. By their
support of the New Poor Law devised in 1834 to
remove the causes of labor unrest, the Benthamites
and their allies incurred the bitter enmity of the great
majority of the working people. The provisions of
this new law were largely the work of Nassau Senior,
Oxford Professor of Political Economy, and Edwin
Chadwick, formerly Bentham's private secretary.
Senior saw the cause of labor troubles in the poor relief
that had encouraged surplus population by guaranteeing a subsistence income. Now the Wage Fund Law,
discovered by McCulloch in 1828 and popularized by
Senior's own *Lectures on the Rate of Wages* (1830)
seemed to demonstrate clearly that the current rate of
wages was the quotient of a wage fund laid aside by the
employer at the beginning of the year (consisting of that
portion of his capital not reserved for his personal use
and for the purchase and upkeep of buildings, tools,
and raw materials) divided by the number of laborers
employed. Thus strikes or violent uprisings to raise
the price of labor were foredoomed to failure, for they
could not draw upon a larger wage fund except at the
expense of the maintenance and expansion of the industry, a draft which would soon defeat its own end by

putting the employer out of business. The artificial wage maintained by doles to the lowest paid laborers permitted a larger working-class to live than the wage funds of agriculture and industry could support, and thus was leading the nation to financial ruin. Hence Senior, supported by Brougham and by popular writers like Harriet Martineau (*Poor Laws and Paupers Illustrated*, 1833–1834), was for abolishing poor relief altogether. But the majority of the Commission drafting the Bill for Poor Law reform favored the less drastic measures proposed by Chadwick, which became law in 1834 after a very brief consideration by Parliament. These abolished out-door relief altogether,[9] but gave aid to those who would renounce regular employment for custody in workhouses, where they were to be fed and lodged more miserably than the most miserable independent laborer without. The feeding project was somewhat difficult to carry out without killing the inmate, since the independent farm hand, according to Chadwick's calculation, " could expect, on the average, to obtain for his own consumption only 17 ozs. of bread per day and $\frac{1}{2}$ ℔. of bacon per week." [10] But there was hit upon the ingenious plan of supplying food sufficient for nourishment, but in forms such as the oatmeal of Oliver Twist, so unpalatable that the laborer would seek the workhouse only in the last extremity of need. Surplus population, the great bogey of the Malthusians, was provided against by segregating the sexes in the workhouses, and by giving the Overseers power to send off agricultural paupers to the factory districts, where labor was more

in demand.   So effective was the new law, that poor
rates fell almost a third during the first five years of
its operation.[11]

The machinery for enforcing the New Poor Law put
into practice for the first time the centralizing theories
of the Benthamites.   The building and management
of the workhouses, and the decision as to the right of
the laborer to relief were taken out of the hands of the
local officials, and given to three Commissioners sitting
in London, who were to establish a uniform policy for
the nation.   The parish divisions were abolished as too
small for efficient administration, and were amalga-
mated into "unions" centering usually about a
market town, presided over by paid local assistants of
the Commissioners.   Thus the laborer found his claim
to assistance no longer enforceable upon the nearest
magistrate through appeals to sympathy or through
threats, but appraised by officials unknown to him, who
were directed by a mysterious and implacable three in-
accessible in London.   These directors of the nation's
policy became the especial objects of popular execration
as "The Three-Headed Devil King," a Malthusian
monster who segregated man and wife in "Bastilles,"
and strangled infants at birth.[12]

Thus the Benthamites lost the popular following
they had gained by their democratic and philanthropic
opinions through a measure that served to reinforce
their land-owning opponents.   The landlords had their
poor rates reduced and their cheap labor assured without
acquiring the odium of personal enforcement of the revised Poor Law.   The Radicals who investigated the

situation of the paupers in the agricultural counties did not enquire into the justice or wisdom of the enclosures that had been taking the last vestiges of land from the common people; to them, as to Bentham, enclosures were wholly laudable means toward efficient farming.[13] Nor did they, so blinded they were by the Wage Fund theory, enquire whether the landlord might raise wages at the expense of his profits. Thanks to them, the aristocracy's hold on the South was all the firmer after a revolt that had cost four hundred and sixty men their freedom.

Notwithstanding these favors, the Tory landlords rather ungraciously began to take revenge for the Reform Act by lending their support to certain unpleasant Parliamentary enquiries into the labor policy of the rising manufacturers who were the backbone of the Reform parties. These enquiries, which had been made sporadically since 1802, received unusual impetus from a series of letters describing what he called "The Yorkshire Slavery" written by Richard Oastler to the *Leeds Mercury* in the autumn of 1830, while the agricultural uprising was at its height. Oastler, steward of a Yorkshire estate, charged that the plight of the children working in the neighboring woolen mills thirteen hours daily, exclusive of meals, was worse than that of the Negro slaves for whose freedom the North had long been a center of agitation. Mill-owners retorted hotly, declaring that twelve hours' labor was necessary to provide for the children's livelihood; that the employing class was noted for its kindliness; and that a reduction of hours would lower wages, throw children out of employment, deprive agriculturists of a market for their wool, raise prices of manufactured cloth to the consumer, and thus deprive British mills of the advantage hitherto enjoyed over the factories springing up on the Continent.   A minority of woolen manufacturers, notably John Wood, a large worsted spinner of Bradford, admitted the general truth of Oastler's assertions, and expressed a desire to reform their own practice if they could be protected from the competition of employers who persisted in over-working children. Oastler's supporters, who also included clergymen like J. R. Bull (Anglican) and J. S. Stephens (Methodist), joined forces with a simultaneous movement in cotton-manufacturing Lancashire, led by the philanthropic employer John Fielden and the intelligent and able workingman John Doherty, secretary of the Cotton Spinners' Union.   In the Northern counties the agitation for Parliamentary Reform became of secondary interest to great open-air mass meetings addressed by these men, who demanded that the central Government, the only power strong enough, should protect the factory children from exploitation.   Michael Sadler, a Tory who had been interested in the plight of child labor since 1823, was elected from a Yorkshire borough to the un-reformed Parliament of 1831 under pledge to introduce a bill limiting labor to ten hours daily.

This he did in March, 1832, in a stirring speech that not only charged almost unbelievably horrible working conditions, but also maintained the justice of government intervention in behalf of even adult labor. His attack on the generally received dogma of " free competition " showed remarkable insight into contemporary industrial conditions: "I apprehend," he said, " the strongest objections that will be offered on this occasion, will be grounded on the pretense that the very principle of the bill is an improper interference between the employer and the employed, and an attempt to regulate by law the market of labour. Were that market supplied by free agents, properly so denominated, I should fully participate in these objections. Theoretically, indeed, such is the case, but practically I fear the fact is far otherwise, even regarding those who are of mature age. Those who argue the question on mere abstract principles seem, in my apprehension, too much to forget the condition of society: the unequal division of property, or rather its total monopoly by the few, leaving the many nothing but what they can obtain by their daily labour; which very labour cannot become available for the purposes of daily subsistence, without the consent of those who own the property of the community, — all the materials, elements, call them what you please, on which labour can be bestowed, being in their possession. Hence it is clear that, excepting in a state of things where the demand for labour fully equals the supply (which it would be absurdly false to say exists in this country), the employer and the employed do not meet on equal terms in the market of labour; on the contrary, the latter, whatever be his age, and call him as free as you please, is often entirely at the mercy of the former.

. . . Hence it is that labour is so imperfectly distributed, and so inadequately remunerated; that one
part of the population is over-worked, while another is
wholly without employment; evils which operate
reciprocally upon each other, till a community which
might afford a sufficiency of moderate employment for
all, exhibits at one and the same time part of its members reduced to the condition of slaves by over-exertion,
and another part to that of paupers by involuntary
idleness." [14] The manufacturing interests in Parliament, declaring Sadler's statements one-sided and inaccurate, obtained the appointment of a Committee for
the collection of full evidence. This Committee, of
which Sadler was chairman, examined eighty-nine witnesses: gentlemen, clergymen, employers, overlookers,
parents of factory children, and very frequently the
child laborers themselves. The weight of this testimony corroborated Sadler's assertions. Children often
began work in the generally unventilated factories as
early as four or five years of age. They had to assume
for extremely long hours bent and cramped positions
which deformed their pliant frames terribly. If they
relaxed their labors from fatigue and sleepishness, they
were often whipped with heavy leather thongs or a
detachable part of the machinery called the billy-
roller,[a] or perhaps met a worse fate by falling into the
unguarded machinery. The simple stories of the
maimed and sickly workers, old before their time, were
an impressive indictment of the system upon which

---

[a] A heavy rod two to three yards long and two inches in diam-
eter, with an iron pivot at each end.

England had built her extraordinary material prosperity.

Joseph Habergam, a seventeen-year-old patient from the Leeds Infirmary, with cruelly bent and twisted legs, testified in part: "I was seven years old when I began work at George Addison's Bradley Mill, near Huddersfield; the employment was worsted spinning; the hours of labour at that mill were from five in the morning until eight at night, with an interval for rest and refreshment of thirty minutes, at noon; there was no time for rest and refreshment in the afternoon; we had to eat our meals as we could, standing or otherwise. . . . I had fourteen-and-a-half hours' actual labor when seven years of age, the wages I then received was two shillings and six pence a week. In that mill were about fifty children, of about the same age that I was. These children were often sick and poorly; there were always, perhaps, half a dozen regularly, that were ill because of excessive labour. . . . We began to grow drowsy and sleepy about three o'clock, and grew worse and worse, and it came to be very bad about six or seven, I still had to labour on. . . . Strapping was the means by which the children were kept at work . . . the overseer is continually walking up and down with the strap in his hand. . . . It was reckoned by the children to be very bad usage; towards the end of the day the flies of the machines would burst their knuckles. Accidents were frequent. The children were not capable of performing the amount of labour that was exacted of them, without perpetual cruelty. . . . One part of the discipline of those mills is profound silence; they will not allow the children to speak; if two are seen speaking, they are beaten with the strap. The masters encourage the overlooker to beat the children in that manner." [15]   Elizabeth Bentley, twenty-three, deformed and incapable of further work, told something of the still more underpaid female labour: " I began to work at Mr. Busk's flax mill when I was six years old. . . .   I was kept constantly on my feet; there were so many frames, and they run so quick, the labour was excessive, there was not time for anything. . . .   Those who were last in doffing were constantly strapped, girls as well as boys. . . . When I left Mr. Rusk's, I then went to Mr. Benyon's factory.   I was about ten years of age, and was employed as a weighter in the card room. . . it was so dusty that the dust got upon my lungs, and the work was so hard, I was middling strong when I went there, but the work was so hard; I got so bad in health, that when I pulled the baskets down, I pulled my bones out of their places.   The basket I pulled was a very large one; that was full of weights, upheaped, and pulling the basket, pulled my shoulder out of its place, and my ribs have grown over it. . . .   As a spinner . . . I got six shillings. . . .   I had not much food to eat, and the little I had I could not eat it, my appetite was so poor.   My food being covered with dust, was no use to take it home . . . I have had experience in wet spinning — it is very uncomfortable.   I have stood before the frames till I have been wet to my skin; and in winter time, when myself and others have gone home, our clothes have been frozen, and we have nearly caught our death from cold. We stopped at home one or two days, just as we were situated in our health; had we stopped away any length of time we should have found it difficult to keep our situations. I am now in the poor house at Hunslet. None of my former employers come to see me." [16]

Such testimony by youthful victims was corroborated by parents of child workers, by overseers, and even by employers. Gillett Sharp, an assistant overseer whose son had gradually lost the use of his legs at the mill, told the affecting story of the death of a girl worker: " Four or five months back there was a girl of a poor man's that I was called to visit; it was poorly.; it had attended a mill, and I was obliged to relieve the father in the course of my office, in consequence of the bad health of the child; by and by it went back to its work again, and one day he came to me with tears in his eyes: I said ' What is the matter, Thomas? ' He said, ' My little girl is dead.' I said, ' When did she die? ' He said, ' In the night; and what breaks my heart is this, she went to the mill in the morning, she was not able to do her work, and a little boy said he would assist her if she would give him a halfpenny on Saturday; I said I would give him a penny.' But at night when the child went home, perhaps about a quarter of a mile, in going home she fell down several times on the road through exhaustion, till at length she reached her father's door with difficulty, and she never spoke audibly afterwards." [17] James Paterson, overseer, gave support to Sadler's charge of " Slavery ": " The children and young persons were sometimes successful in their attempts to escape from labour and confinement. I have gone on horseback and brought them back myself. . . . Those who had made engagements for any length of time, when they ran away, the master, if he could not find them before they got home to their relations, if they had any, he sent after them and put them in gaol. . . . That girl that was sent to prison worked two years for nothing, to indemnify her master for the loss of her time while she was in the course of punishment." [18] Abraham Whitehead, whose business as a clothier had taken him constantly to woolen mills for twenty years, showed how hardly the discipline of factory hours weighed upon the very poor: " I can tell you what a neighbour told me six weeks ago . . . her child works at a mill nearly two miles from home, and I have seen that child coming from its work this winter between ten and eleven in the evening; and the mother told me, that one morning this winter, the child had been up at two o'clock in the morning, when it had only arrived at home at eleven; it then had to stay at the door till the overlooker came to open it. This family had no clock . . . but this has only generally happened when it has been moonlight, thinking the morning approaching." [19] Twenty-one reputable physicians pronounced more than ten hours' work a menace to children's health. C. Turner Thackrah, surgeon to the Leeds Infirmary, went so far as to say: " Children should not work at all — the least time the best." [20] John Wood sent his overseer to testify that in his own mill, where every effort was made to be kind to the children and provide them sanitary quarters, the length of their labor (6 a.m. to 7 p.m.) caused a steady decline in health.

Similar testimony had been brought repeatedly to the attention of Parliament since 1802, but the net result of thirty years' legislation was an Act passed the previous year which forbade the employment of children under eighteen in cotton and silk mills for more than twelve hours a day.[21] There was no regulation of hours in woolen manufacture, from which had come the bulk of the testimony before the Sadler Committee. For the moment, Sadler's efforts seemed doomed to accomplish no better result. The Reform Bill passed, and in the new election Sadler lost his seat in the Whig landslide. The first Reformed Parliament, in which the manufacturing interest had increased its representation, considered the evidence concerning child labor inconclusive, and replaced the Committee by a Royal Commission popularly considered favorable to the manufacturers, which included the Benthamites Edwin Chadwick (of the Poor Law Commission), Dr. Southwood Smith, and John Wilson. The advocates of the Ten Hours Bill, especially the working population of the North, which had seen daring witnesses before Sadler's Committee blacklisted by employers, did everything to obstruct its operations.

Nevertheless, the Commission gathered evidence in a tour through the manufacturing districts with great thoroughness and despatch, and surprised the opposition by presenting a report which declared the existence of evils substantially as great as those published by Sadler and his associates. But it revealed its *laissez-*

faire bias by allowing the propriety of interference in
the case of children only, since they could not be considered free agents like adult workers. This distinction, while unsatisfactory to Sadler's supporters, won
the approval of a majority of the legislators, whom it
enabled to satisfy their consciences without danger to
the pocketbooks of their class. On the basis of this
Report, the Government passed in the summer of 1833
an Act which distinguished sharply between adult and
child labor. Sadler had proposed to prohibit the employment of children under nine, to limit those between
nine and eighteen to ten hours daily, and to forbid
night work to those under twenty-one. The two latter
provisions the Government disapproved as an entering
wedge to the project of rescuing adult men and women
from the tender mercies of the open market, for they
would make it difficult for the factories to maintain
their existing running hours. Hence it reduced the
age limit for night work from twenty-one to eighteen,
and maintained the legal hours of those between thirteen and eighteen at the 1831 Act's provision of
twelve. On the other hand, it followed Sadler in
excluding children under nine from the factories, and
outdid his effort in behalf of those between nine and
thirteen by giving them an eight-hour day, and two
hours' daily schooling at the expense of their employers. And the Government Act made a distinct advance
over Sadler's Bill by providing the first effective machinery for the enforcement of factory regulation.
The local magistrates were reinforced by four itinerant
inspectors appointed by the Central Government, who

were to report unsanitary conditions, unfenced machinery, and failure to provide schooling. Thus the 1833 Act was a triumph for the Benthamite principles of centralization and education for the masses. Its weakness lay, in the failure of its drafters to comprehend what Sadler had seen so clearly; that the adolescent and even the adult laborer was a free agent in name only. And although the Act applied to woolen, flax, and linen, as well as to the previously regulated cotton and silk mills, it was still too narrow in its scope. In the potteries children of six continued to work twelve to fourteen hours, and in the dark tunnels of the mines little savages crawled on all fours drawing tubs of coal by means of chains bound about their middles.

Even such inadequate protection of child labor proved difficult to secure. The inspectors were honest and diligent, but they soon found it necessary to complain that the magistrates of the North, who were very frequently friendly to the mill-owners or under their influence, often punished the most serious infractions of the law with merely nominal fines. Also, in that period before the compulsory registration of births, which commenced only in 1836, it was exceedingly hard to prove that a child was under age. Furthermore, the Government was hostile to the law. In 1836, Poulett Thomson, the President of the Board of Trade, aided by Bowring and other Benthamites and by Peel and the manufacturing interest among the Tories, nearly succeeded in weakening it by an amendment. The following year Nassau Senior, the most influential of the economists, returned from a tour of the manufacturing districts lost in admiration of "the great triumph of Sir R. Arkwright's genius," [22] and trumpeting the praises of the mill-owners. In his published *Letters on the Factory Act* (1837), he voiced exasperation at the demand of the inspectors to be admitted to any part of a factory without notice; as well, he remarked indignantly, assign to the army similar inspectors to ask of enlisted men their grievances. As a crushing argument against further regulation, he presented calculations proving all profit to be made during the last half-hour of an eleven and a half-hour day. During the course of the debate on the Ten Hours Bill in 1847, Bowring stated the typical position of the orthodox Benthamite: "Why continue in this course of helpless legislation? Why struggle, perpetually, to maintain a state of things which the common interest overthrows? What is the use of laws to which you cannot give effect?" [23] Clearly the greatest ineffectuality was the provision for education dear to the Benthamites. The State provided no funds, and the manufacturers, when they acted at all, generally made the schools farces by setting them up in some unused portion of the factory, even the coal-cellar, and appointing anybody as teacher, without regard to intellectual or moral qualifications.[24]

Such skepticism concerning social control of industry and such estimation of profits above human welfare were, however, not shared by all members of the upper classes. There were philanthropists of a less philosophic cast than the Benthamites who could not contemplate heart-rending human misery without believing that there were immediately effective means of putting an end to it. In reaction to the disillusionment and callous individualism that had followed the religious wars of the seventeenth century, there had sprung up since the middle of the eighteenth century an increasing humanitarian spirit. The product of many civilizing forces quietly at work in British society, it was the exclusive property of no party, or class, or creed. It found equal aliment in the Jacobin doctrine of natural rights and in the Christian dogma of the transcendent value of every human soul. The Methodist revivalists who drew tears from brutalized Cornish miners were as much the friends of man as the deists Paine and Godwin and the atheist Bentham. Methodism was largely confined to the lower and lower middle classes, but its zeal was communicated to the upper classes indirectly through the wealthy and influential Evangelical party in the Established Church. So earnest was their desire to remove suffering and moral degradation, that the severely pious Evangelical leaders, such as the great parliamentarian William Wilberforce and Zachary Macaulay, the editor of *The Christian Observer*, did not disdain alliance to this end with every variety of Christian, including the Unitarian, and even with open enemies of Christianity.[25] Wilberforce supported Romilly and Bentham in demanding reform of the criminal law. His successful efforts in the antislavery cause were heartily seconded by *The Philanthropist*, edited by the Quaker William Allen, which had enlisted the pen of James Mill. The gross immorality prevalent in the new factories soon attracted the attention of the Evangelicals to the new wage-slavery. Their representatives in Parliament voted for the elder Sir Robert Peel's 1802 Act limiting to twelve the hours of pauper children in cotton factories, and for the atheist manufacturer Robert Owen's unsuccessful Bill (introduced in 1815), which proposed to extend to woolen and flax as well as cotton factories a day of ten and a half hours for all workers under eighteen, and a prohibition of the employment of children under ten.

But the pietists' quick perception of distress and prompt action to alleviate it were offset by a corresponding slowness to recognize and attempt to remove its causes. For the Christian world-view led to two opposite attitudes toward social injustice. The devout believer might conclude that bad institutions could so degrade immortal souls as to blind them to their one chance of salvation. Or he might with equal logic decide that, since the earth was ordained to be a vale of tears for transient humanity, the pious soul should learn to forget its mundane misfortunes through contemplation of the beatific eternity in which all the saved would be equal. The latter, or other-worldly, attitude consistently pointed to an entire acquiescence in the world as it was. But in philanthropic pietists both coexisted; they admonished the rich to be unwearied in works of charity, and the poor to accept without complaint the lot to which Providence had assigned them. For ten years Hannah More devoted herself to the moral and religious improvement of the exploited coal miners and glass workers of her native

Gloucestershire, and kept them from strikes or other protests against their economic condition. The belligerent Cobbett was infuriated by her tract containing the "account of the celestial death of the Evangelical mouse, who, *though starving*, would not touch the master's cheese and bacon." [26] Wilberforce approved the bloody dispersal of the petitioners in St. Peter's Field,[a] and was the author of the Combination Act of 1799, whose outlawing of labor unions was one of the most important agencies in keeping down wages during the first quarter of the nineteenth century. Cobbett parodied such philanthropists' advice to the masses in the popular couplet:

"Open your mouth, and shut your eyes,
And God will love you, and send you a prize." [27]

By 1830, however, the success of mass meetings of the populace in forcing consideration of Parliamentary Reform had taught many pietists the value of such meetings as means of pressing an unwilling but timorous Parliament to enact more stringent factory regulation. Sadler was an Evangelical, and his strength came from the great gatherings of factory workers addressed by the emotional Methodist orators Oastler and Stephens and the Evangelical clergyman Bull, even more than from Tory landowners jealous of upstart manufacturers. After Sadler's death in 1835 from over-work in the cause, agitation for the enforcement of the 1833 Factory Act, and for the realization of his original purpose of a ten-hour day was carried

[a] See chapter II, p. 71.

on by Short-Time Committees in which the preponderating pietists were associated with labor leaders like Doherty and benevolent mill-owners like Wood and Fielden.[a] These associates and the arguments of hostile manufacturers completed the education of the Christian philanthropists by obliging them to realize that factory conditions were only the most conspicuous, and by no means the worst results of an unjust and wasteful economic system.

Although they saw that the national policy of *laissez-faire* had fostered evils in every field of employment,[28] the Short-Time Committees wisely centered their efforts upon the factories, both because their congregation of large numbers of workers under one roof suited them ideally to governmental inspection, and also because they presented the most obvious examples of injustice. Before steam-driven machinery had immensely multiplied human effort, there was more than a little justification in the maxim that the niggardliness of nature obliged the vast majority of mankind to toil constantly to secure subsistence. But now its use had presented England with an ever-increasing surplus which warranted reduced hours together with a higher standard of living for the masses. Instead, the surplus had gone to swell the pockets of the few who owned machinery and land, while the machine operators toiled as long, and lived more uncomfortably than their fathers in the day of

[a] Wood is said to have spent £40,000 of his private fortune in financing the Short-Time agitation. See Hammond, *Lord Shaftesbury*, p. 13.

domestic handicrafts. The devices hailed as " labor-saving " had been cruelly deceptive. Increased national wealth had been accompanied by decreased welfare, until England faced a frightful deterioration of her human resources and the outbreak of class warfare between the few rich and the wretched many.

The causes of the failure of the masses to win a share in the wonderful increase in production lay in the social organization and intellectual atmosphere of eighteenth century England. The first factory workers came " from the expropriated farms and commons of the cottagers and yeomen, from the shops and homes of petty manufacturers finding economic independence and even subsistence no longer possible, from the hovels of the Scotch Highlands, the mountains of Wales, and the undulating fruitful plains of Ireland, — plains fruitful of human poverty." [29] Broken in spirit and accustomed to a miserably low standard of living, they welcomed the chance of employment even at the scant wages offered by the new industries. The early mill-owners, almost wholly men of little education or refined tastes,[30] but endowed with a narrow, fox-like cunning which served to outwit a competitor or appropriate a new invention, and a brutality that readily disciplined untrained labor in the performance of novel and distasteful tasks, were not inclined to let considerations of justice and humanity stand in the way of their taking the fullest advantage of an unexampled opportunity to get rich quickly. The adult laborer found himself at a disadvantage in competition even with the women and children of his own class. Dr.

Ure has left us a frank exposition of the manufacturer's policy: " On the handicraft plan, labor more or less skilled was usually the most expensive element of production — *Materiam superabat opus;* but on the automatic plan, skilled labor gets progressively superseded, and will, eventually, be replaced by mere overlookers of machines. By the infirmity of human nature it happens, that the more skillful the workman, the more self-willed and intractable he is apt to become, and, of course, the less fit a component of a mechanical system, in which, by occasional irregularities, he may do great damage to the whole. The grand object therefore of the modern manufacturer is, through the union of capital and science, to reduce the task of his work-people to the exercise of vigilance and dexterity, — faculties, when concentred to one process, speedily brought to perfection in the young. . . . It is, in fact, the constant aim and tendency of every improvement in machinery to supersede human labor altogether, or to diminish its cost, by substituting the industry of women and children for that of men." [31]   Ure estimated that as a consequence, there were employed in the cotton, wool, linen and silk industries in 1835 more females than males, and as many of both sexes under eighteen as adults. [32] The premium upon child labor and the low standard of living created a vicious circle by encouraging large families, thereby increasing the supply of labor even beyond the demand stimulated by the rapid expansion of the machine industries. The wild fluctuations of trade during the vicissitudes of the Napoleonic wars, and thereafter the revolutions in

South America and elsewhere which suddenly opened up unfamiliar foreign markets, brought alternate periods of high-pressure work and of unemployment which were most disastrous to the factory hands. During the periods of so-called over-production they lay idle and consumed what meager savings they had made, vividly aware that the warehouses were full of goods they had made yet could not wear or use, and that their employers were living comfortably upon the enormous profits from preceding periods of brisk trade. And during trade booms rush orders often worked them to the limit of endurance, sometimes for thirty-six hours at a stretch, for wages that were indeed twice or thrice those of the farm laborer, yet were in great disproportion to the value of goods they helped produce. As the Continental nations recovered from long-continued warfare and began to build factories, exaggerated fear gave the British mill-owners an excellent opportunity to enlist the national pride in support of their efforts to keep wages at a minimum. So as the nineteenth century advanced, it became the more bitterly clear to the industrial workers that they had jumped from the agricultural and handicraft frying pan into the factory fire.

And in that fire the upper classes were determined to keep them, by force of arms if necessary. In the late eighteenth century they had held it " axiomatic that the wealth and power of the ' nation ' (the nation being characteristically confused with the possessors of the nation's wealth) depended upon a numerous laboring population, whose productive labors were to be

assured by the stimulus of poverty. The more numerous were the laborers, and at the same time the
poorer, — that is, the more dependent on their daily
employments for a subsistence, — the richer and more
powerful would be the ' nation.' " [33]   The custodians
of the national virtue were for the most part in agreement with the maxim stated by a manufacturer: " All
experience proves that in the lower orders the deterioration of morals increases with the quantity of unemployed time of which they have the command." [34]   And
the new economic science was held to demonstrate that
any interference with the " natural laws " of the labor
market would throw the delicate mechanism of commerce and industry so much out of gear as to bring to
the workers eventual injury far outweighing the temporary good.   Indeed, to facilitate the beneficent
working of the " free " market of labor, Parliament
relinquished rapidly the power to fix wages, until the
repeal of the long-disregarded Statute of Apprentices
in 1813–14 relieved the government of the last vestige
of formal obligation to ensure a living wage.   The
outbreak of the French Revolution changed the attitude toward the lower classes from indifference to a
hostility born of fear.   The offer of the French Convention in 1792 to aid any people that would revolt
against its king inspired the British propertied classes
with a dread of an enemy from within as well as an
enemy from without.   The manufacturing regions
especially were dotted with garrisons of troops whose
commanders reported upon the state of popular feeling as if in a conquered province.[35]   They were assisted

by volunteer mounted " yeomanry," largely recruited from mill-owning families, who were retained as the most dependable of government auxiliaries in the period of popular disturbance which followed the Peace. " Policing the poor " was a common expression on the lips of the rich, who discouraged the teaching of the poor to read, lest they take to reading Paine, Cobbett, and other subversive writers. The only educative agency that reached the great masses of the poor was the Sunday School, which taught obedience to powers established as a prime religious duty. Dr. Ure reprimanded " those educational philanthropists who disdain the study of human nature, as it is expounded in the Gospel." [36] For therein they would learn to teach " the first great lesson — one inculcated equally by philosophy and religion — that man must expect his chief happiness, not in the present, but in the future state of existence. He alone who acts on this principle will possess his mind in peace under every sublunary vicissitude, and will not care to scramble with feverish envy for the idle phantoms which the dupes of pleasure and ambition pursue." [37]

Thus society bound the factory worker hand and foot for the convenience of his master. Dr. Gaskell observed in 1836: " No power ever enjoyed by a feudal lord was so operative. It is true that the life of the dependent no longer lies at the mercy of the superior; what may be termed his social existence is however at his disposal. Around many mills a fixed population has arisen, which is as much a part and parcel of the master as his machinery. The rapid improvement in this last has put an end to the necessity of new labourers and thus little colonies of men are found under the absolute government of the employer." [38] They got back much of the wages paid the inhabitants of these colonies by renting them houses and obliging them to patronize the company stores, which generally charged prices above those of the general market. In all factories the operative found himself subject to rigid discipline. He was called to work by the factory bell, and snatched a hasty repast at fixed times. Lateness and clumsiness were punished by severe fines. The tireless, monotonous whir of the machines gave life no variety, no repose. Conversation was generally forbidden during the long working hours. Gloom without intensified the cheerlessness within, for the leaden sky of Northern England was darker for the smoke of clustering chimneys, and chill winds from the sea lashed the windows with frequent rain. Fear of this discipline was one of the chief reasons why thousands continued home manufacture despite the crushing competition of steam-driven machinery, which, continually reducing the value of their product, obliged them to work longer hours than the factory hand, and for less daily income. It was estimated that in 1833 the domestic workers in the cotton industry exceeded the 212,800 employed in the factories; that some 250,000 handloom weavers were keeping up a well-nigh hopeless struggle against 100,000 power looms. [39] The psychology of a large proportion of these home workers was well summarized in the testimony of a girl lace-embroiderer before the Factory Commission of that year: " I like it better than the factory, though we can't get so much. We have our liberty at home, and can get our meals comfortable, such as they are." [40]

The homes to which the exhausted factory workers retired at night were less wholesome and more forbidding than the factories. After mentioning the improvement of housing for the middle classes since the eighteenth century in his exultant account of *The Progress of the Nation* (1838), Porter was obliged to admit that " The improvement . . . has not hitherto been extended in an equal degree to the dwellings of the working classes. These, especially in the large towns, are still for the most part comfortless, and even unwholesome, ill furnished and ill kept, betraying a lamentable want of self-respect in their inmates, with a degree of recklessness which speaks unfavorably for their moral progress." [41] Other observers did not consider the working classes entirely to blame for their own squalor, for their rapid influx into industrial centers had made them an easy prey of extortionate builders. Even Nassau Senior, the determined opponent of factory regulation, recoiled at the sight of the new slums that had grown about Manchester: " When I went through the habitations in Irish Town, Ancoats, and Little Ireland, my only wonder was that tolerable health could be maintained by the inmates of such houses. These towns, for such they are in extent and population, have been erected by small speculators with an utter disregard to everything except the immediate profit. A carpenter and a bricklayer club to buy a patch of ground, and cover it with what they call

houses.   In one place we found a whole street following the course of a ditch, in order to have deeper cellars
(cellars for people, not for lumber) without the expense of excavation.   Not one house in this street
escaped cholera.   And generally speaking, throughout
these suburbs the streets are unpaved, with a dunghill
or a pond in the middle; the houses built back to back,
without ventilation or drainage; and whole families
occupy each a corner of a cellar or a garret." [42]   Conditions were even worse in the dilapidated and decay-
ing dwellings of the Old Town, which had long been
deserted by prosperous Manchesterians.   Cellars were
especially sought after as dwellings by the most miserable of all industrial workers, the handloom weavers,
because a damp atmosphere kept cotton yarn supple.[43]
Thousands of the homeless were packed like sardines
in three hundred public lodging houses; "young men
and young women; men, wives and their children —
all lying in a noisome atmosphere, swarming with ver-
min, and often intoxicated." [44]   Manchester was typical
of the "Great Towns" described with a wealth of
horrible detail which would almost try the credence of
the hardened observer of the present-day slum, by
Frederick Engels, the co-worker of Karl Marx, in his
Condition of the Working Classes in England in 1844.
The condition of this urban proletariat, half-clothed,
and ill-nourished on improperly chosen and often
spoiled food, was of little concern to the municipal
authorities until visits of the Asiatic cholera in 1832–
33, 1848–49, and 1853 made it the center of contagion.
Then, for self-protection, the upper classes appointed

local boards of health, who examined the worst districts but did little to improve them. It was only after 1848 that, largely through the efforts of the Benthamite Edwin Chadwick, the central government began a more effective sanitary campaign.[a] The extent to which these early boards of health were thwarted by the debased state of the populace they tried to serve may be illustrated by the following experience of Charles Kingsley in 1849: " Over the cholera districts of Bermondsey [b] and Oh, God! what I saw! people having no water to drink — hundreds of them — but the water of the common sewer, which stagnated full of . . . dead fish, cats and dogs, under their windows. At the time the cholera was raging, Walsh saw them throwing untold horrors into the ditch, and then dipping out the water, and drinking it! ! " [45]

The ignorance of the lower classes was not confined to sanitation; it was almost complete. " This United Kingdom," wrote Porter, " which boasts itself to be at the head of civilization, has been among the last of the European nations to make any public provision for the instruction of the people." [46] A Parliamentary investigation into the education of the poor in 1818, provoked by the widespread post-war riots, disclosed that in England and Wales only one child in three was

[a] National sanitary reports, by-products of the attempt of the Poor Law Commissioners to get at the causes of pauperism, had been made under Chadwick's direction since 1838.

[b] A suburb of London. Sanitary conditions in London had been improving since the middle of the eighteenth century. See Dorothy George, *London Life in the Eighteenth Century*, 1925.

receiving even a smattering of education, and that only one in thirteen had access to an endowed school. In the mushroom manufacturing cities illiteracy was the rule. Preston, a Lancashire city of 18,000 inhabitants, contained but one endowed school accommodating thirteen pupils, and three private schools giving indifferent instruction to a few others. During the years 1839–41 in the counties of Chester and Lancashire forty percent of the males and sixty-five percent of the females signed the marriage register with a cross.[47] Private philanthropy supplied a few day schools for children under eleven, and there were a few night schools and mechanics' institutes at which factory hands bravely tried to keep awake after a long day's work. But there was no national appropriation for secular education until 1833, when the Benthamites Roebuck and Grote secured a yearly grant of £20,000, increased to £30,000 in 1839. This latter sum was about one-tenth of one percent of the yearly budget, and, as Brougham sarcastically noted, less than one-half the appropriation for building the Queen's stables; it was furthermore doled out in small sums on the condition of large local appropriations, with the result that it seldom benefited the lower classes.[a] " Allowing for irregularity of attendance, the average length of school life rises on a favorable estimate from about one year in 1835 to about two years in 1851 ";[48] but the mutual jealousy of Churchmen and Dissenters, supporting the rival systems of Bell and Lancaster, and the fanaticism

[a] We have noted the failure of the educational clauses of the 1833 Factory Act, chapter IV, p. 142.

of *laissez-faire* doctrinaires prevented the nation from making school attendance compulsory or insuring instruction of good quality before 1870. During the first half of the nineteenth century England contained not a single free lending library of any kind.

" The very essence of our laws," declared Bulwer in 1833, " has been against the social meetings of the humble, which have been called idleness, and against the amusements of the poor, which have been stigmatized as disorder." [49] The result of this paternal care for the morals of the populace was that it sought refuge from monotony, weariness, and squalor in the excitements of gambling, sex, and crime, and in the oblivion of intoxication. In England the number of gallons of spirits on which excise was paid rose from 1,976,000 in 1823 to 7,875,000 in 1837; in Scotland from 2,300,-000 to 6,620,000 during the same period. [50] In Glasgow one house out of every twelve was a public house in 1830; one out of ten in 1840. [50] This without counting unexcised liquor, of which Gaskell estimated that there were more than a hundred secret distilleries, producing 156,000 gallons yearly, in Manchester alone. [51] In Lancashire, crime increased six times more rapidly than population, doubling every five and a half years, while population took thirty to double. [52] The number of crimes against property in England was especially significant, being one to every 779 in the population, as compared to one to 1,804 in France, one to 5,389 in Spain, and one to 7,140 in the Netherlands. [53] The sexual promiscuity of the working

classes was notorious. The early mill-owners and
their sons could take advantage of the opportunities
to debauch their female employees, and put no rein on
the irregularities of the operatives. " In 1828 Francis
Place told D'Eichthal, the Saint Simonian, that when a
friend of his visited a Lancashire mill, the owner had
bid him take his choice among the mill girls." [54]   Hus-
bands frequently permitted wives to add to the scanty
family income by prostitution. " The crowded couch
of incest in the warrens of the poor " threatened the
race with speedy degeneration. Parents sometimes
lived in idleness and vice upon the wages of their exploited children. One of the Commissioners investigating the condition of child laborers in the factories in
1833 found " a conspiracy insensibly formed between
the masters and the parents to tax them with a degree
of toil beyond their strength." The natural alliance
of vicious habits with poverty, ignorance, and excessive
labor shortened the lives of the industrial workers to a
shocking extent. " In Liverpool in 1840 the average
longevity of the upper-classes, gentry, professional
men, etc., was thirty-five years; that of the business
men and better-placed handicraftsmen, twenty-two
years, and that of the operatives, day-laborers, and
serviceable class in general, but fifteen years." [55]   Infant mortality was especially heavy among the laboring
classes. In Manchester in that same year over fifty-
seven percent of the children of those classes died before
the fifth year, as compared to twenty percent of the
children of the higher classes. [55]   Forty was old age for
factory workers in Glasgow. [56]   The problem of the

over-supply of labor was solving itself in accordance with natural law.

It is a testimony to the extraordinary vitality of the human race that the first efforts to replace an economic system so unjust, unregulated, and wasteful by one under social control were made by men so ignorant and degraded as the operatives in the early factories. These efforts arose almost unconsciously from the concentration of population and the division of labor which characterized the new industries. The operatives " were reduced to a common level of wages and working conditions. . . . The individual laborer performed over and over again some fractional and seemingly trifling act having significance only in connection with related acts by other members of the group. In respect alike to his work, to his living conditions, and to the promotion of his welfare, the individual worker was more and more merged into the group. The group concept was literally thrust upon him." [57] Associations of laborers for the purpose of raising wages and improving working conditions date practically from the beginning of large scale machine industry. These associations frequently managed to evade the laws against combinations by masquerading as " box clubs " and " friendly societies " for sick insurance and funeral benefits.[58] But the savage repression of those groups discovered in the attempt to raise their standard of living sometimes resulted in acts of exasperation, such as machine-smashing and throwing of vitriol at particularly detested employers, which confirmed the upper-class opinion that trade unionists were rebels and criminals. " It is in vain," wrote the liberal Gaskell, " that in their rage, worked up to madness by heartless demagogues, by the sight of their famishing children, they have taken the law into their own hands, and dreadful proofs they have given how unfit they were to have wielded it for their own benefit." [59] The repeal of the Combination Laws in 1824 gave immediate rise to so many strikes openly directed and financed by trades unions, that an alarmed Parliament rescinded its action in the following year to such an extent as to grant an illusory freedom only. Penalties were prescribed for " molesting " and " obstructing " the progress of industry, vague terms which permitted the magistrates, who were usually sympathetic with the employers, to proceed against almost any pressure exerted by associated labor. Nevertheless, in 1829 attempts to reduce greatly the wages of cotton spinners met with determined opposition from that upper class of workmen, who had the intelligence and skill to manipulate and repair highly complicated machinery.[60] Aided by small allowances from their local unions, about ten thousand spinners of Manchester and Stockport clung desperately to the decent standard of living to which the comparatively high weekly income of some thirty shillings had accustomed them, and gave a six months' battle before they were obliged to surrender to a combination of their employers. Finding in this defeat the lesson that no local union could succeed against employers' combinations, whose extremest measures no magistrate was known to restrain, John Doherty, secretary of the Manchester Cotton Spinners'

Union, organized in 1830 an ambitious National Association for the Protection of Labor, embracing several different trades. In Doherty, who had begun as a child laborer in a cotton mill, one sees the factory laborers arriving at a conscious social philosophy. Through the journal of the National Association, *The Voice of the People,* which had thirty thousand subscribers, he endeavored to divert working class aims from the destruction and abolition of machinery to the control of the machinery by the workers in the workers' interest, which would employ the new surplus of industry for the general welfare. The death of the National Association, which for a time claimed a million members, in 1832, and of its successor, the Grand National Union, in 1834, testified to the impotence of the workers to gain economic victory against the existing odds.[61] Consequently, though local unions persisted with magnificent courage in strikes whose invariable failure seemed to confirm the contention of the economists that they were scientifically impossible, the most intelligent industrial workers became increasingly interested in a plan of industrial organization eliminating the capitalist altogether, which had been elaborated far beyond Doherty's suggestions by the philanthropic mill owner, Robert Owen.

Owen, the most formidable of the early opponents of the orthodox political economy, was the son of a Welsh saddler, who had risen up through the stages of commercial traveler and foreman to a partnership in a cotton mill which yielded large profits. Thus he resembled the typical mill owner; but he was unlike

him in a thirst for self-education which led him to read
the eighteenth century philosophers, and become a convert to their deistic and humanitarian doctrines.   His
resulting interest in the improvement of society caused
him to think of other things than profits, and take a
greater interest in his " living " than in his " dead "
machinery.   Consequently he determined upon radical
changes in policy when he assumed in 1800 the direction of the mill whose chief owner was his father-in-
law, David Dale.   Dale was a deeply religious Scot
with a reputation for kindliness.   Yet he employed
between four and five hundred pauper children thirteen
hours daily (ten and a half actual working hours), and
had clustered about his mill at New Lanark, at the
remote falls of the Clyde, a mushroom village of
" free " workers and their families, which was notorious for slatternliness, drunkenness, and loose living.
Owen rapidly converted its inhabitants to habits of
decency and thrift.   He discharged the rented pauper
children, refused to employ the children of the other
operatives before they reached the age of nine, and
reduced the working hours of adults from seventeen
to ten.   At the company's expense, he provided schools
for the children, to whom the greed of the parents
left less time for instruction than he desired.   During
an enforced shutdown of the mill in 1806, he continued
to pay full wages.   The protests of his partners against
the curtailment of profits consequent on these innova-
tions made him desire a free hand.   In 1813 he went
to London to seek investors in a frankly philanthropic
enterprise.   The Westminster Radicals came promptly

to his support. Bentham took shares, and Place revised Owen's prospectus, which was published under
the title of *A New View of Society* (1814) and dedi-
cated to Wilberforce, the abolitionist. A full subscription was secured on the understanding that profits
would be limited to five percent, and Owen returned
to New Lanark with full power to institute reforms.
He centered his efforts on education, being as convinced
a Helvetian as James Mill. Instruction, which was
extended until the age of twelve, laid little emphasis
on books, but was of an extremely practical character,
designed to inculcate altruism and recognition of the
greatest happiness principle. The experiment attracted wide attention; from 1814 to 1824 a yearly
average of two thousand persons visited New Lanark.
His success in increasing quantity and quality of production while raising the worker's standard of living,
encouraged him to attempt to convert other manufacturers by arguments from efficiency. The failure of
this attempt obliged him to appeal to the government
as the only power disinterested enough and strong
enough to protect the working population. Largely
as a result of his efforts there was passed in 1819 an
Act of Parliament, applicable to cotton factories only,
which forbade employment of children of less than
nine years of age, and limited the working hours of
those under sixteen to twelve a day (less an hour and
a half for meals), and seventy-two hours per week.
He also agitated for the creation of a Minister of
Labor, and for nationally controlled education and old
age insurance. Having had practical experience of the

falsity of the doctrine of the natural identity of interests, he attacked *laissez-faire* as an obstacle to the greatest happiness of the greatest number. For the competitive system he proposed to substitute a system of coöperation, designed to secure to the workers the greatest possible proportion of the product of their labor, and to raise the level of general well-being by assuring a supply of goods continually in excess of demand. Like Bentham in his younger days, an ineffable bore, he memorialized and button-holed kings, ministers, aristocrats, and potentates, at home and abroad, in the interest of a paternalistic control of economic life.[62]

Like Bentham, too, he at last became disgusted with the unwillingness of the upper classes to assume an effective paternal rôle. His pamphlets and addresses, and the Debating Club which he established in London drew to him a following of intelligent workmen, who in their turn interested him in trades unionism as a stage in the preparation of the proletariat for self-help. Though his activity in founding the Grand National Union bore no immediate fruit, his more original experiment in coöperative stores begun in London in 1832 was the germ of the Rochdale Pioneers, who have had an uninterrupted existence from 1844 to the present time. "Orator" Hunt and other followers of Owen, who had organized demonstrations against the middle-class character of the Reform Bill during the stormy months preceding its passage,[63] formed the backbone of the Chartist movement, which sought to procure for the workingmen the suffrage which they had helped gain for an ungrateful middle class. The most trusted leaders of the unenfranchised millions, they formed what was virtually a second Radical party, intensely hostile to the Benthamite Radicals, whom they detested for *laissez-faire*, the Malthusian principle, and the New Poor Law.

The Owenite Socialists and the trades unionists found themselves associated in the Ten Hours movement of the Short-Time Committees with strange allies, the Tory paternalists. The feudal tradition of a humane paternalism, prominent in Elizabethan legislation, had been almost extinguished by the commercial and individualistic spirit of the eighteenth century. Its revival in the nineteenth century began with three friends sprung from the middle class, who, after a youthful enthusiasm for the cause of the French Revolution, had been convinced by the emergence of Robespierre and Napoleon of the futility of the attempt to better the lot of mankind through political change. In their disillusion and Toryism Wordsworth, Coleridge, and Southey had not ceased to hear

> " The still, sad music of humanity."

Southey, who remained faithful to two cardinal principles of his fallen idol, William Godwin: that the interest of society should take precedence over the self-interest of the individual, and that need was a higher claim to property than conquest, inheritance or even production, continually pointed out the duty of the upper classes to the propertyless and the ignorant during the long period of his *Quarterly* articles (1809–

1839). Especially in a series of articles on *The State of the Poor* (1809–1816) he showed how manufactures tended to collect wealth in masses, not diffuse it, and to render the life of the employed precarious by a continual round of inflation and deflation, and how the condition of the agricultural dependents of his aristocratic readers was scarcely better. At all times he fiercely attacked Malthus's population principle, asking whether all the arable surface of the earth was yet populated and whether the government had done its best to prepare to feed an increasing population. " Great capitalists," he wrote, " become like pikes in a fishpond, who devour the weaker fish." [64] Believing that the only hope of progress lay in the contrary disposition of the powerful to defend their inferiors, he continually urged that the government be highly centralized; that it employ surplus labor on public works, encourage popular education under the Bell system, and, through a revivified State Church, take the civilizing message of the gospel to the poor. Southey helped prepare the Tories for their support of the Factory Acts, and encouraged Robert Owen on meeting him in 1816; but perhaps his most important influence was on Carlyle, who tells in his *Reminiscences* how eagerly he awaited the appearance of the *Quarterly* articles. [64]

Wordsworth was keenly aware of the great changes which were transforming even the physical aspect of his beloved England; how romantic castles and forest footpaths were giving place to macadamized roads and smoky cities. In 1801, when the revolution in his political convictions was yet incomplete, in a letter accompanying a gift of the second edition of the *Lyrical Ballads* he appealed to the great Whig leader Charles James Fox to save the " small independent proprietors of land " of the Northern counties from the new " liberalism " which was depriving them of their patrimonies and obliging them to become factory hands: " You, Sir, . . . have felt that the most sacred of all property is the property of the poor. The two poems, which I have mentioned, (*The Two Brothers* and *Michael*) were written to show that men who do not wear fine clothes can feel deeply." [65] But Fox, who considered poetry an elegant artistic accomplishment entirely dissociated from political and economic life, replied only with remarks concerning metre. In his Tory days Wordsworth deplored in *The Excursion* (1814) the proximity to his beloved Lake Country of cheerless factories, wherein men, women, and children worked in double shifts extended throughout the night by artificial lighting, which defied nature's provision for repose.

> Within this Temple — where is offered up
> To Gain — the Master Idol of the Realm,
> Perpetual sacrifice,

he showed the shades of the prison house descended on the child, dull and stunted, breathing audibly, with lungs and hair filled with cotton lint, exposed to the worst moral influences; and asked if the economists were right in asserting that the nation benefited by exposing its newest generations thus prematurely to the withering light of common day. And the drudging

plowboy, he added, was also dull and prematurely
bent; could not both be educated, and given the unspoiled freedom for which Nature intended them? [66]

The industrial deflation and bad harvests immediately following the close of the Napoleonic wars
brought forth Coleridge's *Lay Sermon addressed to
the Higher and Middle Classes on the Existing Distresses and Discontents* (1817). Coleridge described
vividly a typical factory town, and laid the blame for
the miseries of its inhabitants on the aristocrats, who,
yielding unbecomingly to the " trading spirit " had
enclosed the commons, and on the manufacturers, who,
after encouraging the laborers to multiply like rabbits
while business was brisk, assumed no responsibility for
their care in commercial crises. Believing that " men
. . . ought to be weighed, not counted," [67] and that
" their worth ought to be the final estimate of their
value," [67] he warned that lack of health and prosperity in any portion of the population was a loss to
the nation. With his customary breadth of view, he
pointed out three " positive ends " of a truly wise
state: "1, to make the means of existence more easy to
each individual; 2, to secure to each of its members
the hope of bettering his own condition or that of his
children; 3, the development of those faculties which
are essential to his humanity, that is, to his rational
and moral being." And he closed with a stirring
peroration very like those of Carlyle: " If we are a
Christian nation, we must learn to act nationally, as
well as individually, as Christians. Our manufacturers must consent to regulations; our gentry must con-

cern themselves in the education as well as the instruction of their natural clients and dependents, must regard their estates as secured indeed from all human interference by every principle of law and policy, but yet, as offices of trust, with duties to be performed, in the sight of God and their country. Let us become a better people, and the reform of all the public (real or supposed) grievances, which we use as pegs whereon to hang our own errors and defects, will follow of itself. In short, let every man measure his efforts by his power and his sphere of action, and do all he can do." [68] He spoke to Crabbe Robinson of " what is ironically called free labor," and distributed pamphlets supporting the elder Sir Robert Peel's bill providing for the partial safeguarding of child labor, which passed the House of Commons the following year. But when the Lords threw it out on the recommendation of the economist Lord Lauderdale, he characteristically ceased his efforts in despair. However, in his *Constitution of Church and State* (1828) he made a valuable contribution to economic theory. With an historical insight which the Benthamites conspicuously lacked, he demonstrated that " in the spirit and history of our laws . . . the possession of a property not connected with especial duties, a property not fiduciary or official, but arbitrary or unconditional, was in the sight of our fathers the mark of a Jew and an alien." [69] He furthermore diagnosed with remarkable clairvoyance the ills of the time: " the tillers of the land paid by poor rates, and the remainder of the population mechanized into the engines for the manufactory of

new rich men; yea, the machinery of the wealth of the
nation made up of the wretchedness, disease, and depravity of those who should constitute the strength of
the nation! . . .   Our state policy a Cyclops with one
eye and that in the back of the head; our measures
become either a series of anachronisms, or a truckling
to events instead of science, that should command
them; for all true insight is foresight." [70]   " Has the
national welfare," he asked, " have the weal and
happiness of the people, advanced with the increase of
the circumstantial prosperity?   Is the increasing number of wealthy individuals that which ought to be
understood by the wealth of the nation? " [71]   Con-
demning impartially both the " presumption, temerity,
and hardness of heart in political economy," [72] and the
unhappy preponderance in Parliament of the landed
interest, with its oppressive Game Laws, Corn Laws,
and import duties, he called for a central government
wise and strong enough to preserve the human resources of the nation, and a State Church equipped to
restore the moral tone of a commercialized people
perishing from lack of vision.

Of the same school of philosophic Toryism with
Southey, Wordsworth, and Coleridge was Michael
Sadler, whose clear-sighted argument for state interference in the " free " market of labor has already
been quoted.   In Sadler, in Oastler and the Rev. J.
R. Stephens, mob orators who kept the masses of the
turbulent North in continual agitation, in Sir Andrew
Agnew, their Scotch ally, and in Lord Ashley, who
succeeded Sadler as Parliamentary leader of the fac-

tory reformers, Tory principles were united with evangelical Christian zeal. Lord Ashley carried both paternalism and piety to the pitch of fanaticism. Son of the Tory Earl of Shaftesbury, who possessed extensive estates in Dorsetshire, and nephew by marriage to the Whig Prime Minister Lord Melbourne, he was nevertheless imbued in childhood by an old family servant with a narrow puritanism which detached him from the frivolity, the easy morals, and the cold worldliness of the inner aristocratic circle into which he was born. His exhibition of a heart and a conscience in supporting a reform of the Lunacy Laws while representing a pocket borough in the unreformed Parliament had suggested him to Sir Andrew Agnew, like himself a fanatical advocate of the strict observance of the Sabbath, as one qualified to replace Sadler as Parliamentary champion of the factory slave. Ashley's emphasis upon the moral and religious even more than the physical and mental degradation of the exploited proletariat and his unwavering hostility to universal suffrage, trades unionism, and other means toward the independence of the working classes, by arousing the consciences of men of property while allaying their fears, made him the ideal instrument to persuade Parliament. And the fiery mob oratory of Oastler and Stephens whose tendency he much deplored nevertheless admirably complemented his efforts by stressing the need of forestalling radical by moderate measures of reform. The anti-Poor-Law and Chartist movements furnished the proper pressure for the granting to Ashley of committees to report on the en-

forcement of the 1833 Factory Act and a Royal Commission to report on the employment of children and
young persons in mines and manufactures by the in-
dolent Whig ministry which dragged on an existence
until 1841. The Commission's Report on Mines in
1842 so shocked Victorian prudery and so aroused
social compunction as to force the recalcitrant Tory
Premier, Sir Robert Peel, owner of mines and factories and seventh richest man in the kingdom,[73] to put
through an Act forbidding the employment in coal
pits of women and girls, and of boys under ten. The
economic crisis of 1842, the result of overproduction
and bad harvests occurring simultaneously since 1837,
focussed public attention upon the condition of the
masses. In 1844 Ashley obliged the Peel ministry
to grant a further reduction of the working day for
factory children under thirteen to six and a half hours.
But the final show of strength in regard to the Ten
Hours measure did not come until 1847.

Peel, whose worst side had been exhibited in his
attitude toward factory regulation, had then but recently exhibited his best side in his statesmanlike
repeal, in the emergency of a great Irish famine caused
by the failure of the potato crop, of the Corn Laws
dear to his party. As a consequence he had been
defeated in the summer of 1846 by the secession of a
large group of angry Protectionist Tories. The return of the Whigs to power after a general election
made the time propitious for a reopening of the Ten
Hours' question, for the new Premier, Lord John
Russell, had been converted to intervention in 1844,

and the Tory landowners were eager to retaliate upon the manufacturers for their support of the Corn Law repeal. Unfortunately Ashley had sacrificed his seat in Parliament by his courageous conversion to Free-Trade; but a Ten Hours Bill was introduced afresh in January, 1847, by Fielden, who had operated his own cotton mills on a ten-hour basis since 1836. The division on the Bill cut sharply across party lines. Its chief supporters were: the Tory Protectionists and paternalists, Lord George Bentinck, Lord John Manners, Benjamin Disraeli, and George Bankes, who had been Ashley's fellow-member from agricultural Dorsetshire; new Whig converts, Lord John Russell, Thomas Babington Macaulay, and the Home Secretary, Sir George Grey; liberal manufacturers like Fielden and Brotherton; and free-lance Radicals such as Wakley, Duncombe, and Sir Charles Napier. Its chief opponents were manufacturers fresh from victory over the Corn Laws, headed by John Bright, whose humane management of his own factory caused him to overestimate the humanity of other employers, the Free-Trade Tories Peel and Sir James Graham, and the Benthamites Roebuck, Bowring, Hume, and Brougham (in the House of Lords).

The Benthamite group fought tenaciously for the principle of non-interference in industry. They wished to see the workingman, relieved of the wage-fixing paternalism of the feudal order, transformed into an independent and self-sufficing member of a free community. Although skeptical of the competence of the government to improve directly the

economic status of the poorer classes, they desired that
it improve it indirectly by establishing national education, checking the pauperizing tendency of poor relief,
avoiding war, and providing cheap necessities of life
through Free-Trade and free competition. Education, they thought, would show the laborer that the
key to his welfare lay in the limitation of the numbers
of his family, and would make him fit to exercise the
franchise, which would be an infallible protection from
exploitation. They agreed with Malthus that the
poor " are really the arbiters of their own destiny;
and what others can do for them, is like dust of the
balance compared with what they can do for themselves." [75] They admitted that the contemporary
period of transition from tutelage to autonomy was
bringing much distress to the workers, but they were
confident that much of that distress would disappear
when the abolition of the Corn Laws had time to exert
its full influence. The residual distress was the necessary temporary price of freedom, from which no pana-
cea could relieve the sufferers. Factory regulation was
a will o' the wisp which would lure dupes into servi-
tude under the guise of paternalism, while ruining the
new industries upon which prosperity was based. The
defect of this Benthamite position grew out of that calm
detachment which is the virtue and the vice of the
philosopher. The Philosophical Radicals could maintain their serene Fabianism the more easily because
they had comfortable incomes, and did not come into
intimate contact with the evils of the factory system.
When a legislator announced a visit to a mill, its

owner, like a subaltern expecting an inspection by a superior officer, took care to make everything as attractive as possible, and to escort him through the proper rooms. Thus it is possible to perceive the naïve honesty of Brougham's advice to the working classes during the debates over the 1844 Factory Act: " Make such contracts as you please with your master, carry your labor to the best market, where you can get the greatest share of that abundance which Providence has prepared for you, and employ all the hours of the day in working with perseverance and spirit and honesty, while you retain the power and the will. . . . If we leave the question open, every man had a Ten Hours Bill already; he might work ten hours if he pleased, and no power on earth could make him work more, unless he liked, — no man need work longer than he please." [76]

The trial of strength between these curiously assorted partisans resulted in a decisive victory for the interventionists. A ten-hour day was prescribed for adolescents between thirteen and eighteen, and for women. Incidentally this meant a ten-hour day for adult males also, for women and the children of the protected ages formed so large a proportion of the factory hands that it was found unprofitable to work without them. The attempt to evade this consequence by working women and children in relays was prohibited in 1853.

This interference with the market of adult labor, however indirect in the case of males, was a severe blow to the prestige of the Benthamites. In their zeal for the principle of the natural identification of interests which reigned in Bentham's economics, they had neglected the conflicting principle of the artificial identification of interests which underlay his theory of legislation. They had thus purchased a Free-Trade victory at the price of abandoning their master's major interest in a democratized state which would assure the greatest good of the greatest number. They had left secure the monarchy and the House of Lords, which many thought doomed by the Reform Act, and showed little enthusiasm for the political aims of the Chartists.[77] Thus they assumed the aspect of a capitalistic rather than a humanitarian party, and lost the working-class support which was theirs in the day of their advocacy of Parliamentary reform. The Free-Trade victory that consolidated the agriculturists against them did not win the gratitude of the masses to whom it gave cheap bread, for Free Trade was attached to an abhorrent economic philosophy which established workhouses, discouraged trades unions, and forbade factory regulation. The 1847 Factory Act left the Philosophical Radicals not only unpopular, but discredited. There resulted from the restriction of the hours of labor in factories none of those disastrous consequences to industry which the advocates of uncontrolled competition had so confidently predicted. *Laissez-faire* was to have a long and vigorous future, but the charm of infallibility had departed from it.

Political economy was not the only tenet of the Benthamites which aroused formidable opposition.

Their whole program of scientific adjustment to a changing environment was uncongenial to the national character. Proverbially a conservative and custom-loving race, the English cherished even after the industrial revolution and the Reform Bill the virtues of an agricultural and patriarchal society, with King, Church, Squire, and God over all. With this passing order were associated the glories of a long national history. The Briton was proud of the Saxon stubbornness which had snatched many a victory from the jaws of defeat, of the green fields, the stagecoach, and the fox hunt of merrie England, of the matchless Constitution which grew of itself, without plan, yet was held up by Montesquieu and foreign observers generally to the admiration of the world, of the venerable laws, " broadening slowly down from precedent to precedent." His attitude toward the Radical who bade him renounce these things for a better order of democracy and industrialism was very like that of his descendant of the present day toward the visitor who points out the advantages of the steam radiator over his obsolete open fire of coal. He may grudgingly admit that it is wasteful and inefficient; that it fails of being comfortable, since it roasts one side of the person standing before it and leaves the other to shiver. But he will not abandon it. The open fire has been for time immemorial a national institution; it is agreeable to look upon; it draws the human circle closer, its glowing coals assume a thousand fantastic shapes which lure the mind to reverie. It is not a mere utilitarian device for securing warmth; its value is emotional, spiritual. The word "hearth" brings tears to the eyes of the Englishman in exile.

All that was deepest in this emotional life was threatened by Benthamism. Violent hands were being laid upon the sacred institutions, the fountains of England's feeling were being shut off at their source. The young Gladstone professed to see in the Reform Bill "a certain element of the Anti-Christ." The dialect of the new school was strange and foreign; it spoke of pure reason, logical arrangement, radical rebuilding, a program of progress. Its dangerous weapon was analysis, the dreaded solvent of the great complexes which had formed the basis of communal emotions. Loyalty, which had held hearts true to the lost cause of the Stuarts, duty, given a fresh birth at Trafalgar, conscience, for which Cranmer and Ridley had burned at the stake, patriotism, honor, even love itself, were resolved into elements, made bare machinery. Even at its best, as Keats protested in *Lamia*, philosophy would destroy harmless illusions, change a loving and beautiful maiden back into the serpent form from which she had escaped, and shatter the dream of her lover.[a]

At the same time shrieking and rattling locomotives were invading the sylvan solitudes, factories were polluting earth, air and water, and new, raucous and ugly cities were sprawling over meadow and river bank. Factory operatives, and clerks who trudged from slatternly suburbs to cheerless offices in the city's

[a] Keats and Lamb agreed that Newton had "destroyed all the beauty of the rainbow by reducing it to the prismatic colors."

central roar, felt as keenly as artists and men of letters a homesickness for the scenes of unspoiled nature among which their childhood was passed. In the upper classes, this revulsion from the crudity of a growing industrial civilization took the form of a yearning for the past. The eighteenth century, proud of its "enlightenment," had despised the Middle Ages; in the nineteenth century, many of the wisest and best spirits, aghast at some of the consequences of that enlightenment, began to idealize them as ages of faith, beauty, and virtue. The pomp and pageantry of castle and coronation, the glories and delight of battle in glistening armor before gunpowder made the churl the equal of the knight, the chivalric virtues of courage, loyalty, courtesy to ladies, and kindness to inferiors were restored in the magic canvases of Sir Walter Scott. The thrilling diablerie, the warm sensuous beauty, the naïve religious faith of remote days returned in a *Christabel* and an *Eve of St. Agnes*." Against the Reform Bill leveling, there were opposed pictures of knighthood in its flower, and of a holy and beneficent priesthood which converted many a noble and sensitive soul to conservatism and reaction.

While the Benthamites, who, like most of the educated classes in the eighteenth century, believed that "the proper study of mankind is man," enjoyed the comforts and complexities of urban life, Wordsworth

"in lonely rooms, and mid the din
Of towns and cities"

longed for the calm and freshness of his native Lakes, and Byron sought refuge from the censoriousness and

pettiness of mankind in the solemn fastnesses of the
Alps.   The Benthamites looked upon nature as a soulless mechanism which man ought to control and make
subservient to his civilization, which he ought to regu-
larize like the patterned and pollarded trees of a
French garden.   Wordsworth looked upon nature as a
beneficent spirit which soothed man's troubled soul and
in her unhampered course gave a thousand moral examples for his imitation.   Shelley, found in her beautiful symbols of the highest ideals; Coleridge, evidence of the majesty and glory of the Creator.   And
from admiration of the wonders she performed without the assistance or tampering of man, arose a belief
in institutions which instinctively adjusted themselves
by gradual processes to changing conditions, of constitutions which grew mysteriously like a tree, and were
not invented and manufactured by conscious human
agency and abruptly put in operation, as Bentham
proposed.

"When I look on his cold, clear-cut face," wrote
Kingsley of John Stuart Mill, "I think there is a
whole hell beneath him of which he knows nothing,
and so there may be a heaven above him." [78]   This
was typical of the impression the Philosophical Radicals made upon their opponents, an impression which
was much more just in the case of a Bentham, a James
Mill, and a Ricardo.   These extraverted men, who
carried on the tradition of Voltaire, who sought to
eliminate the personal equation, and see objects in the
dry and clear " light of common day," found themselves in their later years in the alien atmosphere of

Rousseauism, in a lyrical age, in which men cultivated
their feelings and published unabashed the results of
the most searching introspection. Lord Byron, who
displayed through Europe " the pageant of his bleed-
ing heart," Keats, absorbed in the manifold richness
of sensation, Coleridge, the " subtle-souled psycholo-
gist," De Quincey, the dreamer of unearthly dreams,
Hazlitt, the unnoticed neighbor of Bentham, who
poured forth unrestrainedly the romantic illusion of
middle age in a *Liber Amoris,* could not be insensible
to the narrowness of the Benthamite world. For the
most part self-conscious stylists, they smiled at the
inarticulateness and colorlessness of the literature of
the Radical propaganda. Such men could not believe
that those whose experience was confined to the scientific categories, who knew not the heights and depths
of human life, nor communed with nature in her awful
solitudes, could, as they professed, have explained the
universe completely. There were clearly more things
in earth and heaven than were dreamed of in their
philosophy. The Benthamite social science was too
simple a solution of the infinite complexity of society;
the basic average man a mere skeleton or scarecrow.
It seemed probable rather that the universe had not
only not been fathomed, but was unfathomable. And
it was better so, for in an explicable universe there
would be an end of the awe, the mystery, the reverence which contributed so much to the richness of
human experience. It was better to believe that the
world was the manifestation of a God whose ways
were past finding out by the intellect, but were re-

vealed through the immediacy of feeling in moments
of mystic union of human and Divine, and in the
continual voice of conscience.

While the opposition to philosophic Radicalism thus
rested in these reasons of the heart which the reason
did not know, yet the Radical propaganda obliged it
to learn to justify itself in terms of the intellect.
This paradoxical task of using the intellect to define
its own limitations, of finding a logical defense of the
illogical, was indeed difficult, but not insurmountable.
It was first entered upon with success by one who professed to contemn theory altogether: Edmund Burke.
Burke's oft-quoted exclamation " The Age of Chivalry
is gone: the age of economists and calculators has come
instead, and the glory of Europe is extinguished forever," [79] expressed only rhetorical despair, for he
joined battle against " the principles of France " with
an energy which had rallied Whig as well as Tory to
the defense of the *ancien régime*.   Incidentally, despite his protestation of complete empiricism, he had
brought forward a set of conservative principles which
rivaled the principles of the innovators.   These rested
upon a long and fruitful experience in practical politics,
which had convinced him that human society was a
miracle of complexity and delicate adjustment which
the scientific categories were too crude and mechanical
to describe.   " When I hear of simplicity of contrivance aimed at and boasted of in any new political constitutions," he wrote confidently, " I am at no loss to
decide that the artificers are grossly ignorant of their
trade or totally negligent of their duty." [80]   " I must

see the men," he insisted, " I must see the things " ;
and he quoted the authority of Aristotle against those
who expected the geometrical deductive method to
give accurate results in morals and politics.   Though
he conformably affirmed that " nothing universal can
be rationally affirmed on any moral or any political
subject," [81] he permitted himself certain fundamental
axioms which conflicted with those of Bentham.
" Politics ought to be adjusted not to human reasonings but to human nature, of which the reason is but
a part and by no means the greatest part." [82]   Man is
" by his constitution a religious animal." [83]   " The
individual is foolish but the species is wise, and when
time is given to it, as a species it almost always acts
right." [84]   Consequently the habits, the feelings, the
prejudices of mankind, " the moral sentiments
(which) are so nearly connected with early prejudice
as to be almost one and the same thing " [85] had weight
and authority as deposits of the wisdom of the ages.
" Thanks to our sullen resistance to innovation,"
Burke dogmatized in one of his magnificent periods,
" thanks to the cold sluggishness of onr national character, we still bear the stamp of our forefathers. . . .
We know that *we* have made no discoveries, and we
think that no discoveries are to be made in morality;
nor many in the great principles of government, nor in
the ideas of liberty, which were understood long before
we were born, altogether as well as they will be after
the grave has heaped its mold on our presumption, and
the silent tomb shall have imposed its law on our pert
loquacity." [86]

Of a deeply religious nature which had early received the stamp of Roman Catholicism, Burke believed the destinies of men and of nations to be guided
by the Providence of a beneficent and omnipotent God.
" He censures God who quarrels with the imperfections of men," [87] was a principle applied also to venerable
Constitutions like the British, which to touch with violent hands was veritable sacrilege. God's purposes
were actualized through the State and the State Church,
which gave the individual his moral principles, his ends
of life; separated from them the individual was char-
acterless, colorless, aimless. A revolution which
severed ancient ties produced no new society, but " a
number of vague, loose individuals and nothing
more." [88] Seeing what Bentham unfortunately failed
to see, that " the tyranny of the multitude is a multiplied tyranny," [89] he looked with horror at the possibility of any serious Parliamentary reform. In the
aristocracy that Bentham condemned, he found the appointed vice-gerents of God on earth. " There is in
Nature and reason a principle which, for their own
benefit, postpones, not the interest but the judgment
of those who are *numero plures,* to those who are
virtute et honore majores." [90] For long after his
death the authority of Burke was therefore invoked by
the aristocracy and its partisans in support of its dis-
trust of theories and forward-looking idealism; " perhaps the only moral trust with any certainty in our hands
is the care of our own time." [91] Even the moderate
Macaulay coupled his name with Bacon's in support of a wholly empirical and opportunist political

philosophy against the deductive method of James Mill.

Coleridge called himself the heir of Burke, but he believed in the transcendent importance of metaphysics and was capable of recognition of the good contained in radical doctrines impossible to one who, in speaking of the French Revolution, "assumed the expression of a man who is going to defend himself against murderers." [92] In his early twenties he had been fascinated by Hartley's mechanistic materialism, which demonstrated the "corporeality of thought," and had joined heartily in Southey's project of an experiment in Godwinian communism. In his conservatized manhood he found Burke blind to the imperfections of the existing order, and shallow in his pure empiricism, which denied the power of abstract ideas to mold the future. A profound metaphysician, he believed that "an erroneous system is best confuted, not by an abuse of theory in general, nor by an absurd opposition of theory to practice, but by a detection of the errors in the particular theory." [93] Therefore he attempted to demonstrate in *The Friend* (1809–10) that Jacobin tenets were only "half-truths" which needed to be supplemented by Conservative tenets in order to be valuable. So it was with the Radical interpretation of equality. "Do the childish titles of aristocracy detract from my domestic comforts, or prevent my intellectual acquisitions? But those institutions of society which should condemn me of the necessity of twelve hours' daily toil, would make my soul a slave, and sink the rational being in the mere animal. It is a mockery of our fellow-creatures' wrongs to call them equal in rights when by the bitter compulsion of their wants we make them inferior to us in all that can soften the heart, or dignify the understanding." [94]   Likewise with the utilitarian theory of morals: " The character of the agent is determined by his view of action; and that system of morality is alone true and suited to human nature, which unites the intention and the motive, the warmth and the light, in one and the same act of mind " ; [95] and likewise with public spirit and cosmopolitanism: " Let us beware of that proud philosophy which affects to inculcate philanthropy while it denounces every home-born feeling by which it is produced and nurtured. The paternal and filial duties discipline the heart and prepare it for the love of all mankind. The intensity of private attachments encourages, not prevents, universal benevolence." [96]   " Let it be remembered by both parties," he summarized, " and indeed by controversialists on all subjects, that every speculative error which boasts a multitude of advocates, has its golden as well as its dark side; that there is always some truth connected with it, the exclusive attention to which has misled the understanding, some moral beauty which has given it charm for the heart." [97]

An effort at magnanimous mediation characterized also the metaphysics of one who had at one time been both a materialist and a Christian, and who always was torn between rival claims of the heart and the head. In a trip to Germany in 1798–9, he had found in the

Critiques of Kant, who had already attempted to reconcile the conflict of dogmatism and Hume's empiricism,
the resting place which his sorely perplexed mind had
sought. Kant confirmed what his capacity for dreaming
had demanded, and the poetry of Wordsworth had
suggested, that the mind was not passively receptive of
sensations, but helped to create the world which it perceived. From Kant he received also the invaluable distinction between the reason and the understanding, of
which he had made a Fichtean use. The perception of
the Jacobin and the Benthamite, he averred, was limited
because they made use only of the understanding, which
confined them to the mechanical world of phenomena.
But those who used the reason, which fused thought
and emotion in one act of immediate intuition, alone
knew ultimate reality. By such intuition one felt the
moral imperative, and discovered the inner truth of
Christianity beneath the accretions of dogma and the
obsolete language of the Scriptures. By the expression
of this religious position in his *Aids to Reflection* Coleridge became the founder of the Broad Church movement, which appealed neither to tradition, like High
Church Anglicanism, nor to verbally inspired Scriptures, like the Evangelicals and Dissenters. The application of the " reason " to political problems resulted
in Coleridge's doctrine of " ideas." " History studied
in the light of philosophy, as the great drama of an
ever-unfolding Providence " [98] revealed to the initiated
philosopher what Burke was content to leave as a mystery, the " ideas," or ultimate purposes for which God
intended institutions. In the contemporary Hegelian

phraseology, he sought to discover the law of their
development or evolution by an inspection of their
various metamorphoses in the past and present, and
thereby predict the future. In his last important
work, *The Idea of Church and State* (1828), he accordingly found the state to consist of an equilibrium
between the forces of permanence, represented contem-
porarily by the landed interest, those of progress, represented by commerce, industry and the professions, and
the Church, the transmitter to each successive generation
of the traditional culture, the perpetual schoolmaster,
spiritually, morally and intellectually, of the nation.
Thus Coleridge was one of the first to introduce to
England the new philosophy of history, which recognized present and future as organic outgrowths of the
past, and the doctrine of harmonious culture, which was
to oppose the narrowly scientific interests of an indus-
trialized civilization. " But civilization is itself but a
mixed good, if not far more a corrupting influence, the
hectic of disease, not the bloom of health, and a nation
so distinguished more fitly to be called a varnished than
a polished people, where the civilization is not grounded
in cultivation, in the harmonious development of those
qualities and faculties which characterize our humanity.
We must be men in order to be citizens." [99]   Unfortunately Coleridge had neither the clarity of expression nor the vigor of will to make these important ideas
prevail. In him they remained as if in embryo, to be
brought to birth by his disciples, including Hare, Maurice, and Sterling, who were gathered around him in his

latter days at Highgate Hill. Meanwhile, the leadership in the war on Bentham's ideas at which he had aimed was assumed by a man less subtle, original and profound, but much more articulate, and infinitely more energetic and persistent: Thomas Carlyle.

Chapter V

THE APPRENTICESHIP OF A PROPHET.

THOMAS CARLYLE was the son of a master stone-mason of the Scotch village of Ecclefechan, in the dale of Annan, near the English border. The little world to which he opened his eyes in 1795 showed almost no traces of what we call modern civilization. Annandale was a quiet pastureland, full of traditions of the just-vanished border warfare which Scott was soon to make famous. The Carlyle household was such a one as Burns had just described in *The Cotter's Saturday Night*. The father retained the patriarchal authority of the head of the clan. He was a Calvinist of the Calvinists, a member of the " Burghers " that had seceded from the state-established Presbyterianism in order to practice a severer piety. His ten children were brought up in an almost monastic discipline of obedience, poverty, and abstinence from frivolous pleasures. Thomas, the second child, so markedly combined intellectual promise with strength of character that his shrewd but almost illiterate parents determined to run the risk of giving him a college education.

His destination was, of course, the Christian ministry. But the quick-witted youth found much at Edinburgh University, where he matriculated when not quite fourteen years of age, which made him hesitate to accept the parental choice of his career. The influence of the eighteenth century " Enlightenment " was at its height, and religion was a tabooed topic in polite circles. The indifference to Christianity of men whose intelligence and learning he respected first irritated Carlyle, who had been reared in implicit belief in the letter of Scripture and Creed, and then disquieted him. In the summer after his second year at the University he shocked his mother by questions concerning the interpretation of the Song of Solomon and the divinity of Jesus. The Divinity School teachers, mere florid orators without fervid faith or intellectual force, failed to still the "grave prohibitive doubts" which were barring his entry into the Church. Yet it was not easy to renounce a ministerial career. The hearts of his parents were set on it; it was the surest road to a comfortable livelihood. His lack of orthodox zeal would positively recommend him to aristocratic patrons. And there was still open the honest course of upholding the Christian moral code, in which his confidence remained unshaken, against the libertinism into which unbelief had lured many of the emancipated.

Carlyle compromised by choosing the longest road to ordination, that of six terms' *in absentia* study. On the completion of his collegiate course in 1814, he went to the village of Annan to teach mathematics, which seemed to offer the certainty that theology had ceased to give. For a time he tried to persuade himself that "the prevalence of infidelity" was "on the decline" [1] among the upper classes, since its recent spread to weavers and shoemakers was destroying its attraction as a mark of superiority to the prejudices of the vulgar. But Hume's *Essays* prevailed against the temptation of a full pocketbook by appealing to the intellectual pride which was then perhaps the foremost trait of his character. Religious "enthusiasm" was shown to be contemptible, blind zeal without knowledge. In 1817 he definitely abandoned his theological studies. Early in the next year, on reading Gibbon's *Decline and Fall*, which delighted him with its "winged sarcasms, so quiet and yet so conclusively transpiercing and killing dead," Carlyle "first clearly saw that Christianity was not true." [2]

Teaching had meanwhile proved uncongenial. It offered neither the money nor the social position which would persuade a fortune-hunting aunt that he was a fit match for Margaret Gordon, whom he had met at his second teaching post in Kirkcaldy. A fellow teacher, Edward Irving, who had completed his preparation for the ministry and was marking time while awaiting a vacant pulpit, had therefore no difficulty in persuading him to go to Edinburgh, which offered a wider field for ambition. Thither they went together in the fall of 1818. For Carlyle, dependent on meager savings from teaching and the income from private tutoring and articles for the *Edinburgh Encyclopedia*, this fortune-seeking was more perilous than for Irving, who had a profession, money, and influential friends. At the end of a year the latter had gone to Glasgow as assistant to the famous Doctor Chalmers, and left his friend in bare lodgings in a shabby quarter of the city, living almost entirely on oatmeal from the parental farm. The law, for which he was preparing himself, offered little prospect of a livelihood, for Carlyle had as little liking for its practice as Bentham, and was besides " far too sarcastic for a young man," [3] in the opinion of men of influence.

The difficulties of his struggle for existence brought him into increasing sympathy with the laboring classes, whose sufferings he shared. The full weight of the war debt was just being felt, and a disproportionate burden of taxation, high food prices, much unemployment and consequently diminishing wages made the lot of the poor unusually hard. In this lean year, 1819, their discontent was manifest both in Scotland and in England. Workers assembled in the fields of Peterloo, near Manchester, with banners demanding bread and political rights, had been dispersed with bloodshed. At Glasgow a similar manifestation by handloom weavers thrown out of work by machinery had resulted also in a clash with the constabulary. Carlyle heard prominent Edinburgh citizens talking of the necessity of a " cordon of troops." His feelings, confirmed by reports from Irving concerning the condition of the Glasgow poor, were entirely on the side of the weavers. An advocate of Carlyle's acquaintance, " hurrying along, musket in hand, towards the Links, there to be drilled as an item of the ' gentlemen volunteers,' " greeted him with a cheery, " You should have the like of this " (patting his musket). Carlyle puzzled him with the reply, " H'm, yes; but I haven't yet quite settled on which side." [4] He and Irving took joy in the prospect of a repetition of the French Revolution, " Mutiny, revolt," as he noted disapprovingly in his old age, " being a light matter to the young." [5]

But another corollary of the social distress was by no means a light matter to the twenty-three-year-old Carlyle. A world in which force perpetuated man's inhumanity to man challenged his belief in the just order of the universe which had survived the wreck of his Calvinist theology. Without the support of that belief human life seemed a tale told by an idiot, yet he could not honestly reconcile what he saw about him with the existence of a God who was both beneficent and omnipotent, or of any sort of " friend behind phenomena." His favorite *Book of Job* offered no logical solution of this contradiction; and Voltaire's *Candide* demonstrated the absurdity of all solutions which had been proposed hitherto. Carlyle refused to put the problem aside. Confronted with a seemingly inevitable atheism which was abhorrent to his devout nature, he abandoned the law, which permitted little questioning of the established order, and sought a profession which would include thinking out the world-problem as part of his daily task.

This profession he found in letters, to which he had long aspired. Voracious reading in the French and English classics of the pre-war period and in the contemporary Romantic writers, and his college companions' praise of his style had early aroused in him the desire for literary fame, but his Scotch caution had made him doubt his ability to make a living by his pen alone. Now the astonishing successes of Byron and Scott and the prestige of the *Edinburgh Review* seemed to be inaugurating an era in which the man of letters might hope for fortune as well as fame. The failure of more substantial prospects was furthermore making caution less necessary. In 1820 Carlyle threw over tutoring and began what was to be his life's work.

For the moment this decision threw him into even deeper distress. The hackwork which came his way was miserably paid, and he had no longer savings to fall back on. Mental exhaustion from the labor of composition, intensified by anxiety from the menace of atheism and by sympathy for the suffering poor, brought on acute neurasthenia. And this precipitated a dyspepsia to which his monotonous diet of oatmeal had predisposed him; there was an incessant gnawing, as of a rat, at the pit of his stomach. His infatuation for Jane Welsh, who had held him aloof since their meeting in midsummer, 1821, and made him a sport of coquetry, filled to the full " a liberal measure of Earthly distresses, want of practical guidance, want of sympathy, want of money, want of hope." [6]

Within him raged a conflict between heart and head. The work of his skeptical teachers had been less thorough than he believed; they had mastered his intellect, but not his emotions and will. Morality has the persistency of habit, and survives instinctively the loss of its intellectual basis. Carlyle was in the anomalous position of Ibsen's Rosmer, with a Calvinist character left unchanged by the wreck of his Calvinist theology. " At no time was he more the servant of God than when doubting his existence. He listened eagerly for the call of duty: mindful of the parable of the talents, he was impatient to put his capacities to the best use. Had a divine messenger from the clouds or a miraculous handwriting on the wall, convincingly proclaimed to me, *this* shalt thou do, with what passionate readiness, I often thought, would I have done it, had it been leaping into the Infernal Fire." [7] No such command came from heaven. And on earth he found sincere only the voice of Voltaire, which suggested no constructive plan of action. An attitude of refined skepticism was impossible to Carlyle's temperament. He must have faith that the world was just, or further existence would be intolerable. On the solitary walks through Edinburgh streets to which insomnia drove him, Carlyle's disease-sharpened senses assimilated images drawn from the materialistic Lockian philosophy which he was being forced to accept, with memories of the new machinery which he had seen in Glasgow on a visit to Irving, and made of them a veritable waking nightmare. " To me the universe was all void of Life, of Purpose, of Volition, even of Hostility; it was one huge, dead, immeasurable Steam-engine, rolling on, in its vast indifference, to grind me limb from limb. O the vast, gloomy, solitary Golgotha and Mill of Death." [8]

One day in late July or early August, 1822, as he was walking down Leith Walk for a bath in the sea, Carlyle was suddenly delivered from the struggle which was consuming him. It occurred to him to ask himself: " What *art* thou afraid of? Wherefore, like a coward, dost thou forever pip and whimper, and go cowering and trembling? Despicable biped! what is the sum total of the worst that lies before thee? Death? Well, Death, and say the pangs of Tophet, too, and all that the devil and man may, will or can do against thee! Hast thou not a heart; canst thou not suffer whatsoever it be; and, as a Child of Freedom, though outcast, trample Tophet itself under thy feet, while it consumes thee? Let it come, then, I will meet it and defy it." [9] And from that time forth the temper of his misery was changed; " not Fear and whining Sorrow was it, but Indignation and grim, fire-eyed Defiance." [9] The will-to-live had revolted against the doubts that were driving him to suicide. He was given no rational answer to those doubts. His subconscious self demanded that their poison be expelled at once; there would be time enough thereafter to discover why it was poison.

This respite from spiritual suffering had probably been facilitated by a previous relief from the pinch of poverty. Edward Irving, suddenly and brilliantly successful in a London pulpit, had not forgotten his friend. In the spring of 1822 he had presented Carlyle with two pupils, sons of a wealthy British merchant, to be prepared for Edinburgh University. The change in Carlyle's fortunes was great. His pupils, the elder of whom, Charles Buller, was to distinguish himself in Parliament, were charming lads. The two hundred pounds he was to receive yearly were more than sufficient for his modest wants. His duties were light and afforded much leisure for literary efforts, and for the resolution of his doubts, which, although baffled, were still unanswered.

In 1819, while these doubts were gathering force, a friend whose name Carlyle did not preserve for us told him that he would find a constructive solution of his personal problems in the contemporary German literature, then practically unknown in the British Isles. Carlyle, whose curiosity concerning this literature had already been aroused by Madame de Staël's *De l'Allemagne,* immediately began to learn the German language. In 1821 he was reading Schiller and Goethe, who gradually opened to him " a new heaven and a new earth." German literature lured him into the still more unexplored regions of German philosophy. In 1823 he was undecided as to whether Kant's *Critique of Pure Reason* was " a chapter in the history of human folly, or the brightest in the history of human wisdom." [10] But the *Critique of Practical Reason* and the works of Fichte decided him unqualifiedly in the favor of the latter opinion. By 1825 he was certain that Germany had supplied him with the solution for all his problems.

Transcendental philosophy cut the Gordian knot of these problems by giving Carlyle plausible grounds for persuading himself that the universe was really what he desired it to be. It put away all fear of materialistic determinism by seeming to demonstrate that the world of matter had only a contingent existence, and was merely a stupendous punching bag created by Carlyle's own unconscious will, and the wills of his fellow-men, for the development of moral muscle. It pictured the ultimate reality as Universal Spirit, ruling the spirits of men, its finite manifestations, through the infallible dictates of the conscience. It declared time to be a mere figment of the human mind, and thereby removed Carlyle's doubts of the equitable government of the world. A survey of the entire course of human history, which permitted Carlyle to partake in some degree of the eternal contemporaneousness of the Universal Mind, convinced him that substantial justice had been executed in human affairs. That retribution for evil deeds had often been long delayed no longer disturbed him. Confident in the sure march of the Divine law, he could endure the sight of the multitudinous, but ephemeral evils of the present. In the future Divine Justice would execute itself as sternly as in the past; for the history of the world, as said Hegel, was the judgment of the world. The French Revolution was an unmistakable sign to an unbelieving generation that the Ruler of the world was not dead or sleeping; that, in the modern world as in the ancient, retribution, though long delayed, was inevitable. Restored to his belief in a righteous predestination, Carlyle once more felt himself free to act.

The field for his action had meanwhile been immeasurably widened. Fichte had taught him a grandiose conception of the rôle of the man of letters which exceeded even his youthful dreams. In his essay, *The Vocation of the Scholar*, Fichte had revealed the unique mission of the literary man. The laws of the universal mind which governed the universe presented themselves under the guise of different institutions and different events in each succeeding age. It was the function of men of letters, the elect of the race, to detect these laws beneath the temporary symbols which clothed them, and to point them out to their less clear-

sighted fellow men. Of the necessity of such interme-
diaries in his own age and nation Carlyle needed no
persuasion, for he remembered too vividly how outworn Christian dogma and the new dogmatism of
mechanistic philosophy had so largely dominated contemporary thought that it was only by remarkably good
fortune that he had discovered the real meaning of the
universe. He was certain also that the ordeal through
which he had passed in seeking the light had especially
fitted him to guide others to this liberating knowledge.
He therefore seriously and gravely accepted the rôle
of a prophet to his nation and age.

The former Voltairian became a mystic and a seer.
Surrendering himself to his feelings, he bathed in an
infinite ocean of pure spirit, and felt God closer than
breathing, nearer than hands and feet. He saw the
waves of spirit beating against the closed souls of all
men, and longed to be the means of giving them entrance. He longed to show the presence of this life-
giving spirit in Christianity, where it was concealed
only by the opaqueness of the traditional symbols, and
make it comprehensible even to the most humble and
unlettered. He longed to bring to the suffering poor
the good tidings that the Ruler of the world was living
and just, and would not long leave their wrongs un-
righted.

The year 1825, in which he attained this serene certitude of belief, was probably the happiest in Carlyle's
life. Exultation over his release from doubts was
augmented by a newly-won confidence in his ability to
earn a living by his pen, which permitted him to resign

the Buller tutorship. His literary reputation he also owed to his German teachers. A translation of *Wilhelm Meister*, begun at a time when "the syllables of Goethe" excited "an idea as monstrous as the words Gorgon and Chimaera," [11] had unexpectedly found many readers on its publication in 1824. Carlyle's next venture, a *Life of Schiller*, drew a letter of congratulation from Goethe on its appearance in 1825. His growing reputation enabled him to contract with London publishers for an anthology of *German Romance*, upon which he was working when he reached the end of his spiritual struggles. To complete his happiness, Miss Welsh had finally consented to be his wife. But the marriage, which took place in October, 1826, was followed by an unexpected ill fortune. *German Romance* failed to sell. A novel, through which Carlyle was to preach his gospel to the age, was abandoned because of his inability to manage that literary form. The family treasury ran low, and he began to consider removal to the farm of Craigenputtock, part of his wife's patrimony, where living expenses would be less than at Edinburgh, and opportunity for uninterrupted work greater.

From this removal he was momentarily held back by brightening prospects. The *Edinburgh Review* opened its pages to him for a series of articles on German literature, and a professorship at St. Andrews or London University seemed possible of attainment. The *Edinburgh Review* engagement gave him more pleasure, because it enabled him to preach, with German authors as convenient texts, to the *élite* of the British reading public. In the second of his articles, *The State of German Literature* (1827), Carlyle first disclosed himself as an evangelist. An explanation of the works of Kant and Fichte developed into an attack on the philosophy of Locke, which Carlyle, with a true instinct, singled out as the ultimate source of the general unspirituality of British and Scotch thinking, as manifested in political economy, utilitarian ethics, and thinly veiled atheism. He challenged the confident claims of the Lockians by asserting that their entire system of thought was based upon an error of method. An exclusive reliance upon the understanding had led English thinkers into the barren wastes of materialism, while the Germans, through a recognition of the superiority of the reason as an instrument for obtaining the truth, had entered into the Delectable Mountains of the spirit. In an eloquent peroration Carlyle exhorted his readers to renounce their allegiance to logic, and taste the joy of communion, through the immediacy of the feelings, with an immanent God. But such vigorous propaganda, though gratifying to Carlyle's soul, was a definite hindrance to his prosperity. His attack on Utilitarianism provoked the hostility of James Mill and Brougham, and thereby lost him a chair at the projected London University. St. Andrews likewise declined to admit so conspicuously colorful a personality into the sober ranks of its faculty. *Review* articles alone could not maintain Carlyle's household. Craigenputtock was inevitable.

Thither Carlyle removed in March, 1828. There he was to remain, with but short intervals of absence, for six years. The bleak moors accentuated the gloom of his dreadful earnestness and uncertain prospects. He felt the weight of responsibility for the salvation of his countrymen, and could accept no literary employment which did not conduce to that end. From the solitary watchtower of the border farmhouse he continued steadfastly to survey contemporary civilization as a whole, and to appraise the evils for which he must supply the remedy.

For this comprehensive view he was not solely dependent on his extraordinary wide reading. Patronage of the Bullers had enabled him to escape from provincialism. What he had seen of England and France during a trip lasting from June, 1824, to March, 1825, had reinforced his conviction of the necessity of a spiritual renovation of society. In London he had found the Utilitarians the most active school of thinkers, but had conceived for them an instant and violent antipathy. The parents of his two pupils, who belonged to the inner circle of Radicals, he denominated " a cold race of people," living for " external show." [12] The poet Campbell, allied with the Benthamites in the enterprise of founding London University, had " no living well of thought or feeling in him," and a " heart . . . as dry as a Greenock kipper." [13] The English men of letters generally had succumbed to the blight of the prevailing intellectual atmosphere, for Carlyle found " no man of true head and heart among them." [14] In the hope of identifying himself with a movement of reaction against the universal spiritual torpor he sought out the most prominent of the opponents of Philosophic Radicalism. But Coleridge disappointed him by manifesting a weakness of will and a nebulousness of thinking which wholly unfitted him for the leadership of such a forlorn hope.

Paris, still full of memories of the Goddess of Reason, seemed in a worse plight than even London. Carlyle was indignant on seeing " the people sit and chatter and fiddle away existence as if it were a raree show, careless how it go on so they have excitement, ' *des sensations agréables*.' " [15] Dismissing the Parisians with Voltaire's epithet, " tiger-apes," he turned with relief to seeking out spots made memorable by the Revolution.

Birmingham had a novel and portentous aspect which arrested his attention. As a town he found it " pitiful enough; a mean congeries of bricks, including one or two large capitalists, some hundreds of minor ones, and, perhaps, one hundred and twenty thousand sooty artisans in metal and chemical produce. The streets are ill-built, ill-paved, always flimsy in their aspect . . . often poor, sometimes miserable." [16] But the real importance of this " city of Tubal Cain " lay in its iron works. " Torrents of thick smoke, with ever and anon a burst of dingy flame, are issuing from a thousand funnels. A thousand hammers fall by turns. You hear the clank of innumerable steam-engines, the rumble of cars and vans, and the hum of men interrupted by the sharper rattle of some canal boat loading or disloading." [16]

Carlyle had been in retirement only a year when an opportunity to give wide publicity to the ills of the age was thrust unexpectedly upon him. It happened that the Whigs were making a vigorous effort to disown the Radicals, whose reputation as dangerous extremists was frightening away possible supporters of Parliamentary reform. The youthful Macaulay had already furthered this design by establishing a clear distinction between Whig and Radical political theories in a critique of James Mill's *Essay on Government*, contributed to the *Edinburgh Review* of March, 1829, which had exposed the weakness of the deductive method of reasoning in politics. Jeffrey, who was on the point of relinquishing the editorship of the *Edinburgh*, planned to make the close of his long régime memorable by following up Macaulay's success by a violent arraignment of the central Radical dogma of social reconstruction according to the demands of pure reason. He turned to Carlyle as a writer peculiarly fitted by convictions and polemical powers to make such an assault effective; and Carlyle, who had been constantly chafing at the restraint which Jeffrey's cautiousness and skepticism laid upon his pen, accepted the commission with alacrity. He threw discretion to the winds, and made his attack, which appeared in the autumn of 1829, something much more radical and vital than party propaganda. It chose for its first object, not intellectualism, but the industrialism in which the Whig as well as the Radical proclaimed his pride. Vivid memories of the working populations of Edinburgh, Glasgow, and Birmingham had long stirred in Carlyle bitter indignation at the constant assertion by publicists like Macaulay and McCulloch that statistics concerning the production of goods and the balance of trade proved that Great

Britain was enjoying a prosperity unexampled in her annals. He now gave it expression in the demand that such complacent optimists test their facile generalization concerning the vast improvement in the condition of the English people by expanding their statistical premises to include the results of hitherto neglected investigations into " how much better fed, clothed, lodged, and, in all outward respects, accommodated, men now are, or might be." Carlyle confidently predicted that such inquiries into the distribution of the enormous new wealth would belie their optimism, and force them to acknowledge that the acquisition of this wealth had only increased the gulf between the few rich and the vast mass of the population, whose condition had probably been made worse by the introduction of machinery into industry. That this kind of statistics had not been collected he declared to be the fault of the theory of *laissez-faire* subscribed to by both Whig and Radical, which had reduced the duties of the central government from those of a " father," to those of an " active parish constable." This advocacy of governmental regulation of the distribution of the products of industry was the first declaration of Carlyle's social gospel, which had possibly been forming itself even in 1817, when he and Irving, on a walking trip from Kirkcaldy, had visited Robert Owen's model mills at New Lanark. It was thenceforth to absorb an ever-increasing proportion of his attention, until at last it took precedence in his writing over the literary and philosophical gospel given him by the Germans.

For the moment, however, it was presented only in

bare outline before he relapsed into his earlier vein. Praise of a paternal interference in industry illogically developed into scorn of the wider paternalism of Bentham's "patent codes," which were with equal inconsistency supported by the Radical advocates of *laissez-faire*. Carlyle found in the growing confidence in the ability of governmental machinery to mold men into good citizens in spite of themselves the menace of a rapid depletion of the national stock of self-reliance and civic spirit. The prevailing philosophy, which regarded man as the creature of his environment, seemed the fountainhead of such demoralizing influences. Attempts to account for the development of genius, psychological explanations of poetic inspiration, and "natural histories of religion," were not only destroying reverence for the sublime and mysterious elements of human life, but were also removing the inspiration to rise above mediocrity. Contemporary thought was being diverted from "moral science" to "physical science," and morality, deprived of its divine content, was being treated as only the product of profit-and-loss calculation. These cumulative influences were drying up the fountains of national life; all that had been free, natural and spontaneous was cabined, cribbed, and confined. Through being treated as lifeless machinery, institutions were actually becoming it. "The time," Carlyle summarized, "is sick and out of joint. Many things have reached their height."

But Carlyle was young and had the instinct of hope; he was religious and had confidence in God's power to reëndow the dry bones of society with flesh and life.

Indeed, Fichte's lectures *On the Character of the Present Age*, to which Carlyle had probably been indebted for much of his analysis of the evils of the time, had pronounced these evils only a transient phase of the great moral progress of humanity from blind obedience to the authority of church and state to understanding and free acceptance of the Divine plan of history. Therefore among signs of the times he found signs of reviving spirituality. Although "the Millites have come up on the left," "the Millenarians have come up on the right"; extravagant religious enthusiasm was becoming an antidote for Utilitarian analysis. For the liberation of the spirit the influence of the French Revolutions was not spent; the proved inadequacy of political revolution would soon lead it into the right channel of "inward perfection." The reform of society depended upon the individual's willingness to reform his own moral nature. And toward this end Carlyle, in his usual fervent peroration, urged each of his readers to strive.

This declaration of war against the spirit of the age attracted little attention in England, but it received new direction and impetus from an unexpected quarter, from France, a nation which Carlyle had judged to be wholly given over to frivolity. *The Signs of the Times*, reprinted in *La Revue Brittanique*, aroused the interest of the followers of the recently deceased Comte de Saint-Simon. Saint-Simon had been a philosopher-philanthropist of familiar eighteenth-century type, who resembled Bentham and Owen except for the profession of a religion. Overwrought by the storm and stress of the Revolution and the bewildering economic and political changes which resulted from it, he had come to believe himself a Messiah with a God-given mission to reform society, and had gathered about him disciples for the spread of a new Christianity. These disciples reflected the strange dual nature of their master; they were men of excellent scientific training and business experience: Polytechnicians, bankers, physicians, politicians, and promoters ignited by a common religious enthusiasm, men who founded almost simultaneously the first French railway company and a monastery at Ménilmontant, and, while on a wild errand to the Orient to discover " *la femme libre*," saw the advantage of piercing the Isthmus of Suez with a canal. The religion in which Saint-Simon had indoctrinated them purported to be a return to the beliefs and practices of primitive Christianity, but it contained no whit of other-worldliness. It accepted the methods and discoveries of modern science, and proposed to practice the Divine precepts of brotherly love by employing them to bring about " the most rapid possible improvement of the lot of the poorest class." [17] Carlyle's article, which contained the germ of this religion, attracted the attention of these Saint-Simonians when their proselyting zeal was at its highest. One of the youngest and most enthusiastic of their number, Gustave d'Eichthal, directed in July, 1830, a letter to the author of the *Signs of the Times*, congratulating him on his insight into the faults of the age, and urging him to accept the gospel of Saint-Simon, the new Jesus, which was their providentially revealed remedy. With this letter went a package containing Saint-Simon's *Le nouveau Christianisme* and copies of the periodical *L'Organisateur* in which appeared the *Expostion* of the latest developments of his gospel by his followers Bazard and Enfantin.[18]

These writings gave an extraordinary stimulation to Carlyle's thought on social questions. " Received," he noted in his *Journal*, " a strange letter from some Saint-Simonians at Paris, grounded on my little *Signs of the Times*. These people have strange notions, not without a large splicing of truth, and are themselves among the *Signs*. I shall feel curious to know what becomes of them. *La classe la plus pauvre* is evidently in the way of rising from its present deepest abasement. In time it is likely that the world will be better divided and he that has the toil of plowing will have the first cut at the reaping. A man with £200,000 a year eats the whole fruit of 6666 men's labor through the year; for you can get a stout spadesman to work and maintain himself for the sum of £30. Thus we have private individuals whose wages are equal to wages of seven or eight thousand other individuals. What do these highly beneficed individuals *do* to society for their wages? *Kill partridges! Can* this last? No, by the soul that is in man it cannot, and will not, and shall not! " [19]

This grimly-joyful confidence in the inevitable redress of existing social injustices was excited by the discovery of a novel treatise on political economy which gave the prestige of scientific sanction to Carlyle's objections to the orthodox economic theory. This was the *Exposition* of Saint-Simonian ideas in the *Organisateur*, soon to appear in book form as *La Doctrine de Saint-Simon*. Its chief authors, Bazard and Enfantin, well-to-do Parisian bankers, did not have Carlyle's intimate knowledge of the sufferings of the lower classes, but they had the advantage of acquaintance with something resembling the governmental statistics concerning their economic condition whose lack Carlyle had deplored. These they had found in *Nouveaux principes d'Économie Politique*, by the Swiss historian Sismondi. This treatise reverted to the inductive method of economic study which had been so greatly neglected since Adam Smith. It was based on a first-hand study of the phenomena of the manufacturing districts of England and the Continent in 1819, when the widespread suffering caused by an over-production crisis had almost ranged Carlyle on the side of the insurrectionary weavers. Its picture of industrial conditions profoundly moved the preachers of a new Christianity. As Christians they were distressed by the display of man's neglect of his fellow-man; as men of science they were irritated by the manifest inefficiency of the economic organization, or rather, lack of organization. *Laissez-faire* was clearly as wasteful and cruel as that order of nature to which its champions likened it. It was an anachronism in a scientific age, and must give place to that intelligent control whereby man had already compelled the indifferent or hostile forces of nature to minister to his well-being. For a resigned reliance on an unconscious process Saint-Simonians therefore proposed to substitute purposive organization

for the attainment of a clearly-defined goal. That goal
their ethical prepossessions caused them to define as the
greatest possible physical and moral well-being of
every member of society. The primary requisite of
such an organization was evidently the allocation of the
direction of economic life in the hands of those most
capable of stimulating production.

A formidable obstacle stood in the way of this
arrangement: the institution of private property. By
its provisions the tools of production were allotted
according to birth or other accidents, or even to anti-
social trickery and over-reaching, more often than according to ability to produce. The interests of efficient
production consequently seemed to demand the confiscation of all property by the State, and the distribution
of its income to individuals proportionately to their
skill and fidelity in mental and physical labor. They
seemed to demand also the appointment of new " *chefs
de l'industrie*," [20] who would not own a factory any
more than a colonel his regiment, who could not dispose
of their earnings to their children, and whose tenure
of a privileged position in the carefully graduated
hierarchy of labor would not be absolute, but dependent upon their continued capacity and diligence. The
analogy of the military hierarchy seemed to prove that
the abolition of absolute ownership of property and of
the right to testate need not necessarily destroy the
ambition and initiative of the most capable members of
society. Like military officers, they would find ample
reward for their acceptance of responsibility in the field
opened to their executive capacities, in the honor and

deference paid to their rank, in artistic pride in their work, and in their somewhat larger material reward. From the summit of this economic hierarchy a central direction, enlightened by comprehensive statistics, would speedily put an end to the evils which Sismondi had so vividly pictured: the prevalence of privileged and compulsory idleness, the over-production of certain kinds of materials, the over-crowding of certain trades and professions, the neglect and ruin of workers superseded by machinery, and the ethics of warfare which *laissez-faire* had dignified. Freed from excessive hours of labor by the consequently increased efficiency of the productive system, the lowest class could improve itself mentally and morally; the end of economic activity would be achieved.

The Saint-Simonians did not support these proposals by appeals to the scientific temperament and to abstract justice alone; they also employed arguments more likely to convince conservative minds; arguments from legal precedents and from orthodox economic theory. The Saint-Simonians belonged to the philosophic school of historians recently sprung up in Germany and France, who had ceased to disregard the Middle Ages as a barbarous and meaningless interregnum between the Græco-Roman and eighteenth century periods of enlightenment, and had come to consider history as an orderly process of development. Drawing from a knowledge of economic history consequently wider than that of orthodox economists, they were able to demonstrate that property, both in kind and in manner of transmission, had long been subject to legislative modification. For example, property in men, slavery, had been abolished in most European countries, and in France inheritance by primogeniture had been succeeded by equality among heirs of the same degree. Furthermore, the current conception of an indefeasible right of private property, unconditioned by any responsibility to society for its use, was of the most recent growth. The feudal system had made tenure of land by the aristocracy contingent upon the performance of the preëminent social function of stimulating production by protecting the agricultural serf and the burgher against marauding or imperialistic neighbors. Since the national governments had taken over this function, it seemed logical that they, and not the heirs or plunderers of a functionless aristocracy, should possess the land. The absolutist conception of private property could not even be justified by the principles of the political economy which had taken it for granted. The term " rent," which James Mill and his associates had been turning so blithely against the landlords, was equally dangerous to the industrial and commercial capitalists, for it could consistently be expanded so as to include all income from monopoly, from inheritance and every other kind of chance and luck, from interest on loans, and from investments in industries which its recipient did not personally direct.

The Saint-Simonians therefore did not admit any legal or moral obstacle to a revival of the functional conception of property, and the abolition of inheritance, which would put an end to the selfish, irresponsible use of the national wealth by privileged individuals. They believed also that a reorganization of industry on the model of the military organization which had given medieval institutions such astonishing stability and vitality would rescue society from the anarchy into which the succession of equalitarian democracy to feudal militarism had plunged it. Economic liberty would give reality to political liberty, and render superfluous and absurd political government based on universal and equal suffrage and representation of geographical units. The resources of the globe would be pooled in the interest of the greatest good of the greatest number; wars of man against man would be superseded by the intelligent and constructive warfare of united humanity against the forces of nature. Such was the Utopia of Saint-Simon.

Carlyle welcomed this gospel as a clarifier of many ideas which had been struggling for expression in his own mind. He replied to D'Eichthal most cordially, expressing his faith in the coming of an " organic " state of society based on a new religion, a religion growing out of the " deep, mystic, immeasurable sympathy which man has for man," [21] which was the " communion of saints " [21] spoken of in the Apostles' Creed. Although he was unwilling to accept the Saint-Simonian version of this religion as a literal Divine revelation, he avowed his vital interest in the political and economic doctrines to which it led, and his intention to coöperate in the attempt to make them prevail. In this connection he pointed out the independent approximation of his own essays on *Voltaire, Goethe,* and *Novalis* to the Saint-Simonian point of view. A postscript to this letter, written on August 9, 1830, recorded exultantly the arrival in England of the exiled Bourbon Charles X, and rejoiced that D'Eichthal and his associates had plans of permanent reconstruction in comparison with which such political changes were of the utmost superficiality.

As the British Whigs and Radicals, encouraged by this second French Revolution, pressed more strongly their demands for Parliamentary reform, Carlyle likewise looked beneath a superficial Reform Bill to a radical economic reconstruction essentially like that sketched by the Saint-Simonians. He continued his correspondence with D'Eichthal; requested more of their writings; praised them for having discovered, in the " age of steam-engines," [22] that " man is still man " [22] and not a tool to be worn out and thrown away; and blamed them for not having indicated practical means of realizing their ideal of social justice, " To each according to his capacity, to each capacity according to its works." [23] He translated *Le nouveau Christianisme*, and tried to get it published anonymously, with an introduction of his own composition applying it to British conditions. The logic of his own economic situation made him deaf to the expostulations of Jeffrey and Goethe against his association with enemies of the institution of property.[a] Two of his brothers, a farmer and a physician, were unable to earn a living, and the

---

[a] Jeffrey's expostulations against Carlyle's " radicalism " have but recently been published in D. A. Wilson's *Carlyle to " The French Revolution "* (1924), p. 185 ff.

money he advanced them so depleted his slender savings that his economic situation, always precarious, was rendered almost desperate. Such literary employment as his ill-repute as a mystic and a radical still permitted him was badly and slowly paid. Winter threatened the little household at Craigenputtock with worse hardships than it had yet undergone. Anxiety for his own fortunes, pity for those still less fortunate, detestation of rich idlers and wasters, and the exciting prospect of a revolution fraught with incalculable possibilities of good or evil raised Carlyle to the height of prophecy. In September, 1830, amid yellowing leaves and stormy skies which harmonized with his mood, he began to compose his own gospel of social reform. Planned originally to be a short article like *Signs of the Times*, it took such possession of his mind as to expand into a substantial book, whose form reflected the chaotic mental and emotional condition of its author. It likewise burst the strait-jacket of the conventional reviewers' style which Carlyle had hitherto employed, and expressed itself in the *patois* of his boyhood tinged with Germanisms absorbed from his later studies; a strange jargon, by turns bizarre, beautiful, irritating, and powerful, which was thenceforth to be his habitual medium.

The inimitable style of this prophetic book, the irony, the Brobdignagian humor, the pathos, the imagery which have made it live as literature, were Carlyle's; its content was almost entirely a synthesis of the ideas of the German philosophers and the Saint-Simonians. The first of the three books into which it was divided challenged the pretensions of science, and its creature, empirical philosophy. It made capital of the disclosures which the Saint-Simonians, trained scientists as they were, had made of the extent to which professedly objective scientific observations were adulterated by human prepossessions. Like the Saint-Simonians, again, it pointed out the superficiality of Bentham's philosophy, which ignored metaphysical questions. It showed how Transcendental philosophy, for which the problem of knowledge had a meaning, penetrated beneath the phenomenal world to which science confined its observations, and freed the human soul from bondage to a materialistic determinism. Matter, said Carlyle, paraphrasing Fichte, was man's servant, not his master; it had no independent existence, but had been created by man's spirit to supply the resistance necessary for the development of human morality. Man was pure spirit, and subject only to the laws which God had implanted in his conscience; men were " light sparkles floating in the æther of Deity." Carlyle breathed the breath of life into Fichte's rather dry and formal representation of the transcendent world, and by the magic of his words transformed " this so-solid-seeming world " into " an unsubstantial, færy place," which had power to shake the confidence of the most matter-of-fact and skeptical of readers. And to make his hold on the credence of his audience doubly sure, he devoted the second book to a narrative, largely autobiographical, but influenced by *Wilhelm Meister* and Fichte's *Vocation of Man*, of the steps whereby a perplexed human soul rose from slavery to the material world to an assurance of God, Freedom, and Immortality.

In the third and concluding book, Carlyle strove to show how all men could be brought to share in the spiritual rebirth to which a few had attained. He believed he had to do with an age sunk into what Fichte had called " the state of completed sinfulness," [24] at the antipodes of that " state of completed justification and sanctification " [24] for which Providence had destined the world. The actual Church, State, and economic system were obstacles to the life of the spirit; and the Utilitarians, reprehensible in most other respects, were blind instruments of God destined to destroy them. After these anarchists had spent two centuries in destroying and cremating the social organism, Carlyle had faith that a new and good social order would rise miraculously, like the Phœnix, from the funeral pyre. To use another of Carlyle's figures, society, like a serpent, was spending two centuries in sloughing off its old skin, while a resplendent new skin was growing beneath the old. Indeed, Carlyle professed to have glimpses of the nature of this embryonic integument. Saint-Simon's rediscovery of the brotherhood of man and the transcendent importance of human values was providing for a society quite unlike the " Egyptian pitcher of tamed vipers, each struggling to get its head above the others," which was symbolic of the society of his own time. Labor was rising slowly to its destined place of preëminent dignity and honor, and incidentally was preparing the destruction of the system of private property. Upon the ability to do useful work, whether physical or mental, was being selected a ruling class far superior to that chosen by birth, wealth or the ballot box. Its establishment would mean permanent order, for Carlyle believed mankind had an instinctive reverence for heroes, and had never rebelled against real superiors. Prowess in war having ceased to be a title to honor and reward, a world of brothers would thereafter coöperate harmoniously in exploiting the resources of the planet. And to inspire mankind with higher than material aims would arise a new, unorganized priesthood of men of letters, whose works would keep men alive to the spiritual significance of the universe, and reveal God's ever-unfolding plan of history. The perfect social order would be a theocracy, God ruling over a reborn human race. "The Golden Age," Carlyle quoted prophetically from Saint-Simon, " which a blind tradition has hitherto placed in the Past, is Before us."

In the concluding chapter of this remarkable book, which he whimsically entitled *Sartor Resartus*, Carlyle explained the disappearance of Professor Teufelsdröckh, its pretended author, by the suggestion that he might have gone to Paris to confer with the Saint-Simonians. Such an ultimate destination may have been contemplated when, immediately upon the completion of the *Sartor* at the end of July, 1831, Carlyle took it to London for marketing. On the day of his arrival there, he recorded in his *Journal:* " dine in an eating house among Frenchmen, one of whom ceases eating to hear me talk of the Saint-Simonians." [25] The same topic was dominant in his first conversation with his friend Irving a week later. His interest in these social prophets was at its height in early September, when he sought out another " sign of the times," a " new mystic," [26] whom he discovered to have also learned much from them, and actually to have met Gustave d'Eichthal in 1828.

Chapter VI

A REASONING MACHINE.

THAT Mill's *Spirit of the Age* showed any trace of what Carlyle called mysticism seems explicable only on an assumption which Mill himself would have rejected; namely, that the child chosen by the Philosophical Radicals to be made the wholly rational being whom they desired all men to resemble was originally endowed with a deeply emotional, almost poetic nature. Otherwise it would be hard to account for the waves of indignation, admiration, and high aspiration which so often disturb the clear and placid surface of John Stuart Mill's mature prose, and for his *Spirit of the Age*, which was so warm and enthusiastic in tone, ascribed so predominant an importance to the influence of ideas on history, and professed so sublime a faith in the reconstruction of society on the basis of intrinsic merit. If we accept this assumption, we shall have the greater cause to wonder at the efficacy of a system of education which almost succeeded in suppressing entirely this original nature, and subjected it permanently to one of the coolest, most analytic, and most logical of intellects.

With characteristic foresight, Bentham and James Mill had chosen, at the very inception of their united propaganda in 1808–9, a successor who might carry that propaganda far into the century. Since Bentham had no children, their choice had naturally fallen upon the then only son of James Mill, John Stuart, an unsuspecting infant of three years. They determined to make of the boy not only a faithful and untiring champion of the Benthamite faith, but also an indubitable testimony to the validity of the psychology upon which that faith was founded. With sublime and ruthless confidence, James Mill offered his own flesh and blood for an *experimentum in corpore vile* to test Helvetius' theory of the omnipotence of education. By this experiment he intended to produce no mere parrot of the right principles, but a superlatively logical and frictionless mind, which would accept those principles because their inherent justice compelled assent. Bentham cooperated generously, giving the boy books and the freedom of his home; on the occasion of a seemingly serious illness of James Mill in 1812 he proposed to adopt the young hope of Philosophical Radicalism in the event of his father's death. On his recovery, James Mill accepted the offer for a future contingency in a touching letter: " If I were to die any time before this boy is a man, one of the things which would pinch me most sorely, would be, the being obliged to leave his mind unmade to the degree of excellence of which I hope to make it. But another thing is, that the only prospect which would lessen that pain, would be the leaving him in your hands. I therefore take your offer quite seriously, and stipulate, merely, that it shall be made as good as possible; and then we may perhaps leave him a successor worthy of both of us." [1]

The object of such fond solicitude was destined to

be unaware, for ten years, of the high hopes which were centered in him; but he was distinctly conscious of the severity of the discipline preliminary to the achievement of his happy destiny. His childhood was pitilessly snatched from him; for his father would permit no criminal shortening of the all-too-brief period during which a man's efforts are useful to society. Bentham had begun to read Latin and Greek at the age of four; John Mill's earliest remembrance was of learning lists of Greek words. James Mill spared himself no more than he spared his son; he was John's sole teacher, and permitted him to study beside the desk at which he was writing his *History of India*, and interrupt him constantly, while he was in the throes of composition, with inquiries concerning the meaning of Greek words, no Greek-English dictionary being then procurable. From John's fourth year until his thirteenth extended the first stage of his education, which consisted for the most part in storing his mind, which Locke had taught to be then only passively receptive of sensations, with a multitude of facts and impressions from history and literature. Mathematics offered the only diversion from this fare; a diversion not at all to the boy's liking. Of fiction he was permitted very little; biography and books of travel were considered more wholesome and more useful substitutes. When he was eight, Latin, the composition of English verse, and the delegated duty of teaching a rapidly increasing number of sisters and brothers were added to his burdens. Other children he saw but rarely, for he was being protected against " the contagion of vulgar modes of thought and feeling." [2] Consequently he never learned to play. His leisure, which he later described as ample, in spite of his being permitted no holidays, was given to solitary amusements " of a quiet, if not bookish turn," [3] which gave little stimulus to any other kind even of mental activity, than that which his studies called forth. His sole exercise was walking, and that often afforded little relaxation, for his father was wont to accompany him, and catechise concerning his independent reading. It is remarkable that of those who knew him during this period, only Francis Place found John morose and peevish.

By the age of twelve, the boy had read nearly all the Greek and Latin classics, knew the obscurest facts of ancient, and a smattering of modern, history, and had pursued mathematics through the differential calculus. In the year previous, reading aloud his father's *History of India* as an assistant in the correction of the proof sheets had revealed to him the complex problems of civilization and of government. James Mill judged that the period of passive absorption had come to a close, and that John's mind was ready to organize and evaluate the multitudinous impressions which it had received. He was desirous above all things that his son make his generalizations correctly, and avoid what he had continually attacked as the besetting sin of the contemporary British mind: thinking loosely and never pushing a theory to its ultimate consequences; which led the Englishman to the absurdity of professing contradictory opinions, to the apparent hypocrisy of professing those contrary to his practice, and to the in-

effectuality of habitual compromise. He did not share
the then almost universal superstition that mathematical studies would effect this end; for he observed, like
his son after him, that " in mathematical processes, none
of the real difficulties of correct ratiocination occur." [4]
The disciplining instrument which he chose was formal
logic; Aristotle, the Schoolmen, and Hobbes. John
made rapid progress in the art of detecting fallacies.
The complementary art of becoming conscious of the
nature of his own mental processes, and of directing
them into the right paths he found much more difficult, and was thankful for the aid of the Platonic
Dialogues in putting him on his guard against imposing " axioms " and " principles." James Mill's
severity was redoubled at this stage in the educational
experiment; he demanded impossibilities, and was indignant because John could not detect at once the
popular fallacy that something true in theory may need
correction in practice. He also trusted " too much to
the intelligibleness of the abstract," [5] and seldom lightened his pupil's labors by extending the aid of illustrations. But John throve on this regimen, and delighted
his father by thinking independently, and making sound
corrections of the reasoning of Ricardo's extremely
obscure *Principles of Political Economy*, which was put
into his hands when he was thirteen. Seeing the end
of the education thus virtually accomplished, James
Mill sought to reward his faithful pupil by a visit to
General Sir Samuel Bentham, Jeremy's brother, whose
family was spending the summer of 1820 in a château
near Toulouse. To prepare him to conduct himself

properly while in France, it was necessary to reveal the secret of the uniqueness of his education. The proud father therefore took him for a walk in Hyde Park to tell him what he had only remotely suspected, that he had been taught many things which youths of his age did not commonly know; and characteristically followed this flattering announcement with an admonition not to be vain or boastful, for this superiority over his contemporaries was the result of no superlative intrinsic merit, but came entirely from exceptional educational advantage.

The mature John Stuart Mill concurred in this latter judgment, which his father had consistently deduced from the Helvetian dogma. " If I had been by nature extremely quick of apprehension, or had possessed a very accurate or retentive memory, or were of a remarkably active or energetic character, the trial would not have been conclusive; but in all these natural gifts I am rather below than above par; what I could do could assuredly be done by any boy or girl of average capacity and healthy physical constitution; and if I have accomplished anything, I owe it, among other fortunate circumstances, to the fact that through the early training bestowed upon me by my father, I started, I may fairly say, with an advantage of a quarter of a century over my contemporaries." [6] It is tempting to entertain a conclusion which so consoles us in our mediocrity, and presents such boundless possibilities for the improvement of the entire human race, but a less biased examination of Mill's life subsequent to his educational period forbids us the satisfaction of

this self-flattery.   Eight or nine hours' daily study or
writing, rarely interrupted by vacations; many additional hours devoted to political and philosophic discussion, which encroached alarmingly upon his too-little
leisure; prodigies of intensive effort such as that involved in the completion of the 900-page *Political
Economy* in eighteen months, the very bulk of his
writing upon the most abstruse and varied subjects,
[Mill " had always a very humble opinion of (his)
own powers as an original thinker, except in abstract
science (logic, metaphysics, and the theoretic principles
of political economy and politics) "] :[7] could any education have prepared a man of ordinary intelligence and
physical energy to bear so staggering a load?   One
seems forced to conclude that a remarkable experiment
in education was tried, by a happy accident, upon an unusually promising subject, and that Helvetius did not
give us the much-wanted secret of making silk purses
out of sows' ears.   To this inference one is also drawn
by a charming picture of the precocity of John Mill at
the age of three, before educational influences had
begun to count: " When I received your letter on Mon-
day," wrote James Mill to Bentham, " John, who is so
desirous of being your inmate, was in the room, and
observed me smiling as I read it.   This excited his
curiosity to know what it was about.   I said it was Mr.
Bentham asking us to go to Barrow Green.   He desired
to read that.   I gave it to him to see what he would
say, when he began, as if reading — ' Why have not
you come to Barrow Green, and brought John with
you? ' "[8]   Likewise, one finds it hard to accept liter-

ally Mill's claim of twenty-five years' start over his contemporaries. Even if one concede its truth as far as logical training or the acquisition of facts are concerned, one cannot believe, and one's disbelief is supported by Mill's confession that he got nothing out of such works as Plato's *Theatetus,* that the Greek and Latin history and literature studied during the earlier years of childhood was sufficiently comprehended to be of great permanent value. This early curriculum left but little trace in his mature writings, and it seems possible that the same, or a better result could have been achieved in less time when Mill was more mature. It is probable also that the abolition of play in favor of such studies thwarted Mill's best development. He himself ascribed to it only one defect, a clumsiness in manual operations, which, nevertheless, did not approach that of Macaulay, his fellow-prodigy and political opponent, who could never learn to tie his cravat. Yet those who have led the normal life of the boy cannot but feel that Mill lost an invaluable opportunity to understand the human animal at its most naïve, and are inclined to ascribe to the entire lack of exercise of the upper body, such as cricket, swimming, or skating could have given in a pleasant form, the susceptibility to pulmonary disease which shortened his life.

Fortunately, that Spartan education did not wholly shape John Mill's character. It repressed and stunted, but it could not destroy a strong emotional nature. Even at the height of the influence of his father and Bentham, Mill contained potentialities of revolt against the one-sidedness of his training. From time to time

the instincts of the normal boy peeped irrepressibly from
beneath the surface. Mill tells us that in his earliest
reading of English history he " cared little for anything in it but the wars and battles," [9] and had had a romantic preference for far-off countries and events dim
in the obscurity of time. He sympathized patriotically
with England in her war against the American rebels
until his father corrected his judgment. He absorbed
with delight the fairy tales of science, and resented his
father's interference with the imaginative appeal of a
book on Physics by objecting to some of the reasoning
it contained. Bentham's summer home at Ford Abbey,
which he visited for long periods between his ninth and
twelfth years, with its " middle-age architecture,"
" baronial hall," and " spacious and lofty rooms," had
given him " the sentiment of a larger and fuller existence," and a " sort of poetic cultivation," which was
enhanced by the Abbey grounds, " *riant* and secluded,
umbrageous, and full of the sound of falling waters." [10]
At about the same period he was devouring Scott's
metrical romances, which his father, who despised
nearly all the contemporary Romantic school of poets,
had by some chance recommended to him, and it is
consequently interesting to note that the just quoted
reminiscences of Ford Abbey echo the vocabulary of
the Wizard of the North. In his thirteenth year the
romantic poems of Campbell (Campbell was *persona
grata* to James Mill because of his heterodox religious
opinions, and was to be the originator of the plan to
establish the University of London) gave John Mill
sensations which he " had never before experienced

from poetry." [11]   At the time of his trip to France he found "the perfection of pathos" in the "striking opening" [11] of Campbell's highly colored narrative poem, *Gertrude of Wyoming,* whose scene was laid in Pennsylvania:

> On Susquehanna's side, fair Wyoming!
> Although the wild flower on thy ruined wall,
> And roofless homes a sad remembrance bring
> Of what thy gentle people did befall;
> Yet thou wert once the loveliest land of all
> That see the Atlantic wave their morn restore.
>
> Delightful Wyoming, beneath thy skies
> The happy shepherd swains had nought to do
> But feed their flocks on green declivities
> Or skim perchance thy lake with light canoe
> From morn till evening's sweeter pastime grew,
> With timbrel, when beneath the forest brown,
> Thy lovely maidens would the dance renew;
> And aye those sunny mountains half-way down
> Would echo flageolet from some romantic town.
>
> Then, where of Indian hills the daylight takes
> His leave, how might you the flamingo see
> Disporting like a meteor on the lakes.

By sending the boy to France, James Mill unwittingly worked against his own ends. John's conscientious effort to study nine hours a day while with the Benthams was thwarted by the closing of the château library. The boredom resulting from this unwonted deprivation of books drove him to look about him; to walk along the Garonne, to observe peasant customs, to talk to an unexpectedly intelligent workingman. Lady Bentham, a motherly and managing woman, observing his awkwardness, prescribed, to occupy his leisure, riding, fencing, and other physical exercises,[a] most of which he took in the company of her daughters, normal adolescents slightly his seniors. A trip to the Pyrenees with the family stored his mind with ineffaceable images of sublime and terrible beauty. A winter at the University of Montpellier introduced to him " the frank sociability and amiability of French intercourse," [12] which lent an unwonted amenity to his daily life. The French character was a surprise to him; in it emotion had equal rights with intellect. Logical and analytical enough to satisfy even the demands of his own culture, it had also a beauty and a grace which were neglected by the Englishmen he knew. After a year's sojourn in the " free and congenial atmosphere " [13] of the Continent, which quickened his natural adolescent craving for friendship and self-expression, he returned with regret to " the mean and cramped externals of English middle-class life." [14]

The rising tide of John Mill's emotions then might well have burst the carefully constructed dykes of his education, had not his father, with unintentional wisdom, diverted it into the safe channel of Benthamite propaganda. It was very soon after his son's return from France that James Mill put into his hands, as an introduction to his study of the law, Bentham's social philosophy, in the form of Dumont's *Traité de Législa-*

[a] " In none of which, however," Mill remarked, " I made any proficiency." *Autobiography,* p. 40.

tion. The eager youth of fifteen arose from the reading of this work " a different being " inspired by " a creed, a doctrine, a philosophy; in one of the best senses of the word, a religion." [15] Bentham had taken him " to an eminence from which (he) could survey the vast mental domain, and see stretching out into the distance intellectual results beyond all computation " and " the most inspiring prospects of improvement in human affairs. . . . At every page he seemed to open a clearer and broader conception of what human opinions and institutions ought to be, how they might be made what they ought to be, and how far removed from it they now are." [16] Intoxicated by this vision, Mill resolved to be " a reformer of the world." [17] And like a true adolescent, he gathered about him a little group of youths as his fellow apostles for the evangelization of humanity, in the name of Bentham. The members of the Utilitarian society sought to imitate the French *philosophes* of the eighteenth century, and " hoped to accomplish no less results." [18]

The world which he had thus planned to reform presented a very flat surface to this " schoolboy fresh from the logic school, (who) had never conversed with a reality," [19] as he later described himself to Carlyle. Bentham's philosophy won his allegiance principally because it " fell exactly in its place as the keystone which held together the detached and fragmentary parts of (his) belief," [20] a belief which was inherited, not induced from a first-hand study of human life. Ideas and institutions were to him so many irregular bits of colored pasteboard which could and ought to be made to fit into their right places in the map puzzle of human existence. The world was in turmoil only because mankind was not enlightened enough to put them into their right places. Therefore, order, peace, and happiness could be brought about through the education of mankind. As an orthodox Benthamite, Mill believed that morals were only a branch of the intelligence, and that consequently a man would never act in contradiction to his clearly-perceived best interest. The majority of mankind would not object therefore to their own greatest happiness; they needed only to be taught " to believe according to the evidence, and know what was their real interest." [21] When once they knew this, they would enforce it by the peaceful pressure of public opinion on their rulers, who had been consciously exploiting them, and the millennium would be attained. Mill's vanity, for he was then a little vain of a sophistication which he was far from having attained, was appealed to by Bentham's picture of the millennium as the " absence of a certain quality of evil," and no naïve " vision of fulfilled desire." [22] " Perfect happiness," Bentham had stated, " belongs to the imaginary regions of philosophy, and must be classed with the universal elixir and the philosopher's stone." [23] Even after the operation of what Bentham styled " a perfect system of legislation," [24] the powers of nature would still menace mankind, men's passions would continue to clash, men would still suffer from the inequalities of inherited wealth and physical constitution, and numbers of manual laborers would still perform the most disagreeable toil for the smallest recompense.

The incurability of such ills did not appreciably dampen Mill's ardor for Bentham's program of reform, since they menaced almost exclusively the lower classes, with whose joys and sorrows he had no intimate contact, and little concern. There was no limit to his reverence for the most admirable specimens of the race, for a Socrates, a Turgot, but he had no Whitmanic love of "the divine average." Exploited humanity interested him almost entirely because he might gain fame as its deliverer, for his heart glowed at the picture of himself as "a Girondist in an English Convention."[25] It was not sympathy, but desire for personal glory, and the pedagogical instinct, aroused by his teaching of his younger brothers and sisters, which motivated his war on human error.

The intensification of the Benthamite propaganda which began with the institution of the *Westminster Review* in 1824 gave ample scope to John Mill's ambitions. As a principal contributor to the *Review* he had the privilege of offering an intellectual battle which the Tory and Whig "exploiters of the people" dared not refuse to join. He felt that delight of conflict with his peers, of the smashing blow through the buckler of an unjustifiable generalization, of the thrust between weak links of syllogistic armor. He had learned the proud joy of loyalty to a cause which he believed the only true cause, and to its brave champions against great odds. He had an amazing opportunity to indulge in the youthful sport of window-smashing. His leaders bade him pillory dignitaries of church and state, hold sacred no belief, policy, or institution, sit in judgment on the heritage of the past. He gleefully shocked respectability, startled by paradoxes, outraged with frankness. Circulation of a pamphlet advocating birth control brought him in collision with the police.

Ambition, controversy, party loyalty, and unconventionality were, however, the only channels through which his emotions found expression, for the tactics of their adversaries forced the Benthamites further and further into their attitude of hostility to the expression of feeling. "Utility," Mill has recorded, "was denounced as cold calculation; political economy as hard hearted; anti-population doctrines as repulsive to the natural feelings of mankind. We retorted by the word 'sentimentality' which along with 'declamation' and 'vague generalities' served us as common terms of opprobrium." [26] In John Mill, who had had less experience in human relations than his older associates, this intellectual Pharisaism reached its height. He ceased to read poetry, lost interest in music, which had once given him intense delight, and became almost a "reasoning machine." [27] Education had apparently triumphed.

For nearly three years following the first issue of the *Westminster Review*, Mill lived days of single-minded devotion to the Radical cause. He became famed throughout the Kingdom as a prodigy of learning. The most brilliant products of the Universities acknowledged him their equal. The five large volumes of Bentham's important *Rationale of Evidence* bore on their title pages Mill's name as editor. He was admitted into the inner councils of his mature Radical associates, and had the satisfaction of seeing Radical opinions spreading with extraordinary rapidity. Yet the glow of novelty and adventure was cooling with the attainment of his ambitions. He had learned that flaunting red flags did not produce converts to his cause. The increasing demands of an expanding propaganda condemned him more and more to a routine of hard work. The prodigies of labor which he performed during 1825 and 1826 taxed even his iron constitution. Professor Bain was probably right in ascribing to overwork that " dull state of nerves " [28] which caused Mill to ask himself, one day in the autumn of 1826, the momentous question: " Suppose that all your objects in life were realized: that all the changes in institutions and opinions which you are looking forward to, could be completely effected at this very instant: would this be a great joy and happiness to you? " [29]

But the negative answer to this question which plunged Mill into so profound a despair cannot be wholly explained as the result of lowered physical tone. Its ultimate origin must be found, where the *Autobiography* found it, in the inability of Bentham's ideal of human perfection to enlist longer Mill's wholehearted sympathy. The formidable analysis of which continual controversy had made him capable, disclosed the almost exclusively negative character of Bentham's thought. Bentham had concerned himself with the liberation of human life from privation, pain, and error, without conceiving of the desirability of making an addition to its pleasures. He had seemingly never reflected upon the fact that curing a man of a headache may only make him once more a prey of the ennui or anxiety from which the immediate pain of the head-ache had momentarily distracted him. The institution of Bentham's " perfect system of legislation " would therefore deprive Mill of the pleasure of pursuing an ever-receding goal without compensatorially present-ing to the race any permanent possibilities of happiness in which he could contentedly share.

Having realized so clearly that the contemplation of mankind remade would give him no great joy, Mill could no longer deceive himself by maintaining that his reforming zeal was altruistic. Ironically, he acknowl-edged its true aliment to be dreams of the glory which would be his as the author of reforms just at the time when he was coming to know the hollowness of such a reward. His precocious mental triumphs had given him too early a taste of popular acclaim, and its pleas-ures had begun to pall. Hothouse maturing had brought him already, at twenty, to the disillusioning end of first youth, when

> " From that summer's trance we wake to find
> Despair before us, vanity behind."

He concurred in his father's verdict that " Human life (was) a poor thing at its best, after the freshness of youth and of unsatisfied curiosity had gone by," [30] with-out being sustained by his father's faith that " if life were made what it might be, by good government and good education, it would be worth having." [31] The al-ternate exit from his dilemma, through a cultivation of a genuine love for humanity, Mill believed to be completely blocked. According to the associationalist psychology in which he had confidence, the attachment of feelings of pleasure with deeds and thoughts morally good, and of feelings of pain with their reverse, had not been provided for by nature, which had given pleasure and pain only the lower function of indicating automatically the well- or ill-being of the organism. It was entirely artificial, the product of education. Mill was convinced that his father had made the fatal mistake of teaching him to analyze at too early an age, before habit had made this artificial association indissoluble, and had thus given him the unlucky power of severing the bond between his pleasurable feelings and activities for the good of the race. It was now impossible to repair this error, and restore his naïve acceptance of coincident impressions as causally connected. Thus left

> Between two worlds, one dead,
> The other powerless to be born,

Mill fell into a state which he later found exactly described by these lines in Coleridge's *Dejection:*

> A grief without a pang, void, dark, and drear,
> A drowsy, stifled, unimpassioned grief,
> Which finds no natural outlet or relief
> In word, or sigh, or tear.

The bloom had been brushed from life; its uses were weary, stale and unprofitable; its pleasures left him apathetic. He feared that he was becoming a " stock or a stone." [32]

His unexpected release from this state of anaesthesia

by a burst of tears over an affecting passage in Mar-
montel's *Memoirs* gave him an inkling of the cause of
his distress. He learned that the feelings were not
mere impediments to clear thinking, but were necessary to give value to life. He learned also that the
cultivation of the feelings, by which he resolved to
provide thenceforward for the proper balance of his
faculties, could not be pursued in the same direct manner as the cultivation of the pure intellect. Genuine
feelings could not be manufactured at will; they chose
their own season for welling forth from within. The
problem of the cultivation of pleasurable feelings vexed
him, furthermore, with a paradox; for nature had ordained that pleasures fled when pursued, vanished when
examined. He realized that if he asked himself if he
were happy he ceased to be happy; for happiness is
comprised in pleasurable states which are by-products
of the achievement of ends which the will finds worthy.
Nevertheless, he still clung to his inherited belief that
" Happiness is the test of all rules of conduct, and the
end of life." [33] He therefore was not at the end of his
search for readaptation to his environment; he must yet
find ends which were permanent possibilities of pleasure
before he could consider life on a plane higher than the
physical worth the living.

His first impulse was to turn to the arts, which he had
heard praised as ministrants to a rich culture. Music
gave him pleasure, but not the poignant pleasure which
it had given in his childhood. Since the music with
which he was acquainted was dependent for its effects
on tune alone, he almost pardonably concluded that the

charm of music "fades with familiarity, and requires either to be revived by intermittence, or fed by continual novelty." [34] And such continual novelty he believed to be impossible, for the tones of the octave could be combined in only a limited number of pleasurable ways. Consequently, a perpetual succession of musical geniuses could not be expected, and the race's delight from music would have a calculable limit.[a] No permanent possibility of happiness being discoverable in the field of music, and poetry, of which he had unluckily turned to Byron as a representative, having only aggravated his malady by relating the ennuis of a man who, like himself, "had worn out all pleasures," [35] Mill was discouraged anew. His despair assumed a cosmic scope. "I felt," he had recorded, "that the flaw in my own life must be a flaw in life itself," and that "the pleasures of life, being no longer kept up by struggle and privation, would cease to be pleasures." [36] The Spirit of Evil seemed man's friend in disguise; Satan's destruction would involve the destruction of human happiness.

The eventual discovery, after two years of despondency, of the inexhaustible source of pleasure which he sought, came, like the burst of tears which had put an end to the most painful stage of his suffering, entirely by accident. In the autumn of 1828 he glanced at the 1815 edition of Wordsworth's poems "from curiosity, with no expectation of mental relief." [37]

[a] Mill may have got this idea from Bentham; cf. the latter's *Influence of Time and Place in Matters of Legislation*, in Works, Vol. I, p. 294.

These poems performed what he thought impossible, the re-association of his pleasurable feelings with observation of, and participation in, the fortunes of the human race. The edition which accomplished this miracle was as if providentially prepared for that purpose, for it was the first in which Wordsworth arranged his compositions in the order of their reference to the stages of man's life, from earliest childhood, through manhood, to old age, and to glimpses of the immortality beyond. The very first poem, *My Heart Leaps Up When I Behold*, re-introduced Mill to that joy in simple sensation whose freshness had departed from him. A few pages beyond it, *We are Seven* and *To H. C.* (Hartley Coleridge) *Aged Six*, recreated the blissful ignorance of early childhood which lives in harmony with nature, and knows not the existence of death, evil, suffering, or privation. The fragment, later incorporated in the *Prelude*, on the *Influence of Natural Objects in Calling Forth and Strengthening the Imagination in Boyhood and Early Youth*, which presented so vividly the power of mountains, especially in those moments

> When vapors rolling down the valleys made
> A lonely scene more lonesome,

to purify the youthful soul with fear and melancholy, was probably the first of those poems which affected Mill powerfully by recalling the grand and terrible images which the Pyrenees had imprinted indelibly upon his mind. Wordsworth's juvenile *Evening Walk* and *Descriptive Sketches* expanded this theme by describing the hardy and honest population which mountains had nurtured in England, in Switzerland, and in France. The *Descriptive Sketches* must have made an especial appeal to Mill by linking pictures of sublime Alpine scenery with prayers for the success of the Revolution which, at the time of their composition, was promising to make the French mountaineers happy in freedom. But the full creation in Mill of a love for humanity must have come from the great stories, *The Brothers* and *Michael*, in which Wordsworth so impressively fused the joys, and sorrows, and the stoical resignation of the English shepherds with the beauty, majesty, and solemnity of the everlasting hills which nurtured them. The returned sailor, homesick for his native mountains, suddenly confronted by the grave of the brother whom he idolized, and the gray-haired Michael, who spent whole days at the uncompleted sheepfold hallowed by such tragic associations

And never lifted up a single stone,

taught Mill that it was possible to find

A grandeur in the beatings of the heart

even among the humblest of his fellowmen.

The union of the rural sights and sounds which had become dear to him through the long walks on Sundays and holidays which had been habitual since his return from France, with

The still, sad music of humanity,

to which his ears had just been opened, gave him a source of inexhaustible and elevated pleasure which

would be unaffected by the vicissitudes of his own fortunes or those of the world.   He learned also that

> We can feed this mind of ours
> With a wise passiveness,

and recognized the justice of Wordsworth's stricture on
the narrowness of the intensely active, self-conscious
life for which his father had trained him;

> Think you, 'mid all this mighty sum
> Of things forever speaking,
> That nothing of itself will come
> But we must still be seeking?

He was thus enabled to find " real permanent happiness
in tranquil contemplation," " a source of inward joy,
. . . which could be shared by all human beings; which
had no connection with struggle or imperfection, but
would be made richer by every improvement in the
physical condition of mankind." [38]   Even in the most
perfect of Benthamic utopias

> The clouds that gather round the setting sun

could

> Take a sober coloring from an eye
> That hath kept watch o'er man's mortality,

and the simplest human joys,

> A woman's beauty and a child's delight

could lend a transcendent charm to the discovery of a
glow-worm by the roadside.   The poem which closed
the two volumes of the 1815 edition, the glorious *Ode*

on the Intimations of Immortality, gave Mill the greater confidence that he had found the way to the inner peace which he had sought so long, in that it disclosed the fact that Wordsworth had discovered this way to peace in curing himself of the self-same malady; that he, too, had seen "the glory and the freshness" of youth's delights "fade into the light of common day," and had "yielded up moral questions in despair," until he had found compensation in "the years that bring the philosophic mind." "Wordsworth's healing power" did not lose its efficacy with the lapse of time, for Mill records that he "gradually but completely, emerged from habitual depression, and was never again subject to it." [39]

Mill was doubly gratified by this remedy for his despair because it did not demand a renunciation of the type of thinking in which he had been so thoroughly trained. "The delight which these poems gave me," says the *Autobiography,* "proved that with culture of this sort there was nothing to dread from the most confirmed habit of analysis." [40] Mill brushed aside his friend Roebuck's protest that Wordsworthian cultivation of the feelings involved "cultivating illusions." "The intensest feeling of the beauty of a cloud lighted by the setting sun," he remarked penetratingly, "is no hindrance to my knowing that the cloud is vapor of water, subject to all the laws of vapors in a state of suspension; and I am just as likely to allow for, and act on, these physical laws whenever there is occasion to do so, as if I had been incapable of perceiving any distinction between beauty and ugliness." [41] Nevertheless, the spell of Benthamism was broken, for its inadequacy to provide for Mill's happiness had disproved its exclusive claim to his allegiance. Mill was ready to entertain doubts of its infallibility even as a system of abstract thought.

These doubts were confirmed through the influence of new associates with whom Mill came in contact as a result of the continuation of his dispute with Roebuck concerning the merits of Wordsworth. In a consequent two nights' discussion on the floor of the London Debating Society, Roebuck's voluntaristic and Mill's philosophic theories of poetry encountered the distinctively artistic poetic theory of Coleridge's *Biographia Litteraria*, set forth in a brilliant speech by John Sterling, a young man of letters recently come down from Cambridge. Mill's appreciation of Wordsworth astonished Sterling, who had hitherto regarded him " as a ' made ' or manufactured man, having had a certain impress of opinion stamped on (him) which (he) could only reproduce," [42] and therefore incapable of understanding a Conservative poet. At the conclusion of the debate, Sterling impulsively went over to congratulate Mill, and by the personal charm for which he was noted, thawed the reserve which Mill's education had cultivated. Sterling had much to say about the visit which he had recently paid Wordsworth in his Lake Country, and discussions on the common ground of poetry drew the erstwhile opponents rapidly into a friendship, the first warm friendship of Mill's life. Sterling, who had a " genius for friendship," drew Mill into amicable relations with the shy and outwardly

cold Frederick Denison Maurice, Sterling's most intimate companion at the University, with whom Mill had
crossed swords in debate many times during the past
year and a half. Under the new stimulus of a warm
regard for Coleridge's disciples, Mill began to study
once more the political and social opinions of that poet-
philosopher, not as formerly, with the aim of confuting
them, but with the desire to understand why they
should appeal to men of intelligence and character. He
was encouraged in this changed attitude by Coleridge's
declaration that it was the only one proper to a candid
controversialist. " The first duty of a wise advocate,"
Coleridge had written in *The Friend*, " is to convince
his opponents that he understands their arguments and
sympathizes with their just feelings." [43] And Coleridge demonstrated his ability to act on his own recommendation by a sympathetic treatment of the attempt
of the early Jacobinism to reconstruct society on the
basis of pure reason. Coleridge's classification of
Radical tenets, not as worthless errors, but as " half-
truths," which could be combated only by whole truths,
that would include the good which they contained and
add the values they neglected, pleased Mill by cutting
both ways, and being equally applicable to Conservative
doctrines. Maurice's remark " that almost all differences of opinion when analyzed were differences of
method" gave him a fresh and suggestive approach to
the writings of his opponents.

Sterling was admirably qualified to prepare Mill's
mind to receive conservative ideas, for he had himself
gone to Cambridge a convinced Benthamite. Remem-

bering that Niebuhr's *History of Rome* had first shaken his own faith in Radicalism, he introduced Mill, through Coleridge's recently published *Idea of Church and State,* to the new science of history which had sprung up on the Continent. In this work Coleridge followed Bentham in bringing institutions before the tribunal of reason. But Coleridge did not ask, like Bentham, " What is this institution now worth? " Mill found him conducting the examination with an entirely new set of questions: " For what purposes was this institution originally established? Are these purposes still indispensable? If so, can the existing institution be so reformed as to be again capable of fulfilling them? " And he also discovered to his surprise that this historical method of attacking contemporary problems, which the Benthamites had so consistently neglected, did not necessarily justify the existing order of society, but in Coleridge's hands demonstrated the injustice of private property in land and of the diversion of church endowments from their original purpose of National education to their existing function of maintaining and propagating the Christianity defined by the Thirty-nine Articles.

Christianity Maurice and Sterling presented in a new light. They had left Cambridge because they could not conscientiously subscribe to the Articles, they had little respect for the hierarchy, they favored the Reform Bill and the Ballot Box, they denied the literal inspiration of the Scriptures; yet they were wroth at the Saint-Simonians for ranking Christianity as only one among the valuable religions of mankind, they reprobated the Utilitarian ethics, and insisted that the conscience was the direct voice of God. Maurice was even contemplating study for the Anglican priesthood. For an explanation of their puzzling position, Mill's friends referred him to Coleridge's *Aids to Reflection*, and through this work he first came to know a Christianity which he was obliged to respect, a Christianity whose essence was a progressive revelation unfolding as men's minds and hearts became ready to receive it, a Christianity which welcomed examination by reason and exhibited its especial credentials in its capacity to satisfy man's moral and intellectual nature more completely than any other religion, or any system of philosophy.

Coleridge's conceptions of Christianity, of Church, and of State attracted Mill, as Sterling had hoped, to the study of the comprehensive philosophy of history of which they were corollaries. By Niebuhr, Guizot, Michelet, and other representatives of the scientific school of history which originated with Herder, Mill was taught to consider institutions as adaptations to successive stages in the progress of the human mind, a progression which institutions could do comparatively little to hasten or delay. Mill had already come to doubt his father's dogma that "identity of interest between the governing body and the community at large" was "the only thing"[44] upon which good government depended, for he had perceived what Coleridge had pointed out in attacking Rousseau, that nations, as well as individuals, sometimes went mad. He was therefore an easy convert to the theory that institutions could exercise a wholesome educative func-

tion if they were so contrived as to be always slightly
in advance of the culture of the masses. The realization that the "ignorance and want of culture "[45] of the
ruled, not the tyranny of the rulers, was the chief
enemy of the reformer, began to effect a revolution in
his political thinking. The influx of what he with
insight denominated the revolt of the nineteenth century against the deficiencies of the eighteenth did not,
however, sweep Mill loose from his Benthamite moor-
ings. The new conservatives, he saw, clung to their
half-truths as Bentham to his; they rashly and incon-
siderately rejected the skeptical spirit which had done
so much to liberate humanity from its own initial errors.
He maintained, therefore, a neutral position, and
"marveled at the blindness of the antagonists." [46] who
fought for partial views which might be reconciled in a
higher synthesis.

An approximation to this reconciling synthesis Mill
believed he had found in the Saint-Simonian doctrine.
On May 30, 1828, Gustave d'Eichthal, come to study
English civilization and to spread therein the gospel of
Saint-Simon, heard at the London Debating Society
"the discourse of a young man of much worth, Mr.
Mill," which exhibited "altogether unusual modera-
tion, good sense, and learning." [47]   The impulsive
French youth of twenty-four, whom Carlyle has described as "a little, tight, clearly pure lovable *Ges-
chöpchen; a pure martyr and apostle, almost the only
one (not belonging to the past) whom I have met with
in my pilgrimage," [48] immediately sought to convert
the attractive debater, whose "high, martyr, apostolic

spirit," [49] he recognized as akin to his own. In spite of the mood of indifference into which he was then sunk, John Mill received the strange missionary cordially, and promised a consideration of the New Christianity. D'Eichthal returned to France before Wordsworth and the Coleridgeans had opened Mill's mind to new ideas, but he left behind an early work of the then little-known Auguste Comte, who had not yet become estranged from his Saint-Simonian associates, which exerted the conclusive influence in detaching Mill from the Benthamite sect.

The brief *Treatise on Positive Polity* (*Traité de politique positive*), which had originally appeared in 1822 under the more descriptive title, *Plan of the Scientific Operations Necessary for Reorganizing Society*, was as unqualified as Carlyle's *Edinburgh* and *Foreign Review* essays in its denunciation of the negative and anarchical character of the eighteenth century radicalism, but it attracted Mill by the cool logic, the clarity, the conciseness of its manner, which contrasted so markedly with what Mill then considered the "insane rhapsody" of Carlyle. It exposed the essential barrenness of radicalism of the *philosophes* in a single brilliant sentence: " It essentially consists in attributing an organic character to the negative principles which served to destroy the Feudal and Theological System; in other words, it takes mere modification of the Old System as the foundation of the system which is to be established." [50] The so-called Right of Private Judgment was but a reaction to the authoritarian dogmatism of the Church; the so-called

Sovereignty of the People a mere protest against the
pretensions of a Divine Right of Kings. Furthermore,
Comte asserted, both of these counter-claims had become greater obstacles to political progress than the old
faiths which they were destroying. Sovereignty of the
People meant government by the least competent; the
application to politics of the Right of Private Judgment, which implied that any man's political ideals and
opinions were of equal worth with any other's, precluded the possibility of any generally recognized
political philosophy. The Catholic Church had once
been able to enunciate principles which the temporal
rulers were obliged to heed: it was the failure of the
philosophes to assume its rôle of a spiritual power, and
formulate new political principles applicable to the
new social order, which had thrown Europe into intellectual bankruptcy.

The logical remedy for this lamentable condition
lay, therefore, in the rediscovery of the seat of spiritual
power. This Comte, with somewhat of prophetic
clairvoyance, found among men of science. " In Astronomy, Physics, Chemistry, and Physiology," he observed shrewdly, " there is no Liberty of Conscience." [51]
He was certain that scientists had already almost attained the international reputation of infallibility once
enjoyed by the hierarchy, and consequently believed
that a science of politics organized, not by narrow specialists in the particular sciences, but by men broadly
educated in the methods of all the sciences, might
receive the universal recognition once accorded to the
decrees of Church councils. His study of history had

furthermore convinced him that the time was just ripe for the constitution of this new science, which he was later to call sociology. Comte found three stages in what he, in common with the contemporary philosophical historians, called the fated progress of civilization. In the first of these stages, the Theological, man had considered all phenomena, human and extra-human, as caused and controlled by supernatural beings. In the second, or Metaphysical, he had cast aside this anthropomorphism, and considered them the result of abstract forces. In the final, or Positive stage, into which the most advanced nations were just entering, he was abandoning as useless the search for final causes, and was learning to control phenomena by discovering the uniform relationships existing between them. The present was a scientific age, when men were content only with certain, positive, verifiable knowledge. Such knowledge the sciences dealing with matter could already give, and physiological psychology was fast attaining it in the realm of mind. The science dealing with minds in interrelation, the social science, alone was backward, lagging in the metaphysical stage of the Social Contract, after having advanced from the theological stage of the Divine Right of Kings. " Scientific men," Comte urged, " ought in our day to elevate politics to the rank of a science of observation." [52]

The end of this new science would be the prediction of each new step in the fated progress of civilization, and the consequent elimination of social friction in times of transition by convincing the supporters of outworn ideas and institutions of the uselessness of a struggle

against the inevitable. It would plot the facts of history, verified, in accordance with the recapitulation theory, by anthropology and physiology, in charts which
would indicate the ascent and descent of ideas and social
forces. With the completion of an accurate diagram of
the march of mind in the past, and a projection of its
course into the future, the work of the political scientist
would be done, and that of the man of letters would
begin. For men's emotions must be convinced as well
as their intellects; the inevitable must be presented as
the most desirable. And if both thinker and artist
would succeed, the practical man, the man of the street,
would no longer delay improvements by a dogged and
short-sighted defense of his immediate interests and
possessions; the day of bloody revolutions would be
past, and history would thenceforward present a picture
of rapid and orderly progress.

Read in the summer of 1829, after the Coleridgeans
had battered the first breach in his opinion, the *Positive
Polity* was the decisive influence in divorcing Mill from
the Benthamite faith. In reconciling the Benthamic
ideal of a scientifically reordered society with the Cole-
ridgean philosophy of history, it exposed two fatal
defects in what had been hitherto the tactics of the
reforming parties: the attempt to realize immediately
reforms for which the people were not ready, and the
single-minded devotion to liberty of thought, speech
and action, not merely as a primary need of an age of
transition, but as an ultimate and unique ideal for all
time. Comte enabled Mill to look " forward, through
the present age of loud disputes and generally weak

convictions, to a future which shall unite the best qualities of the critical with the best qualities of the organic periods; unchecked liberty of thought, unbounded freedom of individual action in all modes not hurtful to others; but, also, convictions as to what is right and wrong, useful and pernicious, deeply engraven on the feelings by early education and general unanimity of sentiment, and so firmly grounded in reason and in the true exigencies of life, that they shall not, like all former and present creeds, require to be periodically thrown off and replaced by others." [53]   But desertion of the Benthamic fold did not mean entrance into the Saint-Simonian. Mill had had enough of sectarianism.

His replies to the fervent letters by which D'Eichthal, encouraged by his commendation of Comte's *Treatise,* attempted his conversion to the New Christianity, exhibit the judicial quality which was thenceforward to characterize Mill's mind. While praising the originality and soundness of much of Comte's thought, he reminded D'Eichthal that it was a great error to think that " a few striking and original observations suffice to found a positive science," [54] or that Comte's position contained all the truth. He was suspicious of the neatness of Comte's generalizations, for Macaulay's recent strictures on his father's essay on *Government* had made him especially sensitive to the weakness of deductive thinking unchecked by patient and extensive Baconian induction. The progress of the newer, the empirical sciences was slowly sapping faith in a social science based upon mathematical and astronomical methods. He therefore noted several specific instances where Comte's method had led his astray. For example, his highly questionable assumption [a] of continuous social improvement as axiomatic had led him to fly in the face of the historical evidence in asserting that the Middle Ages were a distinct advance on the Graeco-Roman period. Furthermore, the splendor of the ideal of a spiritual power had blinded Comte to grave practical difficulties in the way of its realization. Who would choose the scientific experts who would be social dictators? And how would society protect itself against their misuse of the tremendous power reposed in them? The Saint-Simonian designation of production as the chief end toward which the energies of the contemporary society should be directed stirred Mill to a warm protest. " If M. Comte had been born in England," he wrote, " where this idol, ' Production,' has been placed on the altar and devotedly adored, if he had seen how the disproportionate importance which is attributed to it is the true root of our worst national vices, corrupts the acts of our statesmen and the doctrines of our philosophers, and hardens the soul of our people to such an extent that it is impossible to inspire it with any ardor of intelligence or emotion — he would have understood that a philosophy which makes production the unique end of social union would make irremediable the great social evils which partially menace the present state of civilization; and thus we come to the great practical conclusion of the Saint-Simonian

[a] " Why not admit," he wrote, " that, if humanity has advanced in certain respects, it has retrograded in others? " *Correspondence inédite avec Gustave d'Eichthal*, p. 20.

school, that the direction of the government ought to be placed in the hands of the principal industrials — at least the temporal power, the spiritual power being confided in the savants and artists. I do not know how it may be in France; but I know that in England it is people of that class who are distinguished by the most grudging and bigoted spirit, and the narrowest and most vulgar views concerning everything beyond their business and their families." [55] " Your organization," he summarized in a later letter, " seems impractical, and not desirable if it were practicable, like that of Mr. Owen." [56]

These strictures on the economic system of the Saint-Simonians were based, however, on a misconception of its animating spirit, which was cleared away by a meeting with Bazard and Enfantin at Paris immediately after the Revolution of July, 1830. At their suggestion he read Sismondi, who did more than the Owenite speakers whom he had heard at the London Debating Society in 1825 to convince him of the iniquities of the factory system, of which his life in middle-class circles in the South had permitted him no first-hand knowledge. He consequently ceased to lay entire blame for the misery of the working classes upon a parasitic and prodigal aristocracy, and began to realize " the very limited and temporary value of the old political economy, which assumes private property and inheritance as indefeasible facts, and freedom of production and exchange as the *dernier mot* of social improvement." [57] For the immediate future, however, he still believed that the economic, as well as the moral

and intellectual status of the masses could be most
rapidly improved by changes in the political rather than
the economic system.   An extension of the suffrage
would force the propertied classes, through fear of the
spread of anti-property doctrines among a majority
armed with the ballot, to treat their inferiors more con-
siderately and provide for their education.   National
education, which would enable the masses to protect
their own economic rights through birth control, and
a widely diffused suffrage, which would destroy the
prestige of wealth as the sole passport to political
power, would coöperate in fitting the people morally
and intellectually for an eventual experiment in communism.   The ultimate practicability of communism
he was inclined to admit, partly through the influence
of his former tutor John Austin, now Professor of
Jurisprudence at the University of London, who insisted that history and daily experience offered conclusive evidence of an " extraordinary pliability of
human nature " that exposed the merely temporary
character of " the universal principles of human nature
of the political economists," [58] which were supposed to
chain mankind forever to the competitive system.

Although Mill was thus in entire sympathy with the
immediate political aims of his Radical associates, he
had ceased to regard democracy as anything more than
one of many means to secure the social good, and was
inclined to agree with Austin, who had recently returned
from study in Germany, that there was " infinitely
more care for the education and mental improvement
of all ranks of the people, under the Prussian Mon-

archy, than under the English representative government . . . and . . . that the real security for good
government is ' *un peuple éclairé,*' which is not always
the fruit of popular institutions." [59]   The aristocratic
element in his opinions at this time is clearly revealed
in his articles on *The Spirit of the Age,* which, as he
wrote D'Eichthal on March 1, 1831, exhibited the
catholic influence of the Saint-Simonian doctrine.   In
these he insisted upon the impotence of the average
citizen to contribute anything valuable to the social reconstruction necessary after the accomplishment of a
political revolution.   Specialists alone, the best minds
of the nation, could put politics on the desirable basis
of a science, upon whose basic principles all thinkers
would agree, and thus provide for growth rather than
change, steady improvement rather than revolution
and chaotic transition.   This aristocratic tendency was
strengthened by Mill's pilgrimage, during his summer
vacation in 1831, to the homes of Wordsworth and
Southey in the Lake Country.   Under the spell of
Wordsworth's personality Mill strayed his farthest
from the fold of Liberalism.   With such a " philosophic
Tory " [60] as Wordsworth, who had a remarkable
ability to see both sides of political questions, Mill informed Sterling that he now had more in common than
with the orthodox Radical.   " It seemed to me," he
continued in the same letter to Sterling, " that the
Toryism of Wordsworth, of Coleridge (if he can be
called a Tory), of Southey even, and of many others
whom I could mention, is *tout bonnement* a reverence
for *gouvernement* in the abstract; it means that they are

duly sensible that it is good for man to be ruled; to submit both his body and mind to the guidance of a higher intelligence and virtue. It is, therefore, the direct antithesis of Liberalism, which is for making every man his own guide and sovereign master, and letting him think for himself, and do exactly what he judges best for himself, giving other men leave to persuade him if they can by evidence, but forbidding him to give way to authority; and still less allowing them to constrain him more than the existence and tolerable necessity of every man's person and property renders indispensably necessary. It is difficult to conceive a more thorough ignorance of man's nature, or what is necessary for his happiness, or what degree of happiness and virtue he is capable of attaining, than this system implies. But I cannot help regretting that the men who are best capable of struggling against these narrow views and mischievous heresies should chain themselves, full of life and vigour as they are, to the inanimate corpses of dead political and religious systems, never more to be revived." [61]

This position of isolation between the contending parties was identical with that of Thomas Carlyle, whom Mill had met seven weeks before he thus wrote. "Carlyle," he announced to Sterling delightedly, "has by far the widest liberality and tolerance (not in the sense that Coleridge justly disavows, but in the good sense) than I have ever met in anyone." [62] Under these favorable auspices began the friendship.

Chapter VII

AN ARISTOCRACY OF TALENT.

L A carrière ouverte aux talens (the tools to him who can use them)," Carlyle, in *Sartor Resartus,* proclaimed " our ultimate Political Evangel." Likewise Mill, in *The Spirit of the Age,* announced that " There must be a moral and social revolution which shall, indeed, take away no men's lives or property, but which shall leave to no man one fraction of unearned distinction or unearned importance." The polity at which both thinkers had thus independently arrived before their meeting was no novelty. From Plato on, most disinterested political philosophers had found in it the most satisfying union of justice and social efficiency. What was unusual in its restatement in 1831 was the tone of confidence in the imminence of its realization, which hitherto had kept postponing itself most discouragingly. The miracle of the French Revolution had recently discredited the generally accepted norms of political probability. Napoleon's inauguration of *la carrière ouverte aux talens* in his armies had astounded and frightened the world with its success. Though the Terror and Napoleon's dictatorship had revealed the dangers of transition to a new political order, the French had nevertheless just reaffirmed, by a second revolution, their resolution to extend the Napoleonic principle to civil affairs. England, which had long watched the French experiments with varying emotions, was at last unmistakably determined to bring, whether by peaceful demonstrations or by force, political power and social distinction into closer correspondence to energy and intelligence. It was difficult for young men not to believe in a new dawn of justice.

The passage of the Reform Bill, which seemed sheer Sans-culottism to the Duke of Wellington and his Tory generation of the Great War, gave Carlyle and Mill encouragement, but not satisfaction. Neither had illusions concerning the political capacity of the middle class or the identity of *vox populi* and *vox dei*. To them the reform of Parliament was of doubtful value except in accustoming the national mind to the idea of change; was a mere preliminary clearing of the ground for a radical reconstruction according to the strict Saint-Simonian formula, " To each according to his talent, to each talent according to its works." It was toward this remoter end that they bent their efforts, persuaded, at a time when unusual importance was ascribed to the influence of the individual, that they could contribute much toward its accomplishment.

Although thus agreed upon the general formula of reconstruction, Carlyle and Mill differed in their conceptions of the character of the " aristocracy of the fittest " which was to calculate and direct the nice adjustment of function to ability. Each would have remade the governing class in his own image. Encouraged by the political influence exerted by Byron and Goethe, and supported by Fichte's description of the rôle of the man of letters, Carlyle proposed to place supreme direction in the hands of literary men, who were the channels of a Power more than human. His ideal government was a theocracy. Mill, true to his education, desired government by scientifically trained experts, whose wisdom would be derived from study and experiment, not intuition or revelation. "Of all governments ancient or modern," he wrote in 1835, "the one by which this excellence is possessed in the most eminent degree is the government of Prussia, a most powerfully and skilfully organized aristocracy of all the most highly educated men in the Kingdom." [1] For the immediate future, Mill desired that this aristocracy be composed entirely of young men, for the older generation had shown its inability to adapt its mind to the great social changes which had taken place.

Carlyle and Mill differed also concerning the proper relation of the ruling class to the collective will of those whom they were to uproot and pigeon-hole in so drastic a fashion. Mill did not have Comte's faith in the infallibility of the expert, and consequently advocated the grant of universal suffrage, limited only by an educational test, which would permit every individual, and every class, to defend its own interests. This enlarged electorate would choose as its rulers, Mill believed, "those whom the general voice of the instructed pointed out as the most instructed," "for the experience of ages, and especially of all great national emergencies, bears out the assertion, that whenever the multitude are really alive to the necessity of superior intellect, they rarely fail to distinguish those who possess it." [2] Here Mill's confidence in the multitude

ended, for he insisted that the people's representative
be a true representative, not a delegate, in order that
political questions be not decided " by an appeal, either
direct or indirect, to the judgment of an uninstructed
mass, but by the deliberately-formed opinions of a
comparatively few, specially educated for the task." [3]
Popular vote would thus be a purely defensive weapon,
curbing the possible mistakes or sinister interests of the
political specialist by refusal to reëlect him. Carlyle
had no need of this machinery of checks and balances;
his ideal rulers were infallible. He relied on a great
spiritual revival, of which the fervor of the Saint-
Simonians and the English millenarians was a presage,
to make men again sensible to the voice of God, and
capable of instinctive recognition of, and obedience to,
the ablest and most honest men, who would rule according to the oracles of the inspirited literary priesthood.
" What are all popular commotions and maddest bellowings from Peterloo to the Place-de-Grève itself? "
he exclaimed in *Chartism*. " Bellowings, articulate cries
as of a dumb creature in rage and pain; to the ear they
are inarticulate prayers: Guide me, govern me! I am
mad and miserable and cannot guide myself. . . .
Surely, of all rights of man this right of the ignorant
man to be guided by the wiser, to be, gently or forcibly,
held in the true course by him, is the indisputablest.
. . . Recognized or not recognized a man has his superiors, a regular hierarchy above him; extending up
degree above degree, to heaven itself and God the
Maker, who made His world not for anarchy but for
rule and order."

In spite of the extraordinary stir of change in the air, the obstacles in the way of these ambitious plans of political reconstruction might have dismayed the stoutest heart. The government which the Reform Bill put into power was composed of Whig aristocrats like Lord Melbourne, trained in the mental habits of the old régime, realizing the insecurity of their position, and fearful that any further movement of reform might bring in, as indeed the Poor Law of 1834 did, another Tory ministry. The Commons remained " the best gentlemen's club," [4] steeped in the atmosphere of precedent and inertia, and composed of two rival groups following their respective leaders with the blind loyalty of clansmen. The middle class electorate, with which ultimate power now rested, was largely without a tradition of civic education, and aware only of its selfish interests. At the base of the pyramid lay an unorganized and inarticulate mass of the unenfranchised, leading for the most part a mere animal existence, largely destitute of even the rudiments of an education, and susceptible of being roused by the manipulations of the demagogue into outbursts of blindly destructive hatred of the propertied classes. Such was the nation which was to recognize an aristocracy of talent and submit to being organized by it.

Mill's hopes were staked upon a saving remnant of some twenty Radicals, who had brought the new spirit of change into the reformed Parliament. Their influence promised to have a weight much more than proportionate to their numbers, for they were men of unusual ability. Veteran politicians like Sir Francis

Burdett, John Cam Hobhouse, and Joseph Hume were
reinforced by thinkers of the promise of Grote and
Roebuck, and by clever youths like Carlyle's old pupil,
Charles Buller. Bentham had died a few months after
the passage of the Reform Bill, but the two Mills
remained to assume the rôle of political experts and
direct the energies of the active politicians. Believing
in the unlimited power of reason and persuasion, they
thought that the little band of Radicals could infect
the whole House of Commons with progressive ideas.
Their first enterprise was a triumph. The Poor Law
revision, drawn up by Benthamites, was an admittedly
successful application of scientific ideas to a concrete
social problem. But it brought the Tories back into
power for a few months, and frightened the Whigs
into a firmer resolution to let sleeping dogs lie. John
Mill, with his reliance on reason, ascribed the subsequent check of radical legislation to another cause, the
lack of leadership among the active Radical group, and
attempted to compensate for this lack, since financial
reasons kept him and his father out of Parliament, by
the publication of the *London Review*. He was confident that progressive measures, such as the institution
of a system of national education, legal reforms, extension of the suffrage, and the repeal of the Game
and Corn Laws and other forms of aristocratic privilege, need only to be skillfully and attractively presented in order to convert their opponents. He failed
for a time to realize that for this task of persuasion the
Radical members were peculiarly unfit. Few had the
pleasing manner necessary for gaining the ear of the

House. They tended to be pedantic bores like Grote and Bowring, or hot-tempered fanatics like Roebuck, the inveterate hater of the aristocracy. Partisan jealousy brought them to neglect the strategic opportunity of alliance with Lord Durham and the liberal Whigs which John Mill proposed in 1834. Yet they could not even present a united party front, and were never in better form than when attacking one another. Roebuck and Grote soon quarreled with John Mill. Desertions of the more conservative to the Whigs, beginning with Burdett and Hobhouse in 1835, occurred steadily. The accession of Queen Victoria in 1837 caused a monarchist landslide which deprived nearly all the rest of their seats. Grote, the most doctrinaire and loyal of Benthamites, left Parliament soon thereafter because he saw no use in supporting " Whig conservatism against Tory conservatism." [5] John Mill clung desperately to his forlorn hope. Even in 1838 he stigmatized Francis Place's letter announcing his abandonment of Parliamentary agitation as " a memorial of the spiritless, heartless, imbecility of the English Radicals." [6]

The next year he made a final effort to rally the forces of reform. Confessing that reason could do little, save in the case of exceptional individuals, to persuade men to act contrary to their material interests and class feelings, Mill frankly tried to make one large Reform Party out of all those whose interests made them dissatisfied with the *status quo*, to organize the outs against the ins. " We have a strong faith, stronger than either politicians or philosophers generally have, in the influence of reason and virtue over men's minds," Mill wrote in an article on *The Reorganization of the Reform Party*, " but it is that of the reason and virtue of their own side of the question; in the ascendancy which may be exercised over them for their good, by the best and wisest persons of their own creed. We expect few conversions by mere force of reason, from one creed to the other. Men's intellects and hearts have a large share in determining what sort of Conservatives or Liberals they will be; but it is their position (saving individual exceptions) which makes them Conservatives or Liberals. . . . We must find out who are the Privileged Classes, and who are the Disqualified. The former are the natural Conservatives of the country; the latter are the natural Radicals." [7] The government, he asserted, remained " an oligarchy of landlords," supported by its dependents of the Church, Army, Navy, and Law, by the protected trades, and by " nearly the whole class of rich men," who aspired to own land and found families in their turn. Against these privileged classes could be arrayed a much more numerous but much less homogeneous host of the disqualified. Since " the difficulty of subsisting on the proceeds of a moderate capital, whether in business or at interest, continually increases," the smaller manufacturers and merchants would form the backbone of the new Radical Party. They could count on the support of landlords dependent on manufacturing cities, on peasant proprietors, and on the Scotch, the Irish, and the Dissenters. The most important of potential allies were the deeply-wronged laboring classes, but it would be difficult to bridge the widening gap between them and their employers. "The men of thews and sinews will never give their confidence to a party recommended only by willingness to take from the aristocracy and give to the shopocracy. On the other hand, to propose Universal Suffrage would be to bid adieu to all support from the middle class." Nevertheless, there might be effected a working compromise whereby the middle classes might agree to support the repeal of the Partnership Laws, which made impossible any trial of Owenite socialism, "the actual creed of a great proportion of the working classes," and to try to extend the suffrage to the best class of workingmen. Mill personally considered this extension of the suffrage to be necessary "to keep the middle classes in that salutary awe, without which, no doubt, these classes would be just like any other oligarchy." The time was propitious for the union of the discontented elements; Melbourne was sure to go down before the Conservatives in the next election, and a real Reform Party could wrest from him the leadership of the Opposition.

The calm and judicial tone of this manifesto was scarcely adapted to rouse men to a political crusade; in any case, the expected party showed no signs of springing into being, and Mill retired from political agitation in disgust. But seven years of heart-breaking efforts had made him much more nearly a political expert. They had begun to teach him what he might have learned from Carlyle in 1831; the slight influence of reason on the actions of mankind. And he had meanwhile learned another great political lesson at second hand from another expert. In 1835 he had read the first two volumes of Alexis de Tocqueville's *Democracy in America*, which forced him to question the wisdom of his advocacy of practically universal suffrage. The summaries of the results of a half-century's experiment with democracy by a large and intelligent population: " On my arrival in America I was struck with surprise in discovering to what degree merit is common among the governed, and how rare it is among the governors," " I am acquainted with no country in which there reigns, in general, less independence of mind, and real freedom of discussion, than in America," " the majority lives in perpetual adoration of itself," " the tyranny of the majority," [8] directly contradicted James Mill's *a priori* axioms that the people would respect superior intelligence, and use their political power only in self-defense against misgovernment. Mill was startled by this revelation of the possibility of a tyranny more efficient than that of any despot or oligarchy because supported by a greater mass of power and opinion, of a throned collective mediocrity intolerant of any kind of superiority. Had the Radicals been constructing a Frankenstein's monster which would destroy them?

Mill could not evade this appalling question. Tocqueville's point of view and method of investigation gave peculiar weight to the evidence he presented. The French thinker was not an advocate of a return to feudalism; he believed democracy irresistible and irrevocable. He regarded it with the impartiality with which a scientist regards a natural force, seeking to direct it into channels beneficial to the human race. His manner of arriving at generalizations was likewise unexceptionable; he had connected equalitarian institutions and social phenomena as cause and effect through the inductive-deductive checking which Mill considered indispensable to political thinking. On the other hand, Mill's faith in democracy was too deep-seated to be easily relinquished. In his first published comment on *Democracy in America,* a review executed for the *London Review* a few months after his first reading, he attempted a compromise by accepting Tocqueville's conclusions as substantially true as regards America, but largely inapplicable to English conditions, because British society contained a much larger number of men elevated above the mass by exceptional intelligence and character and capable of commanding respect, and because England had as yet not committed herself to the inferior type of democracy which had dwarfed American statesmen by reducing them from representatives to delegates. Even with the largest extension of suffrage it might still be possible to retain representative government, under which the people, recognizing that political problems were too difficult to be dealt with in their limited leisure, would farm out the business of governing to those who could make politics a profound study and a permanent profession. The securing of " good intentions " on the part of the governing body, Mill reiterated, " is the only purpose for which it is good to intrust power to the people." [9]

These conclusions were only provisional, for Mill

was not content with a superficial investigation of so
formidable a problem. He therefore imitated Tocqueville by making a similar study of British society,
though on a much smaller scale. The results of his
preliminary survey, entirely unaccompanied by any
attempt to refer social phenomena to political causes,
he published in 1836 in the *London Review* as an article
entitled *Civilization*. The salient characteristics of the
contemporary British society he found strikingly similar
to those of the American: an unprecedented increase in
and dissemination of the comforts of existence through
the industrial revolution, a proportional increase of
population and spread of knowledge through newspapers and periodicals, and a great security of life and
property. The defects of the new social order were likewise characteristically American: the predominance of a
newly-rich multitude, oblivious of higher aims than
material comfort, shamefully mendacious in advertis-
ing and adulteration, and vulgarizing by their patronage
literature and the arts; and the corresponding " decay
of individual energy " and " weakening of the influence
of superior minds over the multitude." Mill urged that
an effort be made to restore the dangerously diminishing prestige of the exceptional individual by encouraging
originality through the permission of greater freedom
of discussion at the Universities, by removing of unearned social distinctions, and by forming a guild of the
best authors for the improvement of the popular taste.
The political lessons derived from this investigation
were not immediately formulated. Published in 1840,
when Mill no longer felt himself bound by the tram-

mels of party loyalty, in the *Edinburgh Review,* which gave them the advantage of a wide audience, they revealed an astonishing apostasy. from the old Philosophic Radicalism. The appearance of the two later volumes of Tocqueville's work gave occasion to reconsider the phrase, " tyranny of the majority," which the Tories were then using to great effect against proposals for extending the suffrage. Mill declared that the formidable phrase was being wrongly applied, that the danger which it indicated would arise from the maintenance of the existing character of the electorate, not the admission of the better class of workingmen to the suffrage. De Tocqueville had erred in referring to equalitarianism the evils which he described; they were really the results of the industrial and commercial revolutions, for they existed both in equalitarian America and in semi-feudal England. The United States exhibited them in an exaggerated form only because their population was all middle class. Not democracy, but commercialism and industrialism, and the *bourgeoisie* in which they were incarnated, were the political menace. Mill therefore proposed the partial undoing of 1832. The agricultural population should be stimulated by a system of national education to exert a larger proportional influence in national affairs, and complement the middle class character with its virtues of calm and reflection. The middle class majority in the Commons, still untrained for civic responsibility, should be restrained from hasty and ill-considered legislation by a new Upper House, modeled after the French Senate, whose members, appointed for life, should have previously held important government positions, and by a Committee on Legislation, composed of legal experts, which should have power to formulate the laws, whose initiation, and acceptance or rejection, should alone remain the prerogatives of the lower House as a whole.

Having thus taken up a position unacceptable to all the parties of the time, Mill retired from political theorizing, as well as from active propaganda, for nearly a score of years. But he never ceased to study the political situation, and by his attacks on middle class ideals in his *Principles of Political Economy,* and his investigations in the *Logic of the Social Sciences,* strove to prepare the nation for a period more fruitful in improvement.

Meanwhile Carlyle's efforts to establish a theocracy had fared no better, although they had been aided by greater wisdom and persuasive power.

He was ten years older, and had had more varied social contacts. He knew the average man too well to believe that he would choose as his governor his superior, rather than his like, and therefore took no interest in the agitation for widening the suffrage. He never tired of repeating Pope's couplet,

> For forms of government let fools contest,
> Whate'er is best administered is best.[a]

He had also no confidence in the power of reason to convert rulers into better administrators. " It is not

[a] Bentham had called this " one of the most foolish couplets that ever was written, if written with knowledge." (*Works,* X, 352.)

our Logical Mensurative faculty, but our Imaginative one which is King over us," [10] he observed wisely. And it happened that he was equipped as few men have ever been to act on the will through the emotions. His literary style, with its vividness and fecundity of image, its vigor and clangor as of an alarm bell, was perhaps better adapted to rouse the hearts of men than even he knew. He saw but one way to the best of administrations which his heart desired: the conversion of all men to religion, which would teach them how to rule, and how to obey. The greatest immediate reforms were promised from an appeal to the existing rulers to awake to their awful responsibilities as vice-gerents of God and shepherds of the people. Carlyle therefore endeavored, like Nathan before David, to convict the ministry of the cardinal sin of disregarding the welfare of the lower classes.

Their acceptance of the doctrine of *laissez-faire*, he warned, condemned them from their own mouths, for it was equivalent to a confession of inability or unwillingness to govern. They must beware to act on it further, lest the masses recognize that they had thereby abolished their reason for existence. Before it was too late, they must see the wide-spread want, squalor, and ignorance which their indifference engendered and fostered, and save themselves and the propertied classes from the explosion of wrath and wanton destructiveness which these would inevitably produce. When this sermon, reiterated in *Characteristics* (1831), a review of Ebenezer Elliott's *Corn Law Rhymes* (1832), and *Sartor Resartus* (1834), failed to din itself into the

ears of the self-confident and lethargic ministers, Carlyle called history to the support of his prophecy. In
a vivid recreation of the stupendous drama of the
French Revolution, he showed how God's judgment
had recently descended upon selfish rulers. The *History* (1837) did succeed in attracting attention. It was
acclaimed by all classes as a work of genius, and gave
Carlyle useful prestige as a man of letters. But he
observed bitterly that its message was unheeded, and
thereupon learned the saddest lesson of history: that
nations never profit by history's lessons.

His prophecy meanwhile began to be fulfilled. The
English workingmen broke their silence of despair, and
demanded a part in governing themselves. In the years
immediately following 1836, unemployment, agricultural under-production, and unprecedentedly severe
winters united in intensifying their sufferings. At the
same time the defeat of the Radicals upon the accession
of Queen Victoria, followed by the official statement
by Lord John Russell that the Liberal Party advocated
no further electoral reform, took away the last hope the
workingmen had of receiving a voice in their own affairs
as a free gift of the enfranchised classes. Their only
recourse seemed a threat of force, of whose success the
middle class had given them so striking an illustration
in 1832. Extremists, headed by Feargus O'Connor,
the most powerful mob orator of the time, dominated a
workingmen's convention held in February, 1839, for
the consideration of a People's Charter, which had been
drawn up by the moderates Place and Lovett. It was
decided to support the Charter's demand of five re-

forms by " physical force," if necessary. The hunger-stricken North was prepared to go to any length. The Trades-Unions extended their ramifications. There was secret drilling on the moors; pikes were forged and guns collected. In London, the People's Charter, in the form of a monster petition signed by thousands of workers, was escorted to the Parliament House by a host of workers, with the intent to overawe the legislators by a display of potential force. They resisted troops sent to disperse them, and there was serious rioting. The government nervously concentrated troops in industrial centers.

The general optimism of the upper classes was rudely shocked by this apparition of proletarian revolt. Liberty, Fraternity, and Equality had an ominous sound on British lips. Carlyle knew the moment to be propitious for driving home the lesson of the French Revolution. In his privately printed *Chartism* he boldly declared revolution to be inevitable if the grievances which excited to it were not redressed, and referred pointedly to what had happened when the French rabble had unloosed itself. The time of repentance was short, for " decreasing respect for what their temporal superiors command, decreasing faith in what their spiritual superiors teach (was) more and more the universal spirit of the lower classes."

The ministry preferred to support the *status quo* with the bayonets of the Duke of Wellington. The influence of an inspired literary prophet counted for little among class-conscious politicians distrustful of ideas and of eloquence, and content to repose on the tangible

realities of wealth and privilege. Carlyle had found
the end of the blind alley which Mill had entered; had
discovered men incapable of being moved to rise above
the narrowest conception of their economic interest.
But he was unwilling to retreat as Mill had retreated,
to take the circuitous and difficult route of contributing
to the intellectual and moral improvement of the ruling
classes. His " hairy strength," [11] which made Emerson
wonder at his choice of literature as a vocation, was
impatient with such a policy of watchful waiting.
Temperament urged him to an attempt to break
through the wall which blocked his progress. Instead
of convincing an entire ministry, he would convert one
exceptional politician, who could bend weaker wills in
the Cabinet to his own, and carry reforms in the teeth
of a reluctant majority.

The conception of such a personality was a commonplace of the contemporary romantic literature. Carlyle had long held it in reserve. Already in the *Sartor*
he had noted that the feudal Duke was originally Dux,
leader of his people by right of the coolest head and
the strongest arm. Historical analogy convinced him
that the new forces unloosed by the industrial revolution could only be stabilized by a government alike
rooted in reality, in a personality strong enough to defy
sinister interests and popular clamor alike.

Many of us even in these days of the triumph of the
democratic idea, have moods in which this dream of a
righteous dictator has been tremendously attractive.
To Carlyle it was especially tempting because it lent
support to his conviction of the Divine government of

the world. In the days when the wrongs which were
the cause of Chartism seemed to cry to an unheeding
Heaven, he was alone sustained by a belief that the just
cause would nevertheless eventually triumph. Since
force was the only arbiter of victory upon earth, it followed that " the strong thing is the just thing," that
force was drawn to the support of the right by a sort
of moral gravitation. Of this the French Revolution
seemed the proof. In this light the much abused Mo-
hammedan propagation of doctrines by the sword revealed a sublime confidence in God's control of the
universe. " Very sure," said Carlyle in his second lecture on *Heroes and Hero-Worship* (1840), " that it
will in the long run conquer nothing that does not deserve to be conquered. . . . In this great duel, Nature
herself is umpire, and can do no wrong." Consequently
the sublimely strong man whom he sought as a deliverer of society in his time must have been Divinely sent,
a foreordained co-worker with the literary prophet.
" The certainty of Heroes being sent us; our faculty,
our necessity to reverence Heroes when sent; it shines
like a polestar through smoke-clouds, dust-clouds, and
all manner of down-rushing and conflagration." Like
a Messianic prophet, Carlyle waited on the coming of
one of these Heroes to restore an efficient government.

But how could he recognize the Hero? To this
question Carlyle could never give an unambiguous answer. At times he thought that all honest men would
recognize him instinctively. This would have provoked
a facile and Fabian optimism had it not given birth to
the query: in a world in which knaves were in a large

majority, how could the Hero rally about him the force necessary to his success? This query Carlyle put to himself, and could find no other answer than the admission of the necessity of the slow moral conversion of the multitude. But this answer closed a vicious circle from which the only exit was Mill's patient meliorism. Recklessly Carlyle turned to a more tangible criterion of recognition; that of success. This had the undoubted advantage of being unmistakable, but it led to serious moral difficulties. History was full of examples of the signal success of villains and charlatans. He was forced to a qualification: " Give a thing time; if it can succeed, it is a right thing." But this concession destroyed the validity of success for the guidance of any one generation, and turned the world to uncertainty again. As the necessity of the immediate institution of reforms became more urgent, Carlyle was therefore more and more inclined to disregard the moral objections to the credentials of immediate success. Intensity of conviction that right made might brought him perilously near saying that might made right, something which he always hotly and strenuously denied having said.

With the elaboration of the doctrine of the Hero, Carlyle's propaganda took on new vigor about 1840, when Mill had given up political agitation in disgust. The tone of the lectures on *Heroes and Hero Worship* was highly optimistic, for the lecturer believed that the latent instinct for the discovery and reverence of great men had only to be stimulated into activity. His conviction that " all power is moral " heartened him during the dark days of 1843, when the social distress which had engendered Chartism had come to its worst, and guided him to a brilliant stroke of political strategy. In *Past and Present* he penetrated beneath political machinery to political forces, and eloquently appealed to the Captains of Industry, who were the strongest power in society, to direct their hitherto selfish energies toward the good of the nation as a whole, and become generous patrons and protectors of their employees. If these men of proved capacity had heeded the appeal, and had become a new paternal aristocracy like that in the heyday of feudalism, the course of English, and perhaps of European history might have been changed. But capitalism made the great refusal; and Carlyle, irritated by the general indifference to his most earnest exhortations, was driven toward that side of his doctrine which justified the coercion of a majority impervious to persuasion. The gospel of Heroes, designed to bring peace into the world, brought a sword.

This militaristic emphasis began with the *Cromwell*, in 1845. In this study of a theocracy which had actually been established in England for a space of years, the author's sympathies were too deeply engaged to permit him to judge his hero's acts impartially. History became thinly disguised, or, in Carlyle's parenthethical comments, undisguised propaganda. Every deed of Cromwell, even the massacre of Drogheda, was justified because it led to an end blessed above all others. This attitude was clearly defensible at a time when Christian theologians generally put the stamp of their moral approval upon the narrative which described Joshua's extermination of the Canaanites, men,

women and children, as executed in obedience to the
direct command of God. Carlyle was only more consistent than his countrymen in believing in a God who
had not been dead since the days of the Fathers of the
Church. So convinced was he of the absolute rightness
of Calvinism in the seventeenth century that he could
only see absolute wrongness in its inveterate opponents,
and necessary " surgery " in their extirpation. That
which more definitely disturbed his contemporaries was
his justification of the forcible dismissal of the Long
Parliament. His attack on the time-honored dogma of
Parliamentary supremacy was based upon an argument
familiar to us through its frequent use in the recent
World War; that a large deliberative body was un-
suited for the rapid dispatch of business. The theocracy
was fighting for its life while deliberations dragged on;
and Cromwell had no choice but reluctantly to seize the
reins of power, and save the Cause by vigorous
measures.

At a crisis similar to that which Cromwell faced Carlyle believed England to have arrived in the mid
'forties. The industrial lords refused to reform themselves; endless Parliamentary debates on the " Condition of England Question " got nowhere. Salvation
seemed to lie only in the appearance of another Cromwell. The repeal of the Corn Laws in 1846 apparently
revealed providentially such a man.

Sir Robert Peel, the Conservative Prime Minister,
had unexpectedly broken a deadlock by swinging his
personal following over to the side of the Free Traders,
thus striking hard at the economic interests of the class

which had put him in power. This *coup*, which Disraeli and the die-hard Tories stigmatized as treason, Carlyle hailed as heroic self-sacrifice, something he had hitherto sought in vain among politicians. Here at last was a man who could subordinate class interest to the good of the nation. Carlyle at once sought to instruct Peel in his entire duty as a Hero by sending him, with a congratulatory letter, a copy of the newly published second edition of the *Cromwell*. Peel replied courteously, and thereafter, although they had not been introduced, recognized Carlyle by a nod when they passed each other in the streets. But it was not until March, 1848, that they were brought together. The recent outbreak of a third Revolution in France brought the conversation naturally to the topic on which Carlyle was eager to speak. Peel's talk seemed to prove him " by far our first public man," a bulwark in those " frightful times." [12] The meeting acquired especial dramatic value in Carlyle's mind when he learned later that it had taken place on the very night of the outbreak of revolution in Berlin. During the year that followed, while he had the satisfaction of seeing his prophecies abundantly justified by an epidemic of revolutions which shook every throne of the Continent, Carlyle was maturing a plan of political reorganization which Peel was to carry into effect. When the reactionary forces had finally restored order everywhere, he felt that the propitious moment for constructive change had come, and he struck hard at the existing order with his notorious *Latter Day Pamphlets*.

These likened the condition of Europe in 1850 to its

condition at the fall of the Roman Empire. Outwardly the old order held its own, but within disintegration had become almost complete. Reaction had won only a Pyrrhic victory; the doom of the " order of Routine " was sealed by the inevitability of democracy. In England alone did a semblance of strong government still exist; England might still dam the rising flood of anarchy. But to attain the strength for this Herculean task, she must submit herself to drastic reform. She must let Peel be dictator and make possible a career open to the talents by calling into his cabinet the best and ablest men, irrespective of party, or social rank, or ability to get elected to Parliament. This cabinet must for a time neglect Continental affairs as hopeless, and concentrate on the tremendous problems of domestic administration. The employment problem must be solved by collecting paupers and idlers into industrial regiments organized to make waste places productive. Any population thereafter found superfluous must then be cared for by a colonial office with a vision of empire.

The *Pamphlets* provoked much protest, for they denied specifically the right of government by the consent of the governed. Peel was to use Parliament in a mere advisory capacity, disregarding the majority opinion when his own was supported by a respectable minority, for the popular course most commonly led to a precipice. " Unanimity of voting," Carlyle exclaimed wisely, " that will do nothing for us . . . the ship, to get round Cape Horn, will find a set of conditions already voted for, and fixed with adamantine rigour by the ancient Elemental Powers, who are entirely careless how you vote." The story is told that Carlyle, piqued by Emerson's disbelief in the devil, resolved to prove his reality by exhibiting his handiwork in London. He took Emerson on a tour through slums and vile gin shops, stopping ever and anon with the eager question, " Do you believe in the Devil, noo? " His conclusive proof was reserved to the last; he displayed the House of Commons in session, with a triumphant, " Do you believe in the Devil, *noo?* " This anecdote, even if apocryphal, represents accurately Carlyle's life-long attitude toward the representative body, which exhibited the quality of hero worship possessed by the part of the population exercising the franchise. In the *Pamphlets* especially he loosed against it the full force of his magnificent power of vituperation. It was the " Talking Apparatus," he said, not the thinking apparatus of the nation. It was composed entirely of " Stump Orators " for no modest or honest man would stoop to exercise the odious arts necessary to win the suffrage of " Ten Pound Franchisers, full of beer and balderdash," who were even thus the better men among a nation of " twenty-seven millions, mostly fools." A democracy was clearly incapable of choosing a wise and able executive; the popular subscription of £25,000 for a statue of Hudson, a railroad magnate, unfortunately discovered to be a swindler on the eve of its erection, was a typical expression of the national Hero Worship. Only coercion could save England from worship of the Golden Calf.

The only man in England who could possibly exercise

this coercion was Sir Robert Peel. Peel had been favorably impressed by the *Pamphlets,* and had begun
definitely to cultivate Carlyle's acquaintance early in
1850. Years of propaganda seemed about to have their
reward. Then a fatality destroyed all hopes. On June
29, 1850, Peel was injured by a fall from his horse.
He lived only a few days thereafter. Carlyle had no
heart for further pamphleteering. The nation contained no other man who could do what he hoped from
the great Premier, perhaps the greatest England ever
knew. He could only wait for the improbable chance
that such another might arise. Meanwhile England
would march rapidly toward the fatal goal of Democracy. Alone in Europe, the rising Kingdom of Prussia
showed promise of realizing that order based on the
recognition of talents which England had failed to
achieve. While following the increasing importance of
Prussia with a hopeful eye, Carlyle consoled himself
for what might have been by tracing the course of
political wisdom in the past, in the acts of the founder
of Prussia's power, Frederick the Great.

While Carlyle was thus striving to arrest the advance of democracy because it seemed synonymous with
anarchy, Mill was considering it a very doubtful good
for precisely the opposite reason; because it threatened
to make society too orderly and conventional. During
the fifteen years following his retirement from active
politics Mill had come to believe that De Tocqueville
had been right in ascribing the evils which he had observed in the United States to the influence of democratic institutions. Looking forward to the period when

democracy would be as firmly established as feudalism had been before it, he saw possibilities which appalled him. Since the trinity of revolutionary ideals was composed of incompatibilities, there seemed every likelihood that Equality and Fraternity would stifle Liberty. If unchecked, they might supersede representative government by a Benthamic arithmocracy, under which every man would count for one and for only one, and superior talents for nothing. They might even require men to be "all alike," to conform in opinions, in morals, and even in clothing and domestic habits, to a standard set by the majority. Argus-eyed respectability might be more efficient than the Inquisition in extirpating every form of unorthodoxy. An expression of disbelief in the infallibility of the democratic ideal, a suggestion of even the slightest change in the established form of government, might be immediately hushed by the infuriated mob. The "ancient empire of routine," whose demise Carlyle had just celebrated with joy, would thus be reëstablished with infinitely greater rigidity. Democratized Europe might become as stationary as China.

And the thought of China suggested to Mill another political danger from the opposite quarter. Chinese stationariness was compatible with an actual government by the talents; for was not proficiency in the classics the door to a Chinese political career? Would not, therefore, the supremacy of Carlyle's Hero and his picked subordinates, though undoubtedly promising much immediate good, finally bring on permanent social stagnation? If all distinguished talent were monopolized by the government, would not its policy, deprived of the stimulus of intelligent and vigorous opposition, degenerate into a routine? Certainly the younger generations would find it more than usually difficult to advance new ideas, if the *status quo* were defended by the united efforts of the best of their elders. One good custom might thus corrupt the world.

If neither pure democracy nor rule by all the talents led to social and political progress, was there a road thither? Not primarily through any political machinery, Mill now believed, but through the recognition by the majority that diversity, dissatisfaction, and curiosity were social virtues. Society should not be considered as a piece of mechanism to be controlled from without, but rather (in the terms of one of Carlyle's favorite similes) as a tree, which contains its principle of development within itself, and unfolds freely in sun and air. Mankind had advanced so slowly because it had been content with lesser perfections, and unwilling to tolerate " experiments of living," which might have revealed undreamed of possibilities for good. The principal benefactors of the race were men of genius, whom keener sensibilities, stronger intellects, and more resolute wills had equipped for fruitful discoveries. Therefore, although " persons of genius . . . are, and are always likely to be, a small minority," it was necessary that society " preserve the soil in which they grow." For the development of this belief in the preeminent political importance of the genius, which dethroned from his mind the ideal of the political expert, Mill was largely indebted to *The Sphere and Duties of Government* by Wilhelm von Humboldt, one of the host of German thinkers who had championed the Goethian ideal of human life which Carlyle had found it impossible to assimilate. " The end of man," the youthful Von Humboldt had written in 1804 . . . " is the highest and most harmonious development of his powers to a complete and consistent whole." [13] To facilitate the attainment of this end, he believed it imperative that society permit to the individual " freedom, and variety of situation."

These statements of Von Humboldt formed the text of an inquiry into " the nature and limits of the power which can be legitimately exercised by society over the individual " which Mill began to write in the dark days of the Crimean War, declared, Carlyle asserted, at the command of the newspapers, when the populace was turning to rend its former idols, Cobden and Bright, of Anti-Corn Law League fame, because of their opposition to a conflict which finds few apologists to-day. With the gravely passionate eloquence to which he could rise when deeply moved, Mill besought society to refrain from using its tremendous power of coercion except in self-defense, and to permit, even at the risk of encouraging much fruitless eccentricity, a freedom of discussion and of action which wise and gifted individuals might use to the incalculable enrichment of their fellows. Such a course would involve no serious danger, for society had " now definitely got the better of the individual." If promptly inaugurated, it might render impotent the daily-growing menace of the mob. The need was pressing, for " the greatness of England is now all collective; individually small, we can only appear capable of anything great by our habit of combining; and with this our moral and religious philanthropists are perfectly contented. But it was men of another stamp than this that made England what it has been; and men of another stamp will be needed to prevent its decline."

When this inquiry, grown to a sizable volume, at length appeared in 1859 under the title *On Liberty,* it was ironic that numerous other works of originality and profundity of thought came forth at the same time as if designed to disprove Mill's theory of the stifling of individual energy. *The Origin of Species, The History of Civilization, Essays and Reviews, Adam Bede,* and *The Ordeal of Richard Feverel* attested to England's continued fecundity in genius and in the highest talent, and proved that the intellectual barrenness of the fifties, when Mill thought Ruskin's the only original mind in Great Britain, to have been no sound basis for a generalization as to the blighting effect of industrialism and democracy. Nevertheless, the essay had an immediate effect in encouraging young men of talent to enter into the new paths blazed by these pioneers, and has since served as a valuable warning of the necessity of preserving liberty from the encroaching claims of equality and fraternity.

The reflorescence of genius was but one evidence of a renewed national vigor after a slack period. Domestic politics showed its first sign of life, since the repeal of the Corn Laws, by splitting the Conservatives and conservatizing the Liberals through bringing them into coalition with the Peelites, had stilled party warfare into a mere sham battle. The working classes, having gained through this same repeal cheaper food and shorter hours, and thereby the power and wisdom which they had lacked during the "hungry 'forties," were pressing the more advanced Liberals to demand further Parliamentary reform. In the year which saw the publication of *On Liberty*, Mill supported this demand through the columns of the *London and Westminster Review*; a seemingly inconsistent attitude on the part of a declared enemy of mob rule. But this action seemed to Mill a logical consequence of the central doctrine of his *Liberty*; freedom of discussion. He thought that the nation would gain measurably by calling to its councils all the available knowledge in its borders, of which the specialized trade information, the peculiar psychology, and the economic views and interests which working class representatives could contribute formed no inconsiderable part. Furthermore, it could gain richly in human resources by the development in the working class, through the exercise of political functions, of those qualities of initiative, self-reliance, and civic responsibility which aristocratical rule had hitherto tended to stunt. It was, indeed, partly for this latter reason, that Mill had not claimed for men of genius the right to rule the state, but had demanded for them only "freedom to point the way," to persuade, not force, the nation into the right paths.

These arguments in favor of the extension of the suffrage Mill repeated in expanded form in his treatise on *Representative Government* (1861), the last and most complete exposition of his political theory. In this work Mill chose a House of Commons devoted to " mere talk," which was Carlyle's chief detestation, as the mainspring of his ideal governmental machinery. The Commons, he declared, should be an open forum, in which every opinion should have the fullest possible hearing; in which the whole population, without distinction of class or sex, would be represented. To render innocuous that incapacity for action which Carlyle had clearly seen to be the inherent defect of such a body, Mill provided that it be deprived of all administrative powers. The chief executive should be chosen by the upper house of trained statesmen whose constitution Mill had advocated in his second review of Tocqueville, and should thereafter choose his own subordinates. Even in its own legislative sphere it was not to have an entirely free hand, for the drafting of laws should be the prerogative of the special Committee on Legislation which had been also suggested in the Tocqueville review. To provide against the control of legislation by the unwisdom of the mob, Mill furthermore stipulated that the suffrage, though universal, should not be equal; that those with superior educational qualifications should be given plural votes. The educated minority was to be still further safeguarded by electoral machinery providing for personal and proportional representation, which delighted Mill by seeming to guarantee that men of conspicuous ability could be elected by the nation at large, and that powerful minorities could plead their causes in the Parliamentary forum, side by side with the opposing majority representatives. If all representatives, furthermore, would maintain their personal opinion where it happened to differ from that of their constituencies, and refuse to become mere rubber-stamps of collective opinion, Mill believed that universal suffrage, subject to the checks which he suggested, could be made to yield nothing but benefit to the nation.

To the steadily increasing agitation for working-class suffrage which received a great accession of strength through the growth of a popular press after the repeal of the paper duties in 1860, Mill therefore added the influence of his name and his writings. But even after the death of Lord Palmerston in 1865 relieved the Liberals of a great conservatizing weight and precipitated a general election in which the suffrage was the dominant issue, he had no intention of reëntering active politics. Then an unexpected request by prominent citizens of the original Radical Borough of Westminster that he stand for election as the Borough representative seemed so clear a call of civic duty that he could not conscientiously cling to the retirement which had been half an exile since Mrs. Mill's death in 1857. Yet he consented only on terms which were among the most extraordinary ever stipulated by a candidate, if candidate indeed he might be called. He refused to canvass the constituency or to spend a penny on a campaign, believing such practices unethical, and insisted on giving fullest publicity to his most unpopular opinions, including his advocacy of women's suffrage and his intention to use his seat for the discussion of national problems, without paying much heed to the local inter-

ests of Westminster. At the few mass meetings on the
eve of the election at which he presented himself in
order to reply to questions, he exhibited the same quiet
contempt for the arts of the demagogue. In reply to
a heckler who asked if he did not write in his 1859
article on *Parliamentary Reform* that English workingmen were generally liars, he replied with an unhesi-
tating affirmative which wrung cheers from his working-
class auditors. In spite of all this, he was returned,
and had the privilege which Carlyle was denied in
1850, of advocating his reforms from the floor of the
House. On May 30, 1867, he introduced an amendment to the Disraeli Reform Bill providing for proportional representation, which won the support of certain
rock-ribbed Tories, such as Lord Cranbourne, later
Lord Salisbury. But Mill's own party leaders, notably
Bright, thought the proposal too reactionary, and the
majority of the Conservatives were prejudiced against
it because of the quarter from which it came. Mental
indolence and the fear of popular pressure caused the
defeat of what was probably " the most practical attempt to organize numbers in democracies." [14]   The
more easily comprehensible proposal of woman's suffrage, the second of what were smilingly regarded as
Mill's whims, won over Bright and an unexpected number of supporters before going down to inevitable defeat. Through an amendment to this second Reform
Bill tacked on by the House of Lords just before its
enactment, a makeshift scheme for proportional representation was given a trial in a few constituencies,
notably at Birmingham. In that working-class strong-

hold the very first election brought forth an expedient which completely nullified the design to give representation to a minority. Schnadhorst, a tailor and practical politician like Francis Place, borrowed from the United States the party caucus, and so successfully taught his popular following to divide their vote that they were able to evade what seemed an aristocratic plot to defraud them, and to return the entire slate of members to which they believed their clear majority entitled them. Thus did Mill receive a last lesson as to the impotence of political machinery to restrain political forces. England had planted her feet firmly on the road to arithmocracy.

Carlyle, who had seen from the first the dangers of the 1867 "leap into the dark," must have smiled grimly at Mill's discomfiture. His aged eyes, grown dim with watching for the advent of a Hero, saw the collapse of another of Mill's principles when Forster was forced, in 1878, to capitulate after a bitter fight for his independence, and shrink from a representative into a delegate. Demos had become sure of its power and tolerant only of its flatterers, and an aristocracy of the fittest seemed farther away than ever. Mill was spared this last bitterness; five years before he had been laid to rest at Avignon.

Chapter VIII

THE DISMAL SCIENCE.

IN the eighteen-thirties and 'forties England accepted political economy as a well-established science like Newtonian physics. The founders of political economy had not claimed so much for it; Malthus, indeed, had thought it necessary to protest against this misconception. In the *Introduction* to his *Principles* (1820) he emphasized the affinity of economics to " the science of morals and politics," rather than to the exact mathematical sciences. He condemned especially " the precipitate attempt to simplify and generalize," because there were " few branches of human knowledge where false views may do more harm or just views more good." [1] But such modesty did not content second-rate popularizers like Senior, Whately, and McCulloch. Senior went so far as to assert that political economy was largely independent of facts, and deducible from four irrefragable principles: (1) that every man desires to obtain wealth with as little sacrifice as possible; (2) that population tends to increase in geometrical progression while the food supply increases in arithmetical progression; (3) that manufactures can increase indefinitely; and (4) that land gives diminishing returns to increased intensity of cultivation.[2] A reviewer of the second edition of James Mill's *Elements* advised his readers to " read it as they would Euclid." [3]

The propertied classes chose to accept the point of view of the popularizers. They found it pleasant to be absolved of responsibility for the unlucky; to be told that higher wages would not raise the standard of living among the workers, but would only encourage the reproduction of children who would soon eat away the margin of comfort. Their consciences were further appeased by Nassau Senior's statement that the condition of the industrial worker was clearly superior to that of the primitive savage, and had every chance of becoming even better. Their fears were stilled by the assurance that a man had the right to do what he liked with his own, and that there was a wage-fund law which made impossible the raising of wages by strikes. Considering the poor in their debt for the employment they gave, the well-to-do ate dinners of thankful satisfaction at the better lot to which it had pleased Providence to call them. Knowledge of economic doctrines spread rapidly. In 1816 Mrs. Marcet published *Conversations on Political Economy* with " young Caroline "; [4] James Mill called his *Elements* (1821) " a school-book of political economy." [5] Before 1830 knowledge of economics had become one of the accomplishments of the man about town; the foppish hero of Bulwer's novel *Pelham* (1828) remarks: " I know not why this study has been termed uninteresting. No sooner had I entered upon its consideration, than I could scarcely tear myself from it." [6] It was brought to the nursery by MacVicar's *First Lessons in Political Economy for the use of Elementary Schools.*[7]

The working classes alone were untouched by this

almost universal enthusiasm. McCulloch blamed their
discontent upon " demagogues, and the workshop agitators so frequently met with in the manufacturing districts," who " never fail to take advantage of the
excitement produced by the occurrence of distress to
instill their poisonous nostrums into the public mind,
and to represent the privations of the work-people,
which in the vast number of cases spring from accidental
and uncontrollable causes, as the necessary consequences
of a defective system of domestic economy, having regard alone to the interests of the higher classes." [8]   Ure
ascribed it to a sort of original sin: " Instead of repin-
ing as they have done at the prosperity of their employers, and concerting odious measures to blast it, they
should, on every principle of gratitude and self-interest,
have rejoiced at the success resulting from their labours,
and by regularity and skill have commended themselves
to monied men desirous of engaging in a profitable concern, and of procuring qualified hands to conduct it.
Thus good workmen would have advanced their condition to that of overlookers, managers, and partners
in new mills, and have increased at the same time the
demand for their companions' labour in the market." [9]
Especial efforts to enlighten the workers were made
by The Society for the Diffusion of Useful Knowledge,
in which Brougham was prominent, and by Harriet
Martineau, who sugar-coated *Illustrations of Political
Economy* in the form of thirty tales. This propaganda
informed the laborers that their salvation lay entirely
in their own hands. Willingness to move from place
to place and from industry to industry as glut in one was

accompanied by scarcity in another, thrift during periods of prosperity to provide for periods of unemployment, and, above all, voluntary limitation of their numbers would assure them a comfortable living. But they failed to purchase Miss Martineau's otherwise enormously popular nine volumes in any considerable quantity, and they were inclined to agree with Cobbett that Brougham and his associates were " feelosofical villains." [10] Admonitions from innumerable other sources had no better effect. Inevitable natural law aroused in the workingman no more enthusiasm than the proclamation of the natural carnivorousness of the tiger would arouse in a native of the jungle. The assurance that everything would adjust itself in time did nothing to blunt the edge of immediate hunger. Saving would have been difficult enough to dishearten even men of better education and larger foresight, for wages hovered close to the level of bare subsistence; equally unattainable by unlettered men was that encyclopaedic knowledge of the state of industry which would indicate the exact place in the country or upon the globe at which labor happened to be most in need. And even if this knowledge had been attainable, sufficient money to pay for transportation would still have been lacking. Freedom of contract, where no equality existed, was slavery in disguise. The advice concerning population, however good in theory, was equally one-sided in its application. " These deferred marriages until men had sure means of supporting a family," recollected the labor leader Holyoake, " meant, to nine-tenths of the poor in those days, no marriage at all — or until love had become a weary memory and nature was dead. While the gentleman who lived on the taxation of others could marry when he listed and no one dared tell him ' a large family was a shame.' " [11] No wonder the Owenite leaders considered the political economist " a bitter foe to the laboring classes, enemies (sic) who deserved no mercy at their hands." [12] Disraeli declared boldly that the Queen ruled in reality over " two nations; between whom there is no intercourse and no sympathy; who are as ignorant of each other's habits, thoughts, and feelings, as if they were dwellers in different zones, or inhabitants of different planets; who are formed by a different breeding, are ordered by different manners, and are not governed by the same laws . . . The Rich and the Poor." [13]

Fortunately there were a few who understood the psychology of both these fatally disunited " nations." Of these Thomas Carlyle was the best fitted by experience and by talents for the Herculean task of mediation and reconcilement. While his genius had lifted him to a comfortable social and financial station, he had not forgotten the bitter frugality of his parental home, his struggles at Edinburgh against neglect and hunger, and the desperate self-denial of his Craigenputtock days, when he had written grimly in his journal: " *tout va bien ici, le pain manque*." [14] Neither had he forgotten his fellow-sufferers, the Glasgow weavers, against whom he had refused to shoulder a musket in 1819, and the miserably housed iron workers in the " city of Tubal Cain." Although he had been too poor to carry out his design of traveling throughout England to in-

vestigate the living conditions of the working population in preparation for writing the *Signs of the Times*,
he had done his best to widen his knowledge by diligent
study of Factory Inspectors' and Poor Commissioners'
Reports, which Mill had sent to Craigenputtock in
1833–34, and Ebenezer Elliott's *Corn Law Rhymes*,
which he had pointedly reviewed for the *Edinburgh*.
The increasing distress of the country was brought home
to him by the difficulty with which his brother Alexander won a scant living by agriculture. His letter
congratulating him on a successful passage of the winter
of 1832–33 held out only the slightest hope for a long
continuance of the struggle: " Millions (a frightful
word, but a true one!) millions of mortals are toiling
to-day in our British Isles, without prospect of rest, save
in speedy death, to whom for their utmost toiling,
food and shelter are too high a blessing. When one
reads of the Lancashire Factories and little children
laboring for sixteen hours a day, inhaling at every
breath a quantity of cotton fuzz, falling asleep over
their wheels, and roused again by the lash of thongs
over their backs, or the slap of ' Billy rollers ' over their
little crowns; and then again of Irish Whitefeet, driven
out of their potato patches and mud hovels, and obliged
to take the hillside as broken men — one pauses with
a kind of amazed horror, to ask if this be Earth, the
place of Hope, or Tophet, where hope never comes.
A good practical inference, too, every one of us may
draw from it; to be thankful that with him it is *not*
yet so, to be content under many griefs, and patiently
struggle towards a better day; which even in this world,

cannot fail to dawn for the afflicted children of men. One grand remedy against the worst still lies partly open; America [a] and its forests, where you have only the wild *beasts* to strive against! " [15] The general unconsciousness of the country's plight exasperated him. " Everybody, Radical and other, tells me that the condition of the country — is — improving. My astonishment was great at first, but now I look for nothing' else but this ' improving daily '! Well, gentlemen, I answered once, the poor, I think, will get up some day, and tell you how improved their condition is! " [16]

Chartism was this self-expression of the poor which Carlyle had foreseen, but he did not on that account approve of its political aims. He knew too well the abysmal ignorance of the people; and had read too many of the records of the French Revolution. His *Chartism*, whose varied history we have already traced, appealed, therefore, to the upper classes exclusively, sought to revive in the old aristocracy, and inculcate in the new aristocracy created by " the triumph of cash," the obligation, recognized at least nominally during the Middle Ages, of paternal care of the masses. It exposed the folly of military coercion, the clamping down the lid on the kettle until it would be blown off, and the equal stupidity of " paralytic radicalism," whose reliance on " time and general laws " would quite as surely lead to the same catastrophic result. Carlyle was no enemy of industrialism; no smasher of machinery. He admired the strange new beauty of Man-

[a] Alexander Carlyle finally did emigrate to Canada in 1843.

chester, symbolic of the "triumph of mind over matter." But he prophesied that the whole wonderful industrial edifice would collapse like a house of cards unless it were based upon contented and therefore efficient workers. He reiterated the demand made in all his earlier social writings that the legislators look before they leap, and proceed in scientific fashion by acquainting themselves with the "condition of England." In the preparation of the New Poor Law, why had not the Commission prepared statistics showing the relation of the average wage to the cost of living, the relative constancy of employment in different industries, the mobility of labor, and the opportunities of the laborer to "rise to mastership"? Why had no one asked the obvious question: "Can the workingman of this England of ours, who is willing to labor, find work, and subsistence by his work?" Carlyle condensed the cause of this culpable incuriosity in one of his unforgettable phrases: "Cash payment as the sole nexus between man and man." If masters would cease their endeavor to overreach their servants, and sincerely begin to care for their best interests, Chartism would quickly vanish. With the advent of this fraternal spirit, a Poor Law could be devised to make labor obligatory but not disagreeable, and national and obligatory education on the Prussian model could be instituted to make the workers fit for suffrage in "about two centuries." Carlyle's admiration for England's triumphant surmounting of all social crises in the past inspired him with confidence that these reforms would be accomplished, and he saw in even the emigration forced by overpopulation a possible good, the creation of a glorious British empire.

Carlyle's reputation as a historian insured *Chartism* many readers, but they received it with disappointment or indignation. The government cut off the head of the popular movement by imprisoning its leaders and called for an addition of 5000 men to the standing army. Meanwhile the distress which had given strength to Chartism grew steadily worse. From 1836 to 1842 so-called over-production crises, the result of failure to open new markets, shut down the great majority of the textile factories. Carlyle wrote to a friend of his visit to Manchester in May, 1842: "The most tragic circumstance I noted there was *want of smoke;* Manchester was never in my time third-part as clear." [17] As if by malicious design, during the same period the winters were exceptionally severe, and the harvests scanty. Relief through the importation of foreign grain being cut off by the Corn Laws, the price of food climbed with great rapidity. Wheat, which had sold at £1 19s. 4d. a quarter in 1835, had risen by 1839 to £3 10s. and for several years failed to fall below £3.[18] The increased price of bread alone raised the average family budget by fourteen per cent.[19] This climax of calamities gave the unemployed laborers the choice between starvation and the work-house. In 1842 there were 1,429,000 paupers in England and Wales, about one-eleventh of their total population.[20] In May of that year appeared the terrible Report of the Commissioners upon conditions in the mines, which moved Members of Parliament to tears when summarized in a speech by Lord Ashley.[21]

Consciousness of the misery about him increasingly distracted Carlyle from his study of Cromwell and his times. " What a strange country we are at this hour! " he wrote Thomas Spedding, " Two thousand men and women assembled the other night before the Provost's door in Paisley, without tumult, indeed almost in silence; when questioned as to their purpose, they said they had no money, no food nor fuel, they were Fathers and Mothers, working men and women, and had come out there to see whether they could not be saved alive. The police withdrew to a distance, there were soldiers hard by to have checked any riot. By dint of great efforts the Provost collected a sum which yielded one penny farthing to each, and at sunrise they gradually dispersed again." [22] He explained to Emerson: " About Cromwell, one of my grand difficulties I suspect to be that I cannot write *two books at once*; cannot be in the seventeenth century and in the nineteenth at one and the same moment. For my heart is sore and sick in behalf of my poor generation." [23] In the countryside, he questioned an old man concerning farm laborers: " Do they drink much milk? " " Lord bless you, Sir," the old man replied, " they never see milk! They take a little hot water with salt and pepper mixed to soak their bit of bread in, and breakfast on that." [24] A visit to Cromwell's birthplace at St. Ives presented him with the spectacle of a workhouse filled with able-bodied men idle against their will. On his return home to London he met the same evidences of distress: " Here at Chelsea, for the first time, I notice the garden palings torn up this winter and stolen for fuel — a bitter symptom, for the poor in general

are very honest." [25] As he brooded over the chaos of
the times, his eyes happened to fall upon an account of
a former state of British society almost incredibly free
from the evils he deplored. This was a chronicle in
Latin of the deeds of Abbot Samson of the Monastery
of Saint Edmund's, recently resurrected by the Camden
Society. As he had held up the French Revolution as
a warning to flee from the City of Destruction, so he
now decided to hold up twelfth century England as a
guide to salvation. In December, 1842, he began to
write *Past and Present*.

In that thick pamphlet, written under tremendous
pressure in the space of three months, the social gospel
of Carlyle attained at once its highest development and
most appealing form. With bold and vivid strokes
Carlyle portrayed once more the existing state of
anarchy: the masses helpless, squalid, and uncared for;
the aristocracy pursuing a round of vapid pleasures and
sapping the nation's life with its bread tax; the commercial and manufacturing classes, busy indeed, but
from the motives of buccaneers, piling up useless
pounds like Indian scalps; the government, composed
of windbag stump orators, lazily accepting the " dismal
science " of economics with its gospel of despair, and
permitting multitudes of its subjects to be destroyed in
the cruel game of " the devil take the hindmost." For
such widespread and desperate social disease he professed to have no simple cure-all. The best of
remedies was the most radical; revival of the national
conscience from its appalling lapse into a state where
the " Englishman's hell " was " not making money."

Past and Present was the greatest of Carlyle's sermons, wielding far more influence than any he could have preached in the Scotch kirk. To arouse a conscience which he believed dormant, not dead, he employed, like his fellow prophet Tolstoi, the simplest and most obvious method of appeal. To a professedly Christian nation he repeated the simple ethical precepts of the Bible.

Three Scriptural texts served as an indictment and condemnation of the acquisitive society. " *A man's life consisteth not in the abundance of the things which he possesseth.*" " To whom," commented Carlyle, " is this wealth of England wealth? Who is it that it blesses . . . makes happier, wiser, in any way better? . . . We have the sumptuous garnitures of life and have forgotten to live in the midst of them." " *Am I my brother's keeper?* " " My starving workers," Carlyle imagined the manufacturer's reply, " did not I buy them in the market — did not I pay them every cent I owed them? " Nevertheless, went Carlyle's comment, a fever-stricken Irish widow proved the reality of a close bond of sisterhood when denied aid, by infecting seventeen other human beings. " *We have forgotten God,*" Carlyle concluded. Reckless of retribution, the ruling classes had forgotten that justice was inevitable in a Divinely-governed world. Once again he called them to flee from the wrath to come.

Like Shelley, Carlyle held out the noblest ethical ideals to attract mankind. And he went further and showed that they were not impracticable; that an approximation to them had already been attained on earth.

By quotation from the old chronicle with interpretative comment, he restored the twelfth century past of the Abbey of St. Edmund's with a marvelous skill that surpassed even Scott's. "Feudalism," exclaimed Carlyle, " with a real king Plantagenet, and their living realities, how blessed! " The twelfth century lived in awe of God's laws; its rulers recognized the responsibility of governing. " No human creature then went about connected with nobody, left to go its way into Bastilles or worse, under *laissez-faire*, reduced to prove its relationship by dying of typhus fever." The feudal lord did not dismiss his retainers after the fighting was over or limit his relations with them to cash payment. His very fighting was governed by a chivalrous code of honor whose canons would have outlawed commercial warfare as *Schrechlichkeit*. Feudalism, with all its faults, kept order and human solidarity, because it had a soul, a religion to animate it.

Observers from such opposite points of view as Comte de Saint-Simon and Nassau Senior had already observed that the outward form of feudalism had reproduced itself in the factory system, with its centralization of authority, caste, and discipline; that the " captains of industry " wielded the power which the enfeebled aristocracy had relinquished. Carlyle repeated Saint-Simon's exhortation that they complete their absorption of the functions of the feudal lords by receiving the vital spirit of chivalry, which would straightway supersede their childish scramble for pennies by a noble " war on bare backs " insuring permanent employment to their industrial troops. The laboring classes, he urged, would lose no liberty through conscription by such a beneficent military despotism, except the empty "liberty to starve to death"; wise, just, and kindly superiors would be better judges and sureties of their best interests than they themselves. Eventually, too, they might be granted a share in profits, if this were found not to impair discipline. Against abuses of power they could be guarded by factory and (on the soil) by "furrow-field" inspectors appointed by a strong central government, which would also provide for national education, parks, and systematic emigration. With the economists' cry of "impossible" Carlyle had no patience; "Release those starving souls of workers," he retorted, "and let the cotton industry take care of itself." A repeal of the Corn Laws would, he believed, give England a period of relief during which this projected "organization of labor" could be consummated. The captains of industry had but to choose between class war and peaceful solidarity.

Although the captains of industry chose to continue the more exciting occupation of buccaneering, Carlyle's seed did not this time all fall on stony ground. His continual appeals to men of letters at last were heeded; English literature began to transfer its attention from the problems of the individual to those of the social whole, and to brave the dust and heat of controversy. Ironically, the first man of letters to exhibit Carlyle's influence was one he cordially disliked, Benjamin Disraeli, who adopted his social gospel for a purpose which he had definitely repudiated, the rehabilitation of the hereditary aristocracy. Having been swept into Parlia-

ment, after many unsuccessful candidacies, by the loy-
alist landslide of 1838, this brilliant political adventurer
saw in the new popularity of the throne a rallying point
for forces of reaction, and in the condition of the working population the Achilles heel of the Liberals. In
1839 he had vainly urged the Conservatives to oppose
the Coercion Bill directed against the Chartists. Turning to the pen which he had continually used to ad-
vertise himself during the past decade, he published
in 1844 a political novel, _Coningsby_, in which he made
an impressive review of English history to prove that
the Whigs had brought the existing distress upon the
people, and that the Crown, the only power having no
sinister class interest, had been consistently their friend.
The "Young England" party which he imagined
rallying to the support of these doctrines was not left
a mere speculative possibility. Disraeli was already
gathering about him a following of young Tories, conspicuous among whom were Lord John Manners, second son of the Earl of Rutland, Bailie Cochrane, a
Scotch laird, George S. Smythe, a talented University
man, and W. J. Farrand, a Yorkshireman familiar with
the manufacturing districts. These were representative
of a new generation, which, as the _Edinburgh Review_
admitted, no longer flocked, like its predecessor, to
Utilitarianism, but was inspired by Scott's novels, Carlyle, and the Tractarian movement to a sentimental
attachment to a romantic past. Disraeli, who shrewdly
observed that "even Mormon counts more devotees
than Bentham," estimated highly the potentialities of
this new spirit, whose contagion might sweep the na-

tion. Knowing also the power of literary propaganda, he set Smythe to elaborating the historical arguments of *Coningsby* and the more sentimental Lord Manners to writing poetry in celebration of that golden age of the poor, when

> " On them no lurid light had knowledge spread,
> But faith stood them in Education's stead." [26]

Although the *Quarterly* withheld its support, the powerful *Times* newspaper, then at the height of its prestige, lent its aid to this propaganda. Disraeli set himself to write a novel portraying the widening gulf between the classes, and in its preparation entered into correspondence with the Chartist leader, O'Connell, studied the recent shocking relations of working conditions in mines, and went with Smythe on a tour of personal investigation of the Black Country. The material thus acquired served also for speeches in Parliament laying bare the " condition of England." Disraeli's baffling personality, compounded of Semitic mysticism and a strange irreverence, romantic fancy and a cynical acceptance of facts, eloquence which soared and wit which stabbed, made him a host in himself; the inspiration of his little party, and the dread of his adversaries.

The Whigs were alarmed, and ready to credit " Young England " with a power to arouse the dormant energies of the landowners altogether disproportionate to its numbers. The Tories had been in since 1841, succeeding a Whig ministry highly unpopular because of general indolence and a yearly deficit of two and a half millions of pounds. In spite of the Reform Bill, members of Parliament still came predominantly from landed families, and Manchester could muster but two votes to Buckinghamshire's eleven. The increasing attacks on the industrial system, not only from Carlyle and Disraeli, but also from minor authors such as the Reverend Robert Vaughan (*The Age of Great Cities*), W. C. Taylor (*Tour Through the Manufacturing Districts*), Helps (*The Claims of Labor*), and Colonel Torrens (*Letter to Peel on the Condition of England*), and the passage of a second and more stringent Factory Act in 1844 were disquieting signs of weakness in a party whose strength centered in Manchester and Birmingham. The *Edinburgh Review* saw the necessity of modifying the intransigeance of Nassau Senior, its principal contributor on economic topics, with reviews of a more conciliatory tone. It no longer denied, as the *London and Westminster* continued to do, the existence of grave evils, but only denied their ascription to the competitive system. Here it stood at bay, and claimed that the achievement of really unlimited competition through the abolition of the Corn Laws was their sole and infallible cure. Carlyle's "cash nexus" charge especially rankled. An entire article was devoted to its refutation, and to the statement of the counter claim that the economists and employers were the real friends of labor. The paternalistic program of Young England also touched this sensitive point. A review ridiculing the youthful extravagances of its literary output closed with a grave warning of its power in Parliamentary debate. Against the increasing pub-

licity of working conditions, the rising tide of humanitarianism, and the hostility of men of letters, repetition
of stock economic catchwords began to lose its efficacy.
In a search for a fresh restatement of the case against
paternalism, it was decided to turn to John Stuart
Mill, who was known to be preparing a comprehensive
treatise on political economy. Mill seemed ideally
fitted to advance the new policy of conciliation. His
intimacy with the founders of the science, and the
evidence of his recent *Essays on some Unsettled Questions of Political Economy* (1844) seemed to guarantee essential economic orthodoxy. On the other hand,
his intimacy with Carlyle was equally well-known, and
his article on the *Reorganization of the Reform Party*
(April, 1839) had shown the influence of the latter's
still unpublished *Chartism* in its sympathetic statement
of the grievances of the working classes. "Factory
labor must be left to Mill," wrote the disgruntled
Nassau Senior to the *Edinburgh* editor in the winter
of 1844. "He will be ingenious and original, though
I own I do not quite trust his good sense. He has
been bitten by Carlyle and Torrens, and is apt to
puzzle himself with the excess of his own ingenuity." [27]

The ostensible occasion for the sweeping attack
against paternalism which Mill agreed to make, was a
review of Helps' *Claims of Labor*, a collection of
moral maxims for the guidance of the master in his
relations with his servants.[28] Mill began by com-
mending the philanthropic interest in the condition of
the laboring population which had indeed lately acquired "the attractions of the latest new fashion," but

regretted the accompanying assumption that " the business of doing good can be the only one for which zeal suffices, without knowledge or circumspection." Through the consequent avoidance of the " formidable labor of thought," the philanthropists had failed to comprehend the magnitude of the social problem, which condemned to insignificance the sincere efforts of a few " model manufacturers." Of even greater superficiality were the proposals of the Young Englanders, caricatured by Lord John Manners' suggestion that the aristocrat " play cricket " with the working-man, if indeed they did not cloak a design, which seemed likely because of Young England's championship of the Corn Laws, the Game Laws, and other forms of class privilege, to " assert the right of the poor to protection, in the hope that obedience will follow." Furthermore, paternalists of every sort seemed blind to the manifold evidences that the spirit of the age was wholly against them; that railways and newspapers, by enabling workingmen to unite, and to discuss wages and conditions of labor more intelligently, were making them increasingly unwilling to permit others to decide what was best for them. The drafting of the People's Charter was a clear evidence of their escape from tutelage.

Mill considered it axiomatic that social maladjustment could only be cured through the discovery and removal of its causes. A scientific investigation of the causes of poverty had already been made, he said, by Malthus, who was thus paradoxically the father of the real humanitarian movement. Before Malthus,

poverty had been considered " an ordinance of God " ;
he showed it to be eradicable through the limitation of
population. The Reform Bill, by impressing upon
men's minds the possibility of change, and the Poor
Law, Factory, and other investigations, by putting in
strong light the shocking contrasts of rich and poor,
had brought about the present widespread desire to
improve the lot of the masses, a desire which Carlyle's writings had greatly stimulated. The Young
England principle of paternalism had not superseded
the principle of Malthus as the proper means of fulfilling this as yet ineffective desire. The paternalist
was confronted with the choice of either reducing the
working population to the actual condition of slaves by
taking forcible measures to limit their propagation, or
continuing to stimulate by doles of food and clothing
until the surplus of the rich were consumed and the
whole nation reduced to one level of want. It was
only national education, which would teach self-con-
trol to the poor, that could rescue legislators from
this dilemma.

Thus far Mill had only repeated the typical defence
of Political Economy familiar to his *Edinburgh
Review* readers. But they were not to be spared the
heresy of which Senior was apprehensive. Mill's
mind was far too radical to accept the existing economic system with the resignation with which the
pre-Malthusian generation had accepted poverty, and
to be content with instructing the worker how to adjust himself to it, or even with providing, against the
advice of many of his fellow economists, for its

humane administration through govermental inspection. It had the temerity to require fundamental
alterations in the system itself. In behalf of the farm
laborer he urged not only the abolition of the landlord's special privileges, but also an abrogation of the
costly method of proving and recording land titles,
which would permit the tenant to become a peasant
proprietor. In behalf of the factory hand, he did not
rest with the conversion of Carlyle's gesture toward
profit sharing into its unqualified recommendation, but
pushed his central thesis of the workingman's self-help
to its logical extreme in suggesting the eventual
abolition of the employing class, and the coöperative
association of workers for the manufacture and marketing of their product. For the encouragement of such
an experiment in communism, he advocated the immediate repeal of the law governing partnership, which
made each partner individually liable for damages
assessed against the whole firm. "Given education
and just laws," Mill concluded, "the poorer class
would be as competent as any other class to take care
of their own personal habits and requirements."

A year after the publication of Mill's assault on his
position in April, 1845, Disraeli had killed the hopes
of Young England with his own hand. His dramatic
split of the Conservative Party after Peel's equally
startling decision to reverse his position on the Corn
Laws destroyed that party unity which was indispensable to any movement back to Feudalism. Disraeli's
act was, notwithstanding, consistent and inevitable, for
the Repeal proved conclusively what had never been

very doubtful, that Peel, the Home Minister Sir
James Graham, the rising young Gladstone, and other
Conservative leaders were really class-conscious
capitalists, unwilling to restore the predominance of
the landed interest. Manufactures and commerce were
rapidly overshadowing agriculture, and this shift of
economic power was being reflected in the stature of
public men; Gladstone had written to Lord Manners
in 1843 that the aristocracy did not contain men capable
of the difficult rôle of paternalist. Certainly the Conservative revenge for the Repeal, through the famous
Ten Hour Factory Act of 1847, laudable enough in
itself, showed no statesmanlike rising above party
politics to a legislative program for the good of the
nation as a whole. In 1848, repressed Chartism,
goaded by another general shut-down of factories
during the American cotton famine of 1847–8, and
encouraged by the outbreak of a third Revolution in
France, again lifted up its head, and temporarily united
the upper classes in an attitude of common defense of
private property. " Chartism and Socialism . . . the
political and the social movement, had coalesced; the
Chartists had begun to discuss social questions, the
Socialists had become political." [29]

On April 12, 1848, while London was still excited
over the much-heralded Chartist demonstration which
the Duke of Wellington had quelled two days before,
there were discovered posted throughout the poorer
quarters of the city placards announcing to the workingmen that they had friends among the upper classes
who knew the reality of their wrongs, and who, though

not sympathetic with their desire for immediate suffrage, were eager to prepare them for ultimate citizenship by accelerating their moral and intellectual education. " The Charter," the placards read, " is not bad, if the men who use it are not bad." They bore a surprising signature — " A Working Parson." This signature proved to represent not one, but two clergymen of the Church of England: Frederick D. Maurice, Mill's old acquaintance of the Debating Society days, now Professor of Theology in King's College, London, and Charles Kingsley, a young country rector, together with a layman, Charles Ludlow, an expert student of workingmen's problems. Carlyle's reminder, " We have forgotten God," had united these men in the resolve to revive the social teachings of Jesus, and recover the working class that had been lost to the church. The placards were followed up by a penny newspaper, *Politics for the People* (later *The Christian Socialist* and *The Journal of Association*), in which Maurice, inspired by Coleridge and Carlyle, attempted to persuade the Owenite Socialists that the practice of communism by both the primitive church and the monastic orders proved the church to be their traditional friend, and Ludlow explained the working of the coöperative societies which he had seen multiply in France after the recent revolution. The assumption of the title of Christian Socialist was daring enough, but the youthful and pugnacious Kingsley, to whom the writings of Carlyle were a second gospel, could not be restrained by his older and more cautious companions from exercising his excellent journalistic gift in sensational onslaughts upon the competitive system. The sweatshops which he met with on being transferred to London from a country parish, where the condition of the agricultural poor had wrung his heart, incited him to publish a pamphlet, *Cheap Clothes and Nasty*, exposing the social consequences of the award of government clothing contracts to the cheapest competing tailor, and styling unlimited competition as " cannibalism." His overwrought feelings, exacerbated by his daily ministrations in the slums during the cholera epidemic of 1848–49, found their outlet in the feverish writing of a story of the Chartist movement from the workingman's point of view based on autobiographical material furnished by Thomas Cooper, who had been imprisoned (1842–43) for sedition. No publisher dared accept the completed novel until Carlyle came to the rescue with a letter to Chapman and Hall. *Alton Locke*, chaotic and imperfectly revised, gained by its very incoherence the added vividness of a nightmare. The impression made by this novel upon its appearance in 1849 is more than comparable to that made upon our own generation by Upton Sinclair's *The Jungle*, for Disraeli's *Sibyl* had been practically its sole predecessor in its genre. Kingsley and Maurice came near being unfrocked, but the Chartist cause got a hearing. The delineation of the epic conflicts of the North by Mrs. Gaskell and Charlotte Brontë gave further impetus to the social novel, and the attraction of Charles Dickens, the most popular of contemporary novelists, to the same field with his *Hard Times* (1853) proved it to have established

a vogue.[a]   Meanwhile the testimony of the Christian
Socialists and John Stuart Mill before a Parliamentary
committee had brought about the repeal of the Partnership Laws which stood in the way of experiments
in coöperation.   Although the failing power of the
Church, which was trammeled by dependence upon
vested interests and weakened by its mistaken opposition to science, doomed to failure their effort to recover the workingman for organized Christianity, an
effort which the lamentably short-lived Frederick W.
Robertson had independently made, to the dismay of
his fashionable congregation at Brighton Beach, the
Christian Socialists made a lasting contribution to the
cause of social reform.   This manifested itself in the
increasing disposition of young clergymen to care for
the working class, in the increasing disposition of literature to deal with social themes, and in the success of the
first Workingmen's College which the Christian Socialists had established in 1854, whose example, educative
results, and importance as a center of reform movements have been of great service in improving the lot
of the British masses.

" Read it, thou self-satisfied Mammon, and per-
pend; for it is both a prophecy and a doom," [30] exclaimed Kingsley's Chartist hero concerning the chapter *On the Probable Futurity of the Labouring Classes*
in the recently published *Principles of Political
Economy* by John Stuart Mill.   Yet one looks in vain
for signs of disapproval in the reviews of Mill's work

[a] For a thorough and penetrating study of the social novel see
Le Roman Social en Angleterre, by Louis Cazamian.

in the *Edinburgh* and the *London and Westminster* reviews, which on the contrary praised it as the greatest contribution to Political Economy since Adam Smith. The key to this enigma lay in the strangely dual character of the *Principles*. One may comprehend that character in its simplest terms by supposing Mill to have said, " I will explain carefully the mechanism of the existing economic order: but since I believe that order to be iniquitous, I will indicate how it may be reformed or superseded." Consequently the descriptive portion of the book took the familiar form of a scientific treatise of the Smith-Ricardo tradition. It took for granted the existing economic division of society into the classes of landlords, capitalists, and laborers, and, universalizing for convenience the prevailing psychology of self-interest and the prevailing disposition to permit unlimited competition, attempted to explain in the form of general laws the results of the struggle, under those conditions, between these classes and between individuals within these classes for unlimited material gain. It deduced from the unmodified operation of these forces in the future a tendency of the landlords' rents to increase, of the capitalists' profits to diminish and then become stationary, and of the laborers' wages to remain where they were, near the minimum level of subsistence and reproduction, unless they were disturbed by a change in the birth rate of that class which might be brought about by peasant proprietorship and better education. This was the tone of the first two hundred pages of the *Principles;* and, since the last forty pages of the work were likewise devoted to an exposition of the principle that " *laissez-faire* . . . should be the general practice, every departure from it unless required by some great good, is a certain evil," it was no wonder that professional reviewers read nothing to which they could take exception, and that the general reader, wearied by following the thread of philosophic argument, laid down the work with a feeling that all was orthodox.

Although Mill had begun with the assertion that the so-called laws of Political Economy were based on purposely narrow premises and subject to continual alterations necessitated by their frequent collision with the laws of the larger science of sociology to which economics was subsidiary, alterations which he admonished his readers to allow for in their application of his generalizations to concrete cases, the second part of his design was not apparent until the opening of his second book, which dealt with distribution. At that point he made the revolutionary pronouncement that the laws of distribution differed essentially from those of production in being almost completely dependent on human will. Any partition of the fruits of human labor could be made only " by consent of society " ; any retention of a share was only possible " by permission of society." " In an age like the present (1848), when a general consideration of first principles is felt to be inevitable, and when more than at any former period of history the suffering portions of humanity have a voice in the discussion," Mill believed it to be not unfitting to inquire into the justice and the utility of existing system of distribution.

Mill condensed the result of this inquiry into an impressive indictment. "If . . .," he wrote, " the choice were to be made between Communism with all its chances, and the present (1852) state of society with all its sufferings and injustices; if the institution of private property necessarily carried with it as a consequence, that the produce of labor should be apportioned as we now see it, almost in an inverse ratio to the labour — the largest portions to those who have never worked at all, the next largest to those whose work is almost nominal, and so in a descending scale, the remuneration diminishing as the work grows harder and more disagreeable, until the most fatiguing and exhausting bodily labour cannot count with certainty on being able to earn even the necessaries of life; if this or Communism were the alternative, all the difficulties, great or small, of Communism would be as dust in the balance." Fortunately, however, society could be spared the unpleasant prospect of ridding itself of enormous injustice only through turning itself topsy-turvy by an experiment in Communism. " The principle of private property," Mill continued, " has never yet had a fair trial in any country, for the laws of property have never yet conformed to the principles on which the justification of private property rests." Society could therefore enjoy with comfort the benefits of a gradual revision of the institution of property to bring it in accord with these principles, while experiments with Communism were being carried out on a small scale to ascertain the exact proportion of good and evil which so radical an expedient would entail.

Mill devoted considerable space to speculations concerning the probable practicality and value of these
communistic experiments.   Pure communism, with its
equalization of reward, appealed to what he considered
the strictest standard of justice, but was for that very
reason a less practical " compromise with the selfish
type of character formed by the present standard of
morality " than the systems of Saint-Simon and
Fourier, which attempted " proportioning remuneration to labour."   Both these systems had the advantage
of providing for the worker's security through a minimum wage and permanence of employment, and making labor attractive and more productive through varia-
tion of occupation and the inculcation of the ideal of
service of the social whole.   There were, however,
grave dangers inherent in all these socialistic systems.
There was a political problem for which neither the
Saint-Simonian proposal of an irresponsible despotism,
nor the pure democracy of the Fourierists and Owen-
ites, with its opposite menace of a tyrannical and
ignorant majority, was a satisfactory solution, and the
even more formidable problem of producing the moral
and intellectual revolution which would provide the
altruism and the voluntary control of population which
were indispensable to the success of any economic system not resting on private property.   The peculiar
advantage of the renovated system of private property
which would compete with socialism for the final suffrage of humanity lay in its encouragement of individual initiative and self-expression.   Socialism implied
a " dependence of the individual on the mass " which

might dangerously increase the "tame uniformity of thoughts, feelings and actions" which Mill found already too prevalent in a competitive society. Since "after the means of subsistence are assured the next in strength of the wants of humanity is liberty," it seemed probable that humanity would decide in favor of the system which was "consistent with the greatest amount of human liberty and spontaneity." But this decision lay far in the future; "for a considerable time to come" the economist would be obliged to concern himself with the improvement of the system of private property.

In providing for this improvement, he had no need to be hampered by regard for the so-called sanctity of property rights. "Society," Mill declared, "mainly consists of those who live by bodily labour; and if society, that is, the labourers, lend their physical force to protect individuals in the enjoyment of superfluities, they are entitled to do so and have always done so, with the reservation of a power to tax those superfluities for the purposes of public utility; among which purposes the subsistence of the people is foremost." The legitimate justification of private property he found rather in its gratification of certain fundamental human desires. It gave the individual a comfortable sense of security by guaranteeing him the possession of the fruits of his labor; it satisfied his sense of justice by proposing to proportion remuneration to labor; and it further stimulated his productive effort by promising expression to his affections or pride through bequests to children or friends. He therefore proposed that society continue to gratify the first of these desires without stint and the other two in so far as their mutual inconsistency permitted. This inconsistency could, moreover, be largely obviated if the freedom of bequest were qualified by the abolition of entail, and the limitation of the amount which each individual could inherit, which would rid society of the burden of an unproductive class. Certain peculiar kinds of property should be subject to special regulation. The unearned increment of land, what Ricardo had called rent, should be liable to heavy taxation or confiscation by the government, for " the reasons which form the justification . . . of property in land are only valid, in so far as the proprietor of the land is its improver. In no sound theory of private property was it ever contemplated that the proprietor of land should be merely a sinecurist quartered on it." Other monopolies, such as gas and railways, should be owned or controlled by the government. This control could be extended to all large corporations, were it not for the counterbalancing danger of bureaucracy. By such entirely justifiable measures, Mill believed society could be relieved of most of the enormous dead weight of idlers, and material reward could be made largely proportional to exertion and talent.

Mill was not content to rest with this result, for he believed that " although levelling institutions . . . may lower the heights of society . . . they cannot of themselves permanently raise the depths." In the final analysis, the modified institution of private property could escape no more than socialism the necessity of revolutionizing the social ideals of mankind. "I confess I am not charmed," Mill wrote, "with the ideal of life held out by those who think that the normal state of human beings is that of struggling to get on; that the trampling, crushing, elbowing, and treading on each other's heels, which form the existing type of social life, are the most desirable lot of human kind, or anything but the disagreeable symptoms of one of the phases of industrial progress." The general tendency of society, to make, like McCulloch, "high profits" the "test of prosperity" had made it "questionable if all the mechanical inventions yet made have lightened the day's toil of any human being." "But the best state for human nature is that in which, while no one is poor, no one desires to be richer, nor has any reason to fear being thrust back by the efforts of others to push themselves forward." "It is only in the backward countries of the world that increased production is still an important object; in those most advanced, what is economically needed is a better distribution." Yet "the industrial arts might (continue to) be as earnestly and as successfully cultivated, with this sole difference, that instead of serving no purpose but the increase of wealth, industrial improvements would produce their legitimate effect, that of abridging labour." This would permit "a much larger body of persons than at present, not only exempt from the coarser toils, but with sufficient leisure, both physical and mental, from mechanical details, to cultivate freely the graces of life, and afford examples of them to the classes less freely circumstanced for their growth."

Human energy would find a new outlet in the improvement of "mental culture" and "the Art of Living." To this high end, as well as to the more basic end of raising the status of the masses, neo-Malthusian limitation of population would essentially contribute. "A population may be too crowded, though all may be amply supplied with food and raiment. It is not good for man to be kept perforce at all times in the presence of his species. A world from which solitude is extirpated is a very poor ideal. Solitude, in the sense of being often alone, is essential to any depth of meditation or of character." [31]

Here Mill would have closed his prophecy of the future, but the warm-hearted Mrs. Taylor did not permit him to leave the toiling masses without an especially addressed word of encouragement as to their share in this bright destiny glimpsed from "the present very early stage of human improvement." In obedience to her request grew the chapter *On the Probable Futurity of the Labouring Classes* which had excited Kingsley's enthusiasm. Therein those classes were shown how they could assist in this progressive movement by forming themselves into coöperative associations, which would eliminate class warfare and the waste of the middleman, and by voluntarily limiting their numbers, in which effort they would be aided by better education, and by the increasing disposition of women to liberate themselves from domestic slavery. Thus at length there would come to be no specialized working class, but all classes and both sexes would work together in what Mill, in the final sentence of his *Principles,* called "the legitimate employment of the human faculties, that of compelling the powers of nature to be more and more subservient to physical and moral good."

The two decades which followed the publication of Mill's treatise were the golden age of British capitalism. Profits increased and industry expanded as Free Trade gave British goods victory in the markets of the world. The Conservative Party bent before the logic of events by renouncing Protection in 1852. France was converted to a reciprocity treaty in 1860. The preface to the fifth edition of Malthus' *Essay on Population* suggested to Darwin the theory of the struggle for existence, which repaid the service by seeming to confirm the pretensions of Political Economy to the character of an exact science. Mill's *Principles* became the Bible of the so-called Manchester School, whose eclectic worship limited itself to Mill's clear exposition of the existing economic order, and conveniently ignored his disturbing prophecies. Two years after Mill had testified before a Parliamentary Committee in favor of Coöperative Associations, the *Edinburgh Review* published an attack upon them in the name of Political Economy. Assured of the moral support of society through the conformity of his business practice to the precepts of what fulfilled prophecy concerning the effects of Free Trade seemed to prove a real science, and through the approval of the *Synthetic Philosophy* of Herbert Spencer, the capitalist enjoyed the added felicity of an almost complete cessation of strikes. The workers had for the most part

become convinced that the odds against them were too
great to be overcome, and therefore resigned themselves
to their masters' wills in order to secure that permanence
of employment which would save them from hunger or
the poorhouse. They could accept this rôle of passive
obedience with the more patience because, though
wages had not been increased, the cost of living had
decreased perceptibly from its high level of the " hungry 'forties." The remedial legislation of that trying
decade was giving the nation that breathing space
which Carlyle had predicted for it. Free Trade had
fulfilled its promise of cheaper food, and had given
the masses the unwonted luxuries of soap and glass
windows. Supervision of the national health, made
operative after the cholera epidemic of 1848, and the
Factory Act of 1847, which safeguarded women and
children to some extent, also contributed to the masses'
well-being. The discouraging failure of strikes, which
seemed to confirm the wage-fund law which Mill had
found inescapable, had turned working class effort for
self-improvement into the pacific channels of thrift,
study, and trial of Coöperative Associations, of which
the famous Rochdale Pioneers, founded in 1844, set
an example of conspicuous success. " The long and
short of it is," said Kingsley, satisfied with this gradual progress, in 1856, " I am becoming an optimist." [32]
Mill was not so easily satisfied. While awaiting a general quickening of the social conscience, he was encouraging Holyoake to stand for Parliament as a working-
class candidate. Carlyle, having fruitlessly repeated
his economic gospel in his *Latter Day Pamphlets*, was

grimly holding his peace. *Laissez-faire* reigned in an unbroken *Pax Manchesteria*.

Then a new voice was raised against it from an unexpected quarter. In 1848, that year of revolutions, John Ruskin, the most celebrated of English art critics, was trying to discover why medieval Venice had produced marvels of architectural beauty, and why the architecture of contemporary England was notable for its ugliness. The cause of these antipodal phenomena he believed he had discovered in the psychology of the builders. The medieval building guilds were not contracting companies working for profit and employing hirelings who had no interest in their work, but were professional associations of free workmen with pride in their achievement. A renaissance of British art was therefore possible through the restoration of the professional spirit in master and workman. Carlyle, recognizing the spiritual kinship of *The Stones of Venice* (1851–53) with *Past and Present*, won Ruskin over to his larger program of reform. Maurice induced him to make immediate trial of his ideas in the Workingmen's College, in which he in turn interested his protégés the Pre-Raphaelite artists, including William Morris, who was to be influential in the Socialist movement a quarter of a century later. Ruskin was loath to leave the delectable lanes of *Modern Painters* for the dusty and robber-beset highway of the world. Although he admitted that " the kind of painting they most wanted in London was painting cheeks red with health," [33] and although he shocked a Manchester audience who had innocently invited him to address them

at the opening of an Art Treasures Exhibit in 1857 by
a Carlylian harangue on the social basis of art, it was
only after a wrestle with the devil, comparable with
that of the youthful Carlyle, in a lonely hut among
the foothills of the Alps, that he obeyed the call of
social duty.

Then he struck fiercely at the reigning Political
Economy in a series of articles for the *Cornhill Magazine* entitled *Unto this Last*. The brunt of this attack
fell upon those portions of Mill's *Principles* which had
used for convenience the terminology of the market-
place. Such statements as: " Everyone has a notion,
sufficiently correct for common purposes, of what is
meant by wealth," [34] and the similar limitations of the
term " value," by the express elimination of moral
considerations, to mean value in exchange, were denounced for lending support to the debased materialism of the popular mind. Ruskin, whose life had
been spent in the judgment and enjoyment of aesthetic
values, insisted that there were economic values which
were intrinsic, and independent of supply and the
usual bad taste of the human demand; values which
consisted of life and all which makes life more abundant.[a] He stigmatized the theory and practice of exchange as immoral, as being essentially the art of over-
reaching, the giving of goods of inferior quality in

[a] J. S. Mill had written in 1848: " Happily, there is nothing in
the laws of value which remains for the present or any fuutre
writer to clear up; the theory of the subject is complete." *Principles*, Book III, Ch. 1, Sec. 2, p. 436. No part of the theory has
been more perplexing to later economists.

return for those of a quality relatively superior. This assault, though intemperate, and unfortunate in mistaking Mill for an enemy, pointed out truths which economic theory had hitherto neglected. And along with the polemic was contributed a valuable analysis of the psychology of the laborer, indicating that higher wages, permanence of employment, old age pensions, and other guarantees of the workers' well-being would more than pay for themselves by improving the quantity, and the quality of production. But the value of these contributions was not perceived by the readers of the *Cornhill*, for whom the orthodox economy had the sanctity of a religion, and a storm of protesting letters forced the editor, William Makepeace Thackeray, to suspend the publication of the articles after their fourth installment.

Angered in his turn, Ruskin resolved " to make it the central work of my life to write an exhaustive treatise on Political Economy." [35] Two years later the introductory chapters of this treatise, which Ruskin called *Munera Pulveris*, began to appear in *Fraser's Magazine*, whose editor was Carlyle's friend and future biographer, James Anthony Froude. Ruskin began by considering Political Economy as really *political;* not a science nor an art, but, in a phrase strongly reminiscent of Bentham, " a system of conduct and legislature." [36] The moral end which he believed it should achieve was the greatest happiness of the greatest number, qualified by especial regard for those capable of the finest quality of happiness. And the means to this end which he advocated was government distribution of riches among those best capable of using them, not those best capable of amassing them; for the wise man, as well as the fool, was indifferent to money making. He went even farther, and advocated the discontinuance of the whole industrial system, which seemed inimical to the happiness of the best men of the nation. These best men should perform the necessary agricultural labor for the benefit of their health, and all unpleasant tasks, including the irreducible minimum of industry, should be left to criminals and men of low, servile mentality. This wholesale arraignment of industrialism, like its less radical predecessor, did not go beyond a fourth installment before renewed protests from an outraged reading public moved the publishers of *Fraser's* to overrule Froude, and refuse its further publication. Broken in health, Ruskin sank into a quiescence which he described as " only as if I had buried myself in a tuft of grass on a battlefield wet with blood, for the cry of the earth about me is in my ears continually if I do not lay my head to the very ground." [37] What seemed the folly of the workingmen's renewed demand for the suffrage in 1867 aroused him to write a series of open letters [a] to a workingman acquaintance published in the *Manchester Examiner* and the *Leeds Guardian*, expounding the superiority of a paternalistic system based on initial equality of opportunity. And when the passage of a second Reform Bill put another barrier in the way of paternalism, Ruskin, with an optimism which Carlyle could not share, began to subsidize

[a] Published separately (1867) as *Time and Tide*.

with his own fortune revivals of the guild system which were popularly regarded as the dangerous eccentricities of a madman.

Already in 1848 Mill had foreseen that "at the first panic which arises on the subject of Chartism or Communism" there would be an exhibition of "the intolerant temper of the national mind," whose force Ruskin was to experience. The conditions under which the suffrage was extended in 1867 caused him to foresee the possibility of a future intolerance equal in power but opposite in direction; the intolerance of a proletariat become master of the state through the exercise of its newly-won franchise, and through direct action by strikes. Of the efficacy of strikes he had just been convinced through Thornton's demolition of the wage fund theory by the simple observation that, since the employer did not, as the economists had assumed, wait to enjoy his profits until the end of the year, but took them from the cash on hand whenever it pleased him, the wage fund could be increased at the expense of profits up to the point at which the employer would be driven out of business. To his recantation of this theory published in the *Fortnightly Review* of May, 1869, Mill added interesting speculations as to the use which the working classes might make of the weapon thus shown to be theirs. Though rejoicing that labor unions might thereby force capitalists to institute profit-sharing, he did not fail to mention the possibility of the selfish and irresponsible abuse of their power by the limitation of production through "ca-canny," sabotage, and unjust decrease of the remuneration of executives. The union of the economic power of direct action with the political power of the majority constituted, therefore, a social peril of the first magnitude. Civilization might well be destroyed by a class war; irreconcilable employer against irreconcilable laborer, doctrinaire Political Economy against equally doctrinaire Socialism, a proletarian revolution establishing State Socialism followed by an inevitable capitalistic reaction.

From this vicious circle created by the " conflict of opposite prejudices," Mill saw escape only in an impartial examination, while the working classes were as yet unconscious of the full extent of their power, of the claims of the rival economic doctrines, which might result in the general agreement of the responsible elements of society upon principles which could form a sound basis for economic peace. As a contribution to this highly important intellectual undertaking, he began in 1869 the composition of a comprehensive critique of Socialism which, unfortunately, his death left unfinished. In this work, of which the four completed chapters were published in the *Fortnightly Review* in 1879, he recommended the Fabian policy of a gradual reform of the system of private property, while socialistic and communistic systems were being tried out on a small scale. The system which would finally be adopted, as he had prophesied in 1848, would be that which would prove to be " consistent with the greatest amount of human liberty and spontaneity." But for permanent emancipation from the cruel and wasteful system of individual self-interest, Mill looked to no economic system, but only to a moral revolution, which would " make a common man dig or weave for his country, as readily as fight for his country." [38]

Chapter IX

THE INFINITE NATURE OF DUTY.

BENTHAMITE ethics became notorious through no novelty or originality. Hedonism and utility were commonplaces of eighteenth century speculation. Locke had declared in 1690 that "things . . . are good and evil only in reference to pleasure and pain,"[1] and utility had had a long and worthy pedigree which included the distinguished name of Hume. They were abominated and feared because Bentham used them so effectively as a standard for the destructive criticism of established institutions and codes of behavior. Bentham was clearly conscious of his relation to his predecessors. " When I came out with the principle of utility," he wrote, " I took it from Hume's *Essays*. Hume was in all his glory, the phrase was consequently familiar to everybody. The difference between Hume and me is this: the use he made of it was — to account for that which *is*, I to show what *ought to be*."[2]

The positive law and the predominant code of morals, the " code of honor " of the gentleman, seemed established, not for the greatest happiness of the greatest number, but only for the greatest happiness of the aristocracy. " Custom, blind custom," he exclaimed, " established under the sinister interest of the ruling few, is the guide by which most operations have hith-

erto been conducted." ³ The law, consisting of obso-
lescent feudal customs patched by arbitrary judicial
decisions, and the Acts of an undemocratic Parliament,
seemed to exist for the protection of aristocratic special privileges, such as game preserves, sinecures, exemption of land from taxation, tariffs on agricultural
produce, practical monopoly of the land and of political power. The very terminology of private ethics
had an aristocratic tinge. To be noble was to be of
the nobility; to be gentle, of the gentry. Courtesy
was learned at courts. Liberality, honor and glory
were the prerogatives of wealth, birth, and political
and military power. Loyalty, duty, humility, and
obedience were the virtues permitted to the inferior
classes, for they made them docile and subservient
to their rulers. Prudence, the self-protecting virtue
of the middle class, was sneered at by the aristocracy,
and stigmatized as low and debasing by the church, its
appanage. The theological virtues also exhibited this
class bias. Faith and hope counseled infinite patience
with misrule; charity was a convenient cloak for the
design to keep up the supply of soldiers by encouraging large families among the poor. As Hume had observed, " celibacy, fasting, penance, mortification, self-
denial, humility, silence, solitude, and the whole train
of monkish virtues . . . serve to no manner of purpose; neither to advance a man's fortune in the world,
nor render him a more useful member of society." ⁴

Bentham proposed to transvaluate moral values in
accordance with the greatest good, not of a class, but
of the greatest number. He would remove morals

from the dominion of church and state by rending the veil of mystery and sacredness which had been cast over them. Locke had already cited the well-attested facts of the variability of moral codes with time and race with telling effect against the belief in innate moral ideas, and, by implication, against the belief in the infallibility of the conscience. Bentham had no difficulty in showing that the criterion of taste, which Lord Shaftesbury had helped give vogue, led to even greater moral anarchy. He noted shrewdly that the aristocracy held " as much and as long as possible to the principle of taste, taking furthermore great pains to constitute itself its supreme arbiter." [5] Revelation and sacred books gave just as great scope to the machinations of priests. Furthermore, the Christian evaluation of acts according to the motives of their authors seemed as likely to encourage ill-deeds as good. Good will, for instance, might prompt these five acts, some laudable, others to be condemned; it might prompt a man to help a poor wretch break prison, to expose a practice of bribery, to perjure himself for the sake of a friend, to give false judgment in a friend's favor, or to feed a starving family. But the intellect could give unambiguous and unbiased judgment. Every man was competent to feel and evaluate pleasure and pain, and a calculation of the results of an action could not be falsified by aristocratic influence without danger of detection. There was no need of invidious distinctions of quality among pleasures, no need to value one man's pleasure above another's. Question-begging epithets like lust and avarice need no longer prejudice the judgment. To the anarchy of taste could succeed the certainty of moral arithmetic. The system of utility would bring morals from heaven to earth. It promised that the future history of moral science would parallel the recent history of physical science, would recount a rapid succession of discoveries of moral truths immediately winning the assent of all mankind. And its initial successes; the sudden vogue of the political economy based upon it, the passing of legal abuses it revealed, and a reform of Parliament based on some recognition of the political rights of the majority, gave considerable warrant for Bentham's faith.

Bentham was not content with the formulation of a moral standard; he was eager to apply it to practical conduct. He pursued with persistent hatred relics of chivalry, such as dueling, which interfered with the useful ordering of social life. He pointed out the especial pernicious effect of the ideals of honor and glory on national well-being, and on international relations; how they encouraged the sovereign and aristocracy to live sumptuously at the expense of their subjects, and to wage wars of conquest. Such acts, he declared, " committed in a private capacity, would bear the name of crimes, and be punished as such. . . . Conquest, colonization can serve the interest of a small number of rulers, never those of the mass of the ruled." " But," he asked sadly, " what orator will ever talk of sacrificing glory to interest, honor to prudence? . . . Away with the real, give us the imaginary! That is the cry of patriotism and nationalism." [6]

Under Bentham's influence, the youthful John Mill reviewed a history of chivalry for the *Westminster* in 1826, in order to inquire how the feudal virtues helped or hindered " enlightened and sound principles of moral action." [7] The knight, he discovered, " was so anxious to banish from his motives and his thoughts everything which bore the semblance of his being actuated by the prospect of advantage that his best exploits never sprung from any solicitude to promote the happiness of mankind, but from an abstract, undefined though most influential and sensitive feeling of his knightly honor and renown." Certain knightly virtues, such as fidelity, courtesy, liberality, and justice, were praiseworthy in themselves, " but . . . springing as they did, not from an enlightened mind which perceived their utility, and practiced them only because they were useful, and only so far as they were so, but from a blind and impulsive feeling of duty — often terminated in positive evil." Fidelity was often wasted on a bad cause or a tyrant, liberality had a questionable source and destination, justice was often finicky or mistaken, courtesy to woman a barrier to her self-development and her self-respect. The honor of a gentleman was not tarnished by a lie to a tradesman, or to a foreign nation. James Mill was attracted by the superior excellence of the Aristotelian quartet of virtues; prudence, fortitude, temperance, and justice, which he sponsored in his *Encyclopædia* article on *Education* under the slightly altered form of intelligence, temperance (including fortitude), justice, and generosity. In final analysis, James Mill and Bentham traced practically all virtues to a single parent, prudence.

It was natural that an ethical system developed and championed by bourgeois thinkers, and giving supreme importance to the bourgeois virtues, should recommend itself especially to the great British middle class. Pain and pleasure were concrete realities with which the practical man could deal confidently; calculation, utility, results, and exchange were borrowed from the vocabulary of the business world. " A nation of shop-keepers " scarcely needed Bentham's reminder that " the only interests which a man at all times and upon all occasions is sure to find adequate motives for consulting, are his own," [8] nor that prudence was the supreme virtue. Even opponents of Bentham, like Jeffrey and Macaulay, had derived from their middle class origin and the general atmosphere of eighteenth century speculation, moral standards not dissimilar. Utilitarian ethics spread with the growth of manufactures and banking, and slipped slowly down to color the thinking of the working classes. Even the Established Church could not escape its contagion. Paley, a hard-headed mathematician, who stated that " virtue is, the doing good to mankind, in obedience to the will of God, and for the sake of everlasting happiness," [9] that " we can be obliged to do nothing but what we ourselves are to gain or lose something by " [9] and that we should be guided by " the will of God, as collected from expediency," [9] was the generally recognized ecclesiastical moralist. His *Principles of Moral and Political Philosophy* (1785) had long been used as the text-

book in Moral Philosophy at Cambridge, where it had
the unanticipated effect of preparing the minds of the
undergraduates for a sympathetic understanding of
Bentham's doctrines.

It was therefore no wonder that the alarmed Carlyle thought that the ethics of utility was the deadly
virus which was infecting his generation with materialism. It was no wonder that a view of life so repugnant to all his instincts should attract the full splendor
of his wrath. Believing that there was no time to be
lost if his countrymen were to be saved from spiritual
death, he scrupled to use no means of arousing them
from their perilous slumbers. "Has the word Duty
no meaning," he demanded in one of the most brilliant
pages of *Sartor Resartus*. "Is what we call Duty no
divine Messenger and Guide, but a false earthly Fan-
tasm, made up of Desire and Fear, of emanations
from the Gallows and from Dr. Graham's Celestial-
bed? Happiness of an approving Conscience! Did
not Paul of Tarsus, whom admiring men have since
named Saint, feel that *he* was the chief of sinners; and
Nero of Rome, jocund in spirit (*wohlgemuth*), spend
much of his time in fiddling? Foolish Word-monger
and Motive-grinder, who in thy Logic-mill hast an
earthly mechanism for the Godlike itself, and wouldst
fain grind me out Virtue from the husks of Pleasure,
— I tell thee, Nay! To the unregenerate Prometheus
Vinctus of a man, it is ever the bitterest aggravation
of his wretchedness that he is conscious of Virtue, that
he feels himself the victim not of suffering only, but
of injustice. What then? Is the heroic inspiration we

name Virtue but some Passion; some bubble of the
blood, bubbling in the direction others *profit by?* I
know not: only this I know, If what thou namest Happiness be our true aim, then are we all astray. With
Stupidity and sound Digestion man may front much.
But what, in these unimaginative days, are the terrors
of Conscience to the diseases of the Liver! Not on
Morality, but on Cookery, let us build our stronghold:
there brandishing our frying-pan, as censer, let us offer
sweet incense to the Devil, and live at ease on the fat
things *he* has provided for his Elect! ''

He solemnly pointed man to his true path, leading
in quite the opposite direction; '' *The Fraction of Life
can be increased in value not so much by increasing
your Numerator as by lessening your Denominator.*
Nay, unless my Algebra deceive me, *Unity* itself divided by *Zero* will give *Infinity.* Make thy claim of
wages a zero then; thou hast the world under thy
feet. Well did the Wisest of our time write: ' It is
only with Renunciation (*Entsagen*) that Life, properly speaking, can be said to begin. . . . There is in
man a HIGHER than Love of Happiness; he can do
without Happiness, and instead thereof find Blessed-
ness! Was it not to preach-forth this same HIGHER
that Sages and Martyrs, the Poet, and the Priest, in
all times, have spoken and suffered; bearing testimony,
through life and through death, of the Godlike that
is in Man, and how in the Godlike only has he Strength
and Freedom? Which God-inspired Doctrine art thou
also honored to be taught; O Heavens! and broken
by manifold merciful afflictions, even till thou become

contrite and learn it! O, thank thy Destiny for these; thankfully bear what yet remain: the Self in thee needed to be annihilated . . . Love not Pleasure; Love God. This is the EVERLASTING YEA, wherein all contradiction is solved; Wherein whoso walks and works, it is well with him."

The source of a moral philosophy so strikingly different in spirit, in content, and in expression from that of Bentham was the mystic union with God which Bentham dismissed as impossible. From this transcendent experience Carlyle derived conscience, " the light of your mind, which is the direct inspiration of the Almighty," [10] in following which man could never err. The possibility of draughts at the well-spring of all goodness rendered superfluous and impertinent all attempts at a science of morals. " People did finer actions when there was no theory of the moral sentiments among them," Carlyle noted in his *Journal*. " Nature is the sure guide in all cases." [11] He consistently took " Nature " as the guide of his own conduct. " *The man should bear rule in the house, and not the woman,*" he wrote Miss Welsh, in justification of his refusal to permit her mother to live in his home after their marriage. " This is an eternal maxim, the law of Nature, which no mortal departs from unpunished. I have meditated on this many years, and every day it grows plainer to me " [12] His early Calvinistic conception of a Universe governed by a divinely established and unchangeable system of ethics, which preserved the stars from wrong and upheld the very heavens, yet condescended to illuminate the conscience of the humblest of men, had been confirmed by the authority of Kant and Fichte. Kant's doctrine of the categorical imperative, which demanded unquestioning obedience, reckless of consequences, like that of the Tennysonian Light Brigade, reinforced the effect of the parental discipline of his childhood. His sufferings from dyspepsia and his sharing of the lot of the poor had taught him the falsity of the doctrine that virtue would generally win happiness or earthly reward. Good men were virtuous for virtue's sake. No external sanctions of pain or pleasure could, as he expressed it, regiment a band of knaves into honest men. Furthermore, his temperament, so enamored of superlatives, so vividly alternating between heights of aspiration and depths of despair, demanded a polarity of vice and virtue which precluded any calculation of the relative amounts of good and evil involved in a proposed act. Advocates of the hedonistic calculus seemed so base and vicious that he would not condescend to meet them with argument. His outraged conscience loosed on Utilitarian ethics the vials of its wrath; crudely abusive epithets, unfair caricature, and ugly sarcasm mingled strangely with rapt display of revered symbols which might lift men's gaze from the trough of sensualism. He had no patience with an analysis which tried to tear away the veil from that holy of holies, man's heart, wherein God's spirit was wont sensibly to dwell, and professed to exhibit only a mechanism for the weighing of pains and pleasures.

From this point of view, and from these methods of attack, Carlyle never departed in his subsequent work.

The fervid ethical appeal of *Past and Present* was based on the most familiar Scriptural texts. The brilliant caricature of Utilitarianism as " Pig Philosophy " in the *Latter Day Pamphlets* was only an expansion of an early conception. He never yielded an inch, and continued to the last to assail Benthamite ethics by repeating, under slightly varying forms, the salient images of the famous *Sartor* passages. The effect of these assaults on the popular mind was enormous. If to this day the epithet " utilitarian " retains a somewhat opprobrious connotation, it is to no inconsiderable degree the result of Carlyle's writings.

But Carlyle was not unsupported in his counter-attack on utilitarian ethics. His weapons of satire and preaching were supplemented by the Benthamic weapon of reasoned analysis, which was turned against its employers by Professors of Trinity College, Cambridge, where Charles Austin, Charles Buller and other vigorous young propagandists had established a flourishing Benthamite party among the students. The Dons, alarmed to see many of their charges seduced by doctrines they believed pernicious, began to realize that the University itself, by adopting Locke's *Essay Concerning Human Understanding* and Paley's *Principles of Moral and Political Philosophy* as textbooks, had been preparing students for the acceptance of Benthamic opinions in politics and ethics. Since the Trinity professorship of Moral Philosophy had long been a sinecure, and its present occupant therefore indisposed to exert himself, it was Adam Sedgwick, Professor of Geology, who, in a series of sermons delivered in

December, 1832, opened the assault upon these dangerous books. He endeavored to find a new philosophic basis for morals by, rephrasing the old theory of innate moral ideas in a manner calculated to avoid Locke's withering analysis. He did not assert that the child was equipped at birth with a ready-made set of moral ideas, but only maintained that it was provided with a moral faculty distinct from the intellect and the emotions, which was designed to record, upon contact with impressions from the outer world, that quality of impressions called moral. For evidence of the existence of this faculty Sedgwick adduced the sense of shame in the very young child, and the especial strength of moral convictions in children. Education could not be solely responsible for the development of moral character, for " a faculty of the soul may be called forth, brought to light, and matured; but cannot be created, any more than we can create a new particle of matter." [13] Scripture sanctioned this opinion, for did not Paul write of the law written on the hearts of the Gentiles? A final indication of the falsity of Locke's psychology lay in the pernicious results of Paley's use of it as the basis for an ethical system. Paley's work revealed the " great injury done to moral reasoning . . . from the attempt to assimilate it too closely to the method of the exact sciences," which obliges the neglect of qualitative differences in pleasures, and " brings down virtue from a heavenly throne and places her on an earthly tribunal." [14] The Utilitarian rule, insidiously " flattering to human pride; for man no longer appears as the subject of a law, but presides with the authority of a judge," [15] contradicted the indispensable " law of honor," and even the Scriptures, for " in the revealed history of the dealings of God with man, acts, which under ordinary circumstances would be crimes of the deepest die (sic), have more than once been made tests of obedience or conditions of acceptance." [16] Paley had therefore fallen into the trap of the deist and atheist by attempting to prove that God must be beneficent, for " by what right can man set limits to the moral condition of the Almighty? " [17] From this point of view, the steadfast faith of the martyr must be madness; hence his system, " sterile in great virtues will be fruitful in great crimes." [18] To protect the youth from its debasing influence, Sedgwick urged that Bishop Butler's sermons, which had recently been used supplementarily, be prescribed instead of Paley as reading in moral philosophy.

Sedgwick's attacks failed in their object, and five years elapsed before an abler and more vigorous champion, Professor Whewell, author of *The Logic of the Inductive Sciences*, which was an invaluable aid to John Stuart Mill in the preparation of his *Logic*, renewed the assault in a series of sermons. He repeated substantially Sedgwick's arguments, but guarded his theory of the moral faculty more closely by declaring that only to those possessing the Kantian " good will," which attuned man to the infinite, would it give sure guidance. His third sermon was notable for its highminded rejection of Paley's use of heaven and hell as ultimate moral sanctions. The really good man,

Whewell insisted, did good deeds because he loved them; only the wicked could be influenced by bribes and threats. And, with imaginative insight, he added that heaven would please the righteous only, for the wicked would find nothing there to their taste. This second protest was sufficient to break the inertia that had hitherto held Paley in the curriculum. Butler was substituted as a temporary text, while Whewell, who was presented the Moral Philosophy Professorship in 1838, was preparing a systematic treatise better adapted for pedagogical purposes.

In his first lecture on assuming the chair he outlined a very interesting plan to base ethics on a sound psychology. He proposed to discover inductively from a study of history the fundamental human desires, and deduce from the exigencies of their proper ranking and frictionless coöperation a complete set of rights and duties. But the execution of the plan was less happy than its conception. Whewell limited his field of induction to statutory law, and disdained to test his derived maxims by their results in practice. This legalistic tendency gave a dull and pedantic character to his textbook, *Elements of Morality,* which appeared in 1845. But it served well its immediate purpose by presenting the Cambridge undergraduates with the Tory principles of its author as an antidote to Benthamism. Its contribution to ethical theory was a critique of Bentham's neglect of motives; it was clear, Whewell said, that a man can relieve distress without being compassionate. His later *Lectures on the History of Moral Philosophy in England* (1852) were much more readable, and contained some keen criticisms of Bentham's ethical writings. Even if it were granted that doing good is on the whole more profitable to the individual moral agent than doing evil, what, on Benthamic principles, Whewell demanded, could restrain a man from doing a particular bad act if he were sure, by careful calculation, that its consequences would net him more pleasure than pain? On the other hand, how was it possible to calculate the result of *any* act, in a world of infinitely complex interrelations? Did not Bentham reason in a circle, when he insisted that virtue was itself happiness, yet made happiness the test of virtue? Was not his emphasis, in the *Deontology*, upon public opinion as the chief moral sanction an identification of virtue with mere popular taste? Did he not at best value the material welfare of society above morals and religion?

Even before Whewell had won his fight against Paley, the tide had turned against Benthamism both in the Universities and in the nation at large. The new student generation of the late thirties, as we noted in discussing the phenomenon of Young England,[a] had conceived an enthusiasm for the ideals and institutions of the romantic past rather than for radical reform, for mysticism rather than rationalism. The most prominent manifestation of this change in sentiment was the immense success at Oxford, always the more conservative of the Universities and never committed to Locke and Paley, of the so-called Tractarians, John Henry Newman, John Keble, Hurrell Froude, E. B.

[a] See Chapter VIII, pp. 309–310.

Pusey, and others, who passionately attacked liberalism
of every sort in the name of the Fathers of the Church
and the dogmas of the Middle Ages. There students
took the letter of Christianity seriously, fasted, con-
fessed, and did penance in the cold medieval college
halls. And the Oxford Movement was only one result of a spiritual awakening within the Established
Church which formed part of the great conservative
reaction after the wars with France. Religious revivals, whose special prominence about 1830 'had encouraged Carlyle, had brought forth actively devout
young clergymen who regarded the Church as something quite other than a comfortable profession for
Laodicean younger sons and tutors of noblemen.
Evangelicals like Thomas Chalmers, Edward Irving,
and Daniel Wilson and Broad Churchmen like Thomas
Arnold, Julius Hare, F. D. Maurice, Charles Kingsley, and Frederick Robertson were no more tolerant
than the neo-Catholic Tractarians of the matter-of-fact
intellectualism of a Paley. They had the conviction
of spiritual realities, the fervent piety, the enthusiastic
self-devotion characteristic of authentic Christianity.
These active reformist parties within the Church were
agreed upon an ethical standard typically defined by
Robertson as " what Kant calls ' the categorical imperative ' that is, a sense of duty which commands
categorically or absolutely — not saying, ' it is better '
but ' thou shalt.' Why? Because ' thou shalt,' that is
all. It is not best to do right — thou must do right;
and the conscience that feels that, and in that way, is
the nearest to divine humanity — not that the law was

made, like the Sabbath, for man; but man was made for it. He is beneath it, a grain of dust before it, it moves on, and if he will not move before it, it crushes him." [19] The Evangelicals and Broad Churchmen made headway against Utilitarianism in its middle class stronghold; the Broad Churchmen were even attempting to reach the working class leaders, who were especially embittered against the Church. The most significant men of letters, still feeling the impulse of the great Romantic tradition, supported this ethical position because of its atmosphere of awe and mystery, its rejection of analysis. Carlyle, Dickens, Browning, and Keble solved the most difficult moral problems by saying with Tennyson,

> . . . the heart
> Stood up and answered, ' I have felt.' [20]

The chivalric virtues retained their glamour for the priest and the literary man, who united with the soldier in reverent admiration of the sublime surrender of self to duty which was to be dramatized in the *Ode on the Death of the Duke of Wellington,* and *The Charge of the Light Brigade.* Even in 1835, when the political, religious, and aesthetic reactions against Benthamism had not attained their full force, John Stuart Mill had become so much aware of the superficiality of the Radical triumphs, and the overwhelming strength of the opposition to Utilitarian ethics, as to be moved to plead that " It deeply concerns the greatest interests of our race, that the only mode of treating ethical questions which aims at correcting existing maxims, and rectifying any of the perversions of existing feeling should not be borne down by clamor." [21]

Mill's alarm was intensified by his knowledge of fatal defects in Bentham's statement of the Utilitarian position. The great crisis in his mental history which had taught him the necessity of the cultivation of the feelings, and the understanding of the psychology of his opponents, had exposed Bentham's ethical system as a half-truth, the product of insufficient knowledge of human nature. This criticism he set forth in *Remarks on Bentham's Philosophy* published in 1833 under Bulwer-Lytton's name in the latter's *England and the English*. Bentham, he pointed out, was not only unaware that human motives were innumerable, but omitted from his *Table of the Springs of Action* even the prominent motive of "conscience or feeling of duty," which, if only a product of association, was nevertheless an undeniable psychological fact. He assumed that a man was only deterred from an action by fear of the pain *resultant* upon its commission, and failed to notice that he might also experience deterrent pain *antecedent* to it, " that the idea of placing himself in such a situation is so painful, that he cannot dwell upon it long enough to have even the physical power of perpetrating the crime." [22] " Not only may this be so," Mill insisted, " but unless it be so, the man is not really virtuous. The fear of pain *consequent* upon the act cannot arise, unless there is deliberation, and the man as well as ' the woman who deliberates,' is in imminent danger of being lost." [23] Bentham did recognize the existence of dispositions, but failed to

lay stress upon it, and by his " superior stress . . .
upon the specific consequences of a class of acts, rejected all contemplation of the action in its general
bearings upon the entire moral being of the agent." [24]
His atomic philosophy represented each class of acts
as " insulated " from the others, although daily experience showed that " no person can be a thief and a
liar without being much else." [25] But the worst and
most dangerous of his narrownesses was his practical
denial of the possibility of cultivating genuinely
altruistic feelings, and his tactless use of the word
" interest " to denote social as well as self-interest.
" I regard," commented Mill, " any considerable increase of human happiness, unaccompanied by changes
in the state of the desires, as hopeless: not to mention
that while the desires are circumscribed in self, there
can be no adequate motive for exertions tending to
modify to good ends even those external circumstances.
No man's individual share of any public good which he
can hope to realize by his efforts, is an equivalent for
the sacrifice of his ease, and of the personal objects
which he might attain by another course of conduct." [26]
Bentham's doctrine would thus defeat his own end of
reform and turn men to " miserable self-seeking."
" It is by such things," Mill concluded, " that the more
enthusiastic and generous minds are prejudiced against
all his other speculations and against the very attempt
to make ethics and politics a subject of precise and
philosophic thinking." [27] If a new ethical system were
to inspire public confidence, it would be necessary for
its author " first to have, and next to show, in every

sentence and in every line, a firm unwavering confidence in man's capability of virtue." [28]

Mill therefore found himself obliged to defend from their friends as well as their enemies what he believed to be " the only methods of philosophizing from which any improvement in ethical opinions can be looked for." [29] During nearly twenty, years of accumulating experience and deepening insight into the human heart culminating in the publication of his *Utilitarianism* in 1863, he endeavored to free the scientific approach to ethics from its unfortunate historical associations and present it in a manner acceptable to those who had experienced the richness of the moral life. The most pressing need was to keep it from being " borne down by clamor." To this end were written his replies to Sedgwick (1835) and Whewell (1852).[a] He had little difficulty in defending Locke against Sedgwick's feeble arguments in favor of an innate moral faculty, which would bind mankind forever to a fixed moral code, insusceptible of improvement or change " from the progress of intelligence, from more authentic and enlarged experience, and from alterations in the condition of the human race," [30] but he admitted that much of Paley was indefensible. Not only was Paley false to the scientific position by making utility binding only because it happened to coincide with the will of God, and by using it to defend, not correct, the low moral ideals and practice of his time, but (and here Mill meant Bentham also,

[a] Published in *The London Review* for April, 1835, and in *The Westminster Review* for October, 1852.

though he did not mention him), he failed to gen-
eralise from a sufficiently comprehensive survey of the
materials of ethics, did not take into account the subjective as well as the objective results of an action,
and, misled by legal analogies, believed moral conduct
wholly, the product of individual self-interest. But
Sedgwick himself offered no better moral guidance;
Christianity, upon which he had reliance, only prepared
the heart, did not prescribe specific duties. These,
Mill insisted, must be reasoned about. Although it
was true that no one could forsee *all* the results of an
action in a society infinitely complex, yet one could
calculate closely enough for practical purposes. Calculation did not necessarily cause fatal hesitation in the
face of action; " on the same principle, navigating by
rule, instead of by instinct, might be called waiting for
the calculations of astronomy. There seems no absolute necessity, of putting off the calculations until the
ship is in the middle of the South Sea." [31] The ignorance and misrepresentation, the vague rhetoric of
Sedgwick, a geologist who had ventured outside his
field, Mill considered " a fair enough sample of the
popular arguments against the theory; his book has had
more readers and more applauders than a better book
would have had, because it is level with a lower class
of capacities." [32] " The contemners of analysis," Mill
added, " have long enough had all the pretension to
themselves. They have had the monopoly of the
claim to pure and lofty and sublime principles; and
those who gave reasons to justify their feelings have
submitted to be cried down as low and cold and de-

graded. We hope that they will submit no longer; and not content with meeting the metaphysics of their more powerful adversaries with profounder metaphysics, will join battle in the field of popular controversy with every antagonist of name and reputation, even when, as in the present case, his name and reputation are his only claims to be heard on such a subject." [33]

For this reason Mill covered much the same ground again in joining issue with Whewell, who had appropriated " to his own side of the question all the expressions, such as conscience, duty, rectitude, with which the reverential feelings of mankind towards moral ideas are associated," and had dubbed Utilitarianism " dependent morality " in order to give his own the connotative prestige of the adjective " independent." [34] He vaguely commented on Whewell's debt to the new apriorism of Kant, but was on surer ground in exposing the futility of his attempt to find a rational proof for the first principle of his system, which finally obliged him to take refuge in such impotent dogmatism as: " In regard to the Supreme Rule, the question Why? admits no further answer. Why must I do what is right? Because it is *right*." [35] The concrete moral precepts displayed in Whewell's *Elements of Morality* failed to convince Mill that the opposing school had the superior moral inspiration it claimed. The *Elements* enjoined as sacred duties " reverence for superiors even when personally undeserving (i. 171–7) and obedience to existing laws even when bad." [36] They advocated legislation punishing disbelievers in a deity and in the

providential government of the world for their willful
blindness to truth. " The morality of the individual,"
Whewell had written, " depends on his not violating
the law of his nation. . . . The laws of the State are
to be observed, even if they enact slavery." [37] He was
shocked at Bentham's belief in divorce at the consent
of both parties, and his classing kindness to animals as a
moral obligation. " We are bound to men by the universal tie of human brotherhood," had been his comment on the latter position, " we have no such tie to
animals. We are to be humane to them because we are
human, not because we and they alike feel animal pleasures." [38] Such, Mill commented, was " the deification
of mere opinion and habit," [39] to which the moral faculty theory led.

But he did not hold up Bentham's ethics as a shining
example of the superior results of the opposing theory.
The death of his father since the publication of the
Sedgwick article had relieved him of the necessity of a
loyal silence concerning Bentham's demerits. But he
did defend him from certain misrepresentations contained
in Whewell's *Lectures on the History of Moral Philosophy*. The Utilitarian formula, he pointed out, did not
enjoin the promotion of the greatest happiness of
the individual, but that of the greatest number. Bentham did not say that public opinion defined moral
obligations; he only regarded it as the most powerful
sanction for enforcing them. He did not reason in a
circle concerning happiness and virtue, for the associ-
ational psychology explained how " the good of others
becomes our pleasure because we have learnt to find

pleasure in it." [40]   The real defects of Bentham's ethics,
Mill asserted, lay in quite another region, which he proceeded to indicate by repeating the substance of certain
observations he had already made in greater detail in
his essay on Bentham in 1838.[a]

These observations, incorporated in an essay which
had been Mill's first public avowal of apostasy from
the Benthamite sect, were an amplification and refine-
ment of the critique of Bentham's moral philosophy
contributed anonymously to Bulwer-Lytton's work in
1833.   The originality of Bentham's work, Mill had
declared, lay not in its hedonism nor its doctrine of
utility, but in its " application of a real inductive philosophy to problems of ethics," [41] which brought clarity
and precision into controversies by testing moral theories
with reference to concrete situations.   But in his application of this method had lain Bentham's greatest source
of weakness.   He had failed to make anything like a
complete examination of the data of ethics before writing his own treatises.   He knew little of human nature
from his own experience, and had made no attempt to
learn more from others.   He was contemptuous of the
speculations of those who had not employed his method,
and did not examine those vast stores of moral materials, of which, as Mill had noted in his reply to Sedgwick, " a large proportion have never yet found their
way into the writings of philosophers, but are to be
gathered, on the one hand, from actual observers of
mankind; on the other from those poets and novelists,

[a] Published in *The London and Westminster Review* for August,
1838.

who have spoken out unreservedly, from their own experience, any true human feeling." [42] He entirely lacked the dramatic imagination " whereby one mind understands a mind different from itself, and throws itself into the feelings of that other mind," [43] and wantonly dismissed as " vague generalities " " the whole unanalyzed experience of the human race." [44] Thus he was thrown back entirely upon his own experience, and that was the reverse of rich. " He had neither internal experience nor external," wrote Mill from intimate knowledge, " the even, quiet tenor of his life, and his healthiness of mind, conspired to exclude him from both. He never knew prosperity and adversity, passion nor satiety: he never had even the experiences which sickness gives; he lived from boyhood to the age of eighty-five in boyish health. He knew no dejection, no heaviness of heart. He never felt life a sore and weary burden. He was a boy to the last. Self-consciousness, that demon of the men of genius of our time, from Wordsworth to Byron, from Goethe to Chateaubriand, and to which this age owes so much both of its cheerful and its mournful wisdom, was never awakened in him. How much of human nature slumbered in him he knew not, neither can we know. . . . His own lot was cast in a generation of the leanest and barrenest men whom England had yet produced; and he was an old man when a better race came in with the present century. He saw, accordingly, in man, little but what the vulgarest eye can see; recognized no diversities of character but such as he who runs may read." [45] Consequently, " the sense of *honor* and per-

sonal dignity — that feeling of personal exaltation and
degradation which acts independently of other people's
opinion, or even in defiance of it; the love of *beauty*,
the passion of the artist; the love of *order*, of congruity,
of consistency in all things and conformity to their
end; the love of *power*, not in the limited form of
power over other human beings, but abstract power, the
power of making our volitions effectual; the love of
action, the thirst for movement and activity, a principle
of scarcely less influence in human life than its opposite,
the love of ease — none of these powerful constituents
of human nature are thought worthy of a place among
the *Springs of Action*." [46]   Likewise, " man is never
recognized by him as a being capable of pursuing
spiritual perfection as an end; of desiring, for its own
sake, the conformity of his own character to his standard of excellence, without hope of good, or fear of evil,
from other source than his own inward consciousness." [47]
Finally, Bentham considered what Mill defined as the
strictly *moral* quality of action, that depending on their
" foreseeable consequences," [48] as their sole quality,
neglecting their two other qualities of beauty and
lovableness, or the reverse, which ought to affect profoundly our attitude toward the persons performing
them.

This extraordinary narrowness of outlook Mill found
to have seriously affected the value of Bentham's ethical writings. His only work concerning itself wholly
with personal morality, the *Deontology, or Science of
Morals*, unfortunately so largely rewritten by Bowring that Mill refused to consider it a wholly authentic

work, revealed a most disappointing preoccupation with
" the *petite morale,* . . . and that with the most
pedantic minuteness, and on the *quid pro quo* principles
which regulate trade." [49]   And his writings on legislation and government neglected almost entirely the
function of institutions in improving the national character. Mill was obliged to admit that Bentham's philosophy was sound only in so far as it taught " the
means of organizing and regulating the merely *business*
part of the social arrangements." [50]

Significantly, Mill failed to answer the accusations
of Sedgwick and Whewell that an ethical system which
failed to recognize qualitative distinctions in pleasure
necessarily debased its adherents' characters. This was
probably because Mill's mind had long been unsettled
concerning this question, for in his *Diary* for March 23,
1854, we find him confessing: " Quality as well as
quantity of happiness is to be considered; less of a
higher kind is preferable to more of a lower. Socrates
would rather choose to be Socrates dissatisfied than to
be a pig satisfied. The pig probably would not, but
then the pig only knows one side of the question: Socrates knows both." [51]   By this final concession, Mill
took from Utilitarianism the similitude to " pig philosophy " which had repelled many lovers of virtue.
But at a tremendous price: the sacrifice of Bentham's
dream of an exact science of morals. Moral arithmetic
was not competent to measure differences in the quality
of pleasure, or in the beauty or lovableness of acts;
these could only be measured, and then imprecisely, by
the undemocratic instrument of taste. Bentham, with

a salutary instinct for the protection of his mental peace, would not tolerate the words " good and bad taste " in his hearing; Mill opened his ears to the opinion of the world, and largely unconsciously, permitted the realm of conduct to slip from the domination of judgments concerning fact and quantity into that of judgments concerning value, which possess no unanimity or fixity. Likewise, fuller participation in the moral life of his time caused him to renounce his early feud against the chivalric virtues, and claim their finer spirit as the precious birthright of an aristocracy of talent in a non-military society. What remained distinctive in his re-vised Utilitarianism was only a denial of the existence of any mental content not derived from experience or any special moral faculty capable of interpreting ex-perience, an emphasis on results and reasoning, and an independence both of supernatural sanction and of Scriptural revelation.

The indispensability of such a system as a supplement to, and a corrective of, the Christian Scriptures, Mill attempted to demonstrate by a critical examination of New Testament precepts. In *On Liberty* (1859) he boldly contradicted the common assertion that Christian ethics were " the whole truth " and " a complete doc-trine of morals." The Gospels, he declared, contained no precise moral legislation. Jesus presupposed the existing Talmudic code, and endeavored to raise it and spiritualize it by the pronouncement of inspiring gen-eralities, often paradoxical and impossible of literal obedience. Professed Christians did not commonly turn the other cheek to the smiter, nor take no thought for the morrow, nor sell all their goods to give to the poor. The Judaising followers of Jesus had felt the incompleteness of his precepts, and had supplemented them from the barbarous code of the Old Testament. Their Hellenizing opponents, particularly Saint Paul, had accommodated them to the Graeco-Roman statutes, " even to the extent of giving an apparent sanction to slavery." What was generally known as Christian ethics was of still later date, and largely the deposit of Church tradition of the first five centuries of the Christian era. And New Testament ethics was not merely incomplete; it was imperfect. It had " all the characters of a reaction," and was in great part only " a protest against Paganism." " Its ideal is negative rather than positive; passive rather than active; Innocence rather than Nobleness; Abstinence from Evil, rather than energetic Pursuit of Good; in its precepts (as has been well said) ' thou shalt not ' predominates unduly over ' thou shalt.' " Its doctrine of passive obedience would make political progress impossible. " It is in the Koran, not the New Testament, that we read the maxim — ' A ruler who appoints any man to an office, when there is within his dominions another man better qualified for it, sins against God and against the State.' What little recognition the idea of obligation to the public obtains in modern morality is derived from Greek and Roman sources, not from Christian; as, even in the morality of private life, whatever exists of magnanimity, highmindedness, personal dignity, even the sense of honor, is derived from the purely human, not the religious part of our education and never could have grown out of a standard of ethics in which the only worth, professedly recognized, is that of obedience." Mill charged the so-called Christian morality with the tendency to form "a low, abject, servile type of character, which, submit itself as it may to what it deems the Supreme Will, is incapable of rising to or sympathizing in the conception of Supreme Goodness." "I believe," he concluded, "that other ethics than any which can be evolved from exclusively Christian sources, must exist side by side with Christian ethics to produce the moral regeneration of mankind." And these other ethics, to attain their best quality, should be the results of individual "experiments of living," unchecked by religious intolerance or civil coercion, save where society was unavoidably obliged to act in self-defense. Thus and thus only could ethics rest on a comprehensive empirical basis, and become truly scientific.

This reasoned protest against the one-sidedness of Christian ethics had a strong immediate influence because it coincided with the prevailing feeling of the working class. Thomas Cooper, in his portrayal of the terrible sufferings of the Leicester stocking weavers in the late 'thirties, has recorded a typical expression of the workers' sense of the incompatibility of Christian faith and hope with the interests of their class: "A poor religious stockinger said: 'Let us be patient a little longer, lads, surely God Almighty will help us soon.' 'Talk no more about thy Goddlemighty'; was the snarling rejoinder; 'there isn't one. If there *was* one, he wouldn't let us suffer as we do.'"[52] The early trades-unionists and labor agitators saw the most dangerous of hostile propaganda in the clerical exhortations to patience and obedience. The clergy, connected for the most part by birth and by interest with the propertied classes, alienated the laborers further by their undisguised hostility to coöperation and socialism. The writings of Kingsley, Maurice, and Robertson contain ample evidence of the extent to which the unpropertied classes were lost to the Church. Popular morality was for the most part unguided; an amalgam of local custom with lingering Christian maxims, or with the rationalism of the cheap press. The penny literature, which had a large and rapidly increasing circulation, was at its worst crudely atheistic in a quaint eighteenth century manner. Its more enlightened manifestations were the dogmatic determinism of Robert Owen, and the secularism of John Jacob Holyoake. Holyoake's penny pamphlet *Secularism* (1854), an interesting evidence of the penetration of the masses by Utilitarianism and Positivism, vigorously voiced the protest of the labor leaders against the passivity and humility of Christian ethics: " Every penniless man, woman, and child is the property of the capitalist, no less than is the slave in New Orleans. Society blockades Poverty, scarcely leaving it escape. The artisan is engaged in an incessant struggle against wrong and injustice — then what has he, the struggler, to do with Christianity, which tells him not to resist evil — which fetters him with an arbitrary faith — which denies saving power to good works — which menaces him with eternal damnation? " Mill had a direct influence on this secularist movement through the lectures and pamphlets of the notorious atheist Charles Bradlaugh, who had a large working-class following during the 'sixties and 'seventies. In a two-penny pamphlet in which he called Mill " the profoundest social philosopher, the truest friend of the working classes of our day," Bradlaugh echoed the position taken in *On Liberty*. " To the inculcation of poverty of spirit," he wrote, " I object as strenuously as I do to the teaching contentment under poverty. Poverty of spirit is no virtue. Honesty of spirit, manliness of spirit, bold, uncompromising determined resistance to wrong and assertion of right, should be taught in lieu of that poverty of spirit which allows the proud and haughty to trample upon, and oppress the highest human rights." Bradlaugh's skill as a popular lecturer and his spectacular and finally successful attempt to enter Parliament, from which he was excluded after four successive elections on the ground of his inability to take the oath on the Bible, attracted much attention to these ethical views. Nor was Mill's influence confined to the masses. His opinions penetrated the intellectual classes through John Morley and Samuel Butler, and were not without welcome even among the clergy. Charles Kingsley wrote him that the reading of *On Liberty* made him " a clearer-headed and braver-minded man on the spot," [53] and the whole school of " muscular Christians " associated with him applauded Mill's encouragement of the more virile virtues, which, by a natural reaction, are perhaps too much emphasized in modern ethical thought.

If the ethics of the New Testament could be called

inadequate, those of the Old Testament were much less
defensible. Mill characterized them in *On Liberty* as
" barbarous and intended only for a barbarous people,"
and advanced clergymen were criticising them ad-
versely. Notably, the American preacher, Theodore
Parker, had adopted an evolutionary conception of the
Old Testament, as marking only a stage in the moral
education of the race. However, against this " sickly
and sentimental morality which talks of the ' ferocious '
God of the popular theology, which is indignant at the
faith of Abraham, which shudders over the fate of the
Canaanites, which prides itself in discovering imperfections in the laws of Moses," [54] religious conservatism
raised up a champion in Richard Mansel, a Professor
of Moral and Metaphysical Philosophy at Oxford.
Just as Mill was publishing his strictures upon it, Mansel was attempting, in the *Bampton Lectures* of 1858,
to put the Divine Morality as portrayed in the Hebrew
Scriptures beyond the reach of human criticism by borrowing from Sir William Hamilton, the Edinburgh
eclectic philosopher, the powerful new weapon of the
Kantian criticism, which was slowly coming to be known
in the British Isles. He rejected as inconsistent the
Kantian discovery of ultimate reality in the moral law,
and removed absolute morality beyond human comprehension by the barrier of the Kantian antinomies.
God's perfect morality, the noumenon, he asserted,
could not be known by finite man, whose knowledge
was confined to phenomena. But for man's guidance
God had graciously left the Scriptural record, which
was suited to his finite comprehension. That this some-

times recorded as commands and actions of the Deity things repugnant to human feelings offered but one more of the many insoluble metaphysical problems involving infinity. Man should regard them best as "moral miracles" whereby "the Almighty is regarded as suspending for special purposes, not the eternal laws which constitute His own absolute nature, but the created laws which he imposed at a certain time on a particular portion of his creatures."

This confident cutting of the knot of controversy deeply impressed Oxford audiences, and the rumor went abroad that orthodoxy had taken up a new and impregnable position. But the blade of the Kantian criticism cut both ways. Thomas Huxley, whose agnosticism had been confirmed by Hamilton's *Essay on the Unconditioned*, urged the geologist Lyell to read Mansel's argument "as a piece of clear and unanswerable reasoning." "Although," he added gleefully, "regarding the author as a churchman, you will probably compare him, as I did, to the drunken fellow in Hogarth's ' *Contested Election*,' who is sawing through the signpost at the other party's public house, forgetting he is sitting at the other end of it." [55] This glee was shared by Herbert Spencer, who saw in the doctrine of an unknowable God a means for the liberation of the social sciences from theological interference. Liberal theologians, on the other hand, were quick to see the danger of a theology which would rob the church of the popular appeal of anthropomorphism. Maurice, who had warmly defended Jehovah's dealings with the Canaanites against Sterling's humanitarian objections, and Kingsley, who had taxed his invention in discovering enormities of vice on the part of those unlucky aborigines which would be sufficient to convince the working-class readers of *Politics for the People* of the necessity of their extirpation by Divine command, found their position exposed from the rear. Maurice, whose faith had always been based on the immanence of God in man's moral nature, and the consequent identity of divine and human morality, hastily and hotly accused Mansel of meaning " either that there is no moral indignation in the human bosom against the confusion of our God and Father with Moloch and Siva; or . . . that moral indignation is good for nothing." [56] Maurice's moral indignation found support in an unexpected quarter. Mill was not so pleased at the free scope which Mansel was giving to the social sciences as not to perceive that he was at the same time depriving the moral maxims evolved by the human race in its social experience of much of their dignity and obligatory force. He therefore at once attempted to prevent the spread of Mansel's doctrine by cutting at its roots in a thorough *Examination of Sir William Hamilton's Philosophy*. In the course of this work he became so wroth at the picture of Mansel's deity demanding, under threat of his omnipotence, conduct repugnant to the feelings and contrary to the reason of mankind, that he exclaimed: " I will call no being good, who is not what I mean when I apply that epithet to my fellow creatures; and if such a being can sentence me to hell for not so calling him, to hell I will go." [57]

Mansel wittily described this outburst as " an exhibition of taste and temper," and coolly disposed of Maurice's arguments, which were from the heart rather than from the head; but the spirit of the age denied him a victory by abolishing the terms under which he conceived the problem. In 1864, Bishop Colenso, a dealer in the new black art of Biblical higher criticism, showed by mathematical tests that the slaughter of myriads of Canaanites, so long a stumbling block for tender consciences, was unhistorical. And in 1859, practically unnoticed by the controversialists, had appeared the revolutionary *Origin of Species*, which corroborated Theodore Parker's theory of the progress of morals, and united with the geological evidence in bringing into serious doubt the infallibility and literal inspiration of the Scriptures, upon which Mansel's argument rested. The Church was immediately put upon the defensive, and the field was free for a humanistic theory of morals.

Mill took advantage of this favorable opportunity to press the claim of the principle of utility to be the soundest basis for such a humanistic system. In the same *Fraser's Magazine* which had brought out *Sartor Resartus* thirty years before, he published a series of articles entitled *Utilitarianism* (1863), which championed a purged and spiritualized form of the very ethical doctrines which had enraged Professor Teufelsdröckh. It was a tribute to the weight and persuasiveness of Carlyle's objections, that Mill devoted the larger part of his space to an attempt to clear away these (as he styled them) misconceptions, which were the " chief obstacle " to the favorable consideration of the Utilitarian ethics. He gave ground to the accusation of " pig philosophy " by publishing for the first time his admission of qualitative difference in pleasures, but dismissed Carlyle's denial of the possibility of happiness as a palpable exaggeration, and admitted only in a qualified sense the necessity of the opposed principle of " *Entsagen.*" Self-sacrifice as an end in itself was not a moral motive, for its practice as a universal rule would be suicidal folly. But self-sacrifice for the sake of increasing the sum of happiness in the world deserved all the praise which Carlyle had bestowed indiscriminately. " Though it is only in a very imperfect state of the world's arrangements," Mill wrote, in one of his most intimate and noble paragraphs, " that any one can best serve the happiness of others by the absolute sacrifice of his own; yet so long as the world is in that imperfect state, I fully acknowledge that the readiness to make such a sacrifice is the highest virtue which can be found in man. I will add, that in this condition of the world, paradoxical as the assertion may be, the conscious ability to do without happiness gives the best prospect of realizing such happiness as is attainable. For nothing except that consciousness can raise a person above the chances of life, by making him feel that, let fate and fortune do their worst, they have not power to subdue him: which, once felt, frees him from excess of anxiety concerning the evils of life, and enables him, like many a Stoic in the worst times of the Roman Empire, to cultivate in tranquillity the sources of satisfaction accessible to him, without concerning himself about the uncertainty of their duration any more than about their inevitable end." The common belief that the Utilitarian was incapable of self-sacrifice Mill attributed to a confusion of the greatest happiness principle with the principle of self-interest. The true interpretation of the greatest happiness principle was quite the contrary; " between his own happiness and that of others, utilitarianism requires him to be as strictly impartial as a disinterested and benevolent spectator. In the golden rule of Jesus of Nazareth, we read the complete spirit of the ethics of utility." And such devotion to the interests of humanity could not justly be called godless, unless God was conceived as not desiring the happiness of mankind.

That this universal happiness is the sole criterion of human action and therefore the sole standard of morality, Mill attempted to demonstrate. " Each person's happiness," he argued, " is a good to that person, and the general happiness, therefore, a good to the aggregate of all persons." Furthermore, it was the sole good, for virtue, its only competitor, could be shown by analysis to be itself in disguise. That the weakness of the first step in this proof should have escaped so trained a logician is astonishing. Later moralists, who have profited by the development of psychological science, are wont to give more weight to Mill's secondary argument that the social feelings of mankind, and the feelings of pain and pleasure, have at least as much right to be called innate as any alleged *a priori* moral principles.

Upon these feelings of social solidarity Mill also relied for the enforcement of the Utilitarian rule. To conscience or the categorical imperative he denied any

other character than that of a subjective feeling in the
human mind. Their "mystical character" he explained as the result of "associations derived from
sympathy, from love, and still more from fear; from
all the forms of religious feeling; from the recollec-
tions of childhood and of all our past life; from self-
esteem, desire of the esteem of others, and occasionally
even self-abasement," which constitute "a mass of feeling which must be broken through in order to do what
violates our standard of right, and which if we do
nevertheless violate that standard, will probably have
to be encountered afterwards in the form of remorse."
The conscience was furthermore so subservient to the
influences of education in its widest sense as to be an
extremely untrustworthy guide; for "there is hardly
any theory so absurd or mischievous that it may not,
by means of these influences, be made to act on the
human mind with all the authority of conscience." The
common belief that a system of morals which thus denied the supremacy of the conscience could have no
very strong influence on human conduct, Mill flatly
contradicted. The danger seemed rather that the social
feelings of mankind, which every progress in civilization tended to strengthen, might become too powerful
and "interfere unduly with human freedom and indi-
viduality." For evidence in support of this novel position Mill referred doubting readers to Comte's *Traité
de politique positive* [a] which had "superabundantly
shown the possibility of giving to the service of hu-

[a] Not the 1824 essay discussed in Chapter VI, but the mature
treatise published 1830–42.

manity, even without the aid of a belief in a Providence,[a] both the psychological power and efficacy of a religion; making it take hold of human life, and color all thought, feeling and action in a manner of which the greatest ascendancy ever exercised by a religion may be but a type and forecaste." Thus in ethics, as well as in politics and economics, Mill was finally confronted by " the vital problem of the future " with which he had grappled in *On Liberty;* that of " the nature and limits of the power which can be legitimately exercised by society over the individual."

The development of Mill's ethical thought shows most clearly what has been often called his tendency to compromise. But it can scarcely be called compromise in its usual meaning of yielding to expediency. Otherwise, for example, Mill would not have clung to the unpopular tenet of hedonism, when hedonism had ceased to have a more than nominal place in his ethics. It is more properly an intellectual honesty, which accepts truth regardless of its source or its effect upon partisan conflict. As a result of this candor, *Utilitarianism* is much less a statement of the strictly Utilitarian theory than a summary of the results of British moral philosophy during the preceding century. There is a certain finality in the treatise, in that it closes what one may call the pre-biological epoch of ethical investigation.

Mill's essay on *Nature,* completed in 1858, a year before the publication of *The Origin of Species,* brings

[a] Mill permitted to his Utilitarian a belief both in a Providence and in God. Cf. *Utilitarianism,* Chapter III.

us into the atmosphere of the new epoch. The purpose of this essay was to show how the reference to " nature " as an ethical standard tended to confuse and pervert moral judgments. It was popularly supposed that proving an act to be " unnatural " was equivalent to proving it to be bad; that living in accordance with the " laws of nature " was living the good life.. Mill held that the word " nature " used in this ethical sense derived most of its force from foreign associations, was ambiguous in its meaning, and in each of its significant meanings was a false guide for human conduct. To support these charges, he made a separate examination of the moral import of each meaning of the term.

He first considered nature as signifying the non-human world, or at least " everything which is of itself, without voluntary human intervention." The word had been thus understood by eighteenth century deists, who, having denied the infallibility of the Scriptures, had sought to read God's rules for man's guidance in the spontaneous activities of the universe which He had created, a universe whose marvelous orderliness the Newtonian physics had just revealed. Orthodox theologians did not disdain to borrow the " natural religion " thus discovered to support and supplement Scriptural revelation, in spite of the warning of Bishop Butler that the created world gave evidence of so much evil and suffering that it was greatly inferior to the Scriptures as a proof of the wisdom and goodness of an omnipotent God. Paley's *Natural Theology* (1802) proved the existence of God by the argument from design, using the famous analogy that the existence of a watch proves that of a watchmaker, and adduced many examples of beneficent animal adaptations as indications of the kindly provision of the Creator. The notion that the spontaneous course of external nature was a model for man to imitate became a commonplace of romantic literature. Wordsworth knew

> . . . that Nature never did betray
> The heart that loved her,

and that

> One impulse from a vernal wood
> May teach you more of man,
> Of moral evil and of good
> Than all the sages can,

and Ruskin deified unspoiled nature, the teleology of a beneficent God. But even in this optimistic atmosphere some devout souls were perplexed by the spectacle of the reckless mutability of inanimate matter, and the hideous struggle for existence in the animal and vegetable kingdoms which was being presented by geology and biology. Tennyson, aghast at

> . . . Nature, red in tooth and claw
> With ravin,

was forced to ask

> Are God and Nature then at strife,
> That Nature lends such evil dreams?

And just as these lines were appearing in *In Memoriam*, F. W. Robertson could not restrain a cry of terror on chancing upon an innocent victim of a sort of adaptation not mentioned by Paley. " The evidence of goodness and wisdom in the external world is very question-able," he wrote in September, 1850, " in some moods, at least. I found a caterpillar the other day writhing in anguish, and perforated with maggots, which had come from the eggs of an ichneumon fly. It perfo-rates the skin of the living animal, leaves its eggs, and the grubs eat the creature alive by degrees. Is that goodness? Wonderful contrivance, certainly; but I should not accuse the understanding of any one who preferred to believe in the Fate of the Stoics necessitat-ing this rather than Omnipotent Will. I know that with the doctrine of the Cross, and the glimpse which it gives us into the grand law of the universe — Sacrifice, conscious and unconscious, for the life of others — this does not startle me; but I profess that I have never yet found an argument from the understanding, or a hint of it, which can make it pleasant to believe in a God who has made such a provision as this." [58] John Stuart Mill had never received that original bias in fa-vor of the beneficence of creation which thus divided the minds of Tennyson and Robertson, for before his birth Bishop Butler's *Analogy* had set his father on the way to the conclusion that it was " impossible to believe that a world so full of evil was the work of an Author com-bining infinite power with perfect goodness and righteousness." [59] Therefore he had no hesitation in pronouncing much of the non-human world unfit for human imitation: " In sober truth, nearly all the things which men are hanged or imprisoned for doing to one another, are nature's every-day performances. Killing, the most criminal act recognized by human laws, Nature does once to every being that lives; and in a large proportion of cases, after protracted tortures such as only the greatest murderers whom we read of ever purposely inflicted on their living fellow-creatures. If, by an arbitrary reservation, we refuse to count anything murder but what abridges a certain term supposed to be allotted to human life, nature does this to all but a small percentage of lives, and does it in all the modes, violent or insidious, in which the worst human beings take the lives of one another. Nature impales men, breaks them as if on the wheel, casts them to be devoured by wild beasts, crushes them with stones like the first Christian martyr, starves them with hunger, freezes them with cold, poisons them by the quick or slow venom of her exhalations, and has hundreds of other hideous deaths in reserve, such as the ingenious cruelty of a Nabis or a Domitian never surpassed." That men were generally so unwilling thus to condemn the ways of the cosmos, Mill attributed not only to the influence of religion, but also to the feeling of their insignificance before the greater natural phenomena. To that feeling of awe with which the voice out of the whirlwind overwhelmed Job, he denied the character of moral, since it was much more akin to terror than to admiration of excellence. " Those in whom awe produces admiration may be æsthetically developed," he remarked acutely, " but they are morally uncultivated."

But there were those who admitted this opposition of nature to man, yet approved of it as a providential provision for the testing of his moral fiber. We have seen how Carlyle regarded it in this light, and applauded the forced renunciation of pleasure which turned men to virtue. This view permitted him to look with equanimity on the struggle for existence, assured that it would result in the survival of the morally fittest. " I will allow a thing to struggle for itself in this world," he asserted, " with any sword or tongue or implement it has, or can lay hold of. We will let it preach, and pamphleteer, and fight, and to the uttermost bestir itself, and do, beak and claws, whatsoever is in it; very sure that it will, in the long run, conquer nothing which does not deserve to be conquered. What is better than itself, it cannot put away, but only what is worse. In this great Duel, Nature herself is umpire, and can do no wrong." With like confidence, Browning exhorted:

> Then welcome each rebuff
> That turns earth's smoothness rough,
> Each sting that bids nor sit nor stand but go!
> Be our joys three parts pain!
> Strive, and hold cheap the strain;
> Learn, nor account the pang; dare, never grudge the throe!

Carlyle realized, however, that this faith in the justice of the universe, which he had reached only after prolonged wrestling with the problem of the existence of evil, was not an easy one. He rebuked Emerson's pupil, Margaret Fuller Ossoli, who exclaimed to him dramatically, " I accept the universe! " with a dry, " Gad, you'd better." Mill found it impossible to recognize a world filled with such terrible struggles as a school of virtue and justice. " If the maker of the world *can* all that he will," he reasoned, " then he wills misery, and there is no escape from the conclusion.

The more consistent of those who have deemed themselves qualified to vindicate the ways of God to man have endeavored to avoid the alternative by hardening their hearts, and denying that misery is an evil. The goodness of God, they say, does not consist in willing the happiness of his creatures, but their virtue; and the universe, if not a happy, is a just, universe. But waiving the objections to this scheme of ethics, it does not at all get rid of the difficulty. If the Creator of mankind willed that they should all be virtuous, his designs are as completely baffled as if he had willed that they should all be happy: and the order of nature is constructed with even less regard to the requirements of justice than to those of benevolence. . . . If it be said that God does not take sufficient count of pleasure and pain to make them the reward or punishment of the good or the wicked, but that virtue is itself the greatest good and vice the greatest evil, then these at least ought to be dispensed to all according to what they have done to deserve them; instead of which, every kind of moral depravity is entailed upon multitudes by the fatality of their birth; through the fault of their parents, of society, or of uncontrollable circumstances, certainly through no fault of their own."

There remained for examination another important meaning of the word nature; human nature unperverted by civilization. Many deists, in reaction to the orthodox Christian doctrine that man was tainted with original sin and by nature wicked, had declared that man had been created wholly good, and might become so again if he gave free play to his instincts and unre-

flecting impulses. Rousseau's picture of the impeccable
" natural man " had become a commonplace of the
Romantic literature and philosophy. Fichte appealed
to the " natural sense of truth in man," [60] and regretted
his initiation into the self-conscious intellectual life;
" I weep in vain for the lost innocence of soul which
can never return to me again." [61] In the same spirit,
Carlyle declared that " people did finer actions when
there was no theory of the moral sentiments among
them. Nature is the sure guide in all cases." [62] Mill,
who was temperamentally hostile to the exaltation of
instinct over reason, had little difficulty in showing that
this deification of undisciplined human nature was based
on false anthropology and false psychology. Anthro-
pological investigation had shown that " savages are always liars," as well as uncleanly and cowardly. Furthermore, " in the times when mankind were nearer to
their natural state, cultivated observers regarded the
natural man as a sort of wild animal, distinguished
chiefly by being craftier than the other beasts of the
field, and all worth of character was deemed the result
of a sort of taming; a phrase often applied by the ancient
philosophers to the appropriate discipline of human
beings. The truth is that there is hardly a single point
of excellence belonging to human character, which is
not decidedly repugnant to the untutored feelings of
human nature." Undoubtedly most instincts of the
race were " directed to things needful or useful for its
preservation," or it would have disappeared from the
earth. But destructiveness, domination, and other selfish instincts which had helped man to supremacy

among animals, were handicaps in his civilized state. They must be extirpated or controlled, if they were not to " fill the world with misery, making human life an exaggerated likeness of the odious scene of violence and tyranny which is exhibited by the rest of the animal kingdom, except in so far as tamed and disciplined by man."

Mill therefore saw neither in the world of matter, nor in the world of living organisms, including the instinctive nature which man shared with the animals, any evidence of the moral gravitation whereby Carlyle believed power came to the aid of virtue. To accept success as a criterion of morality seemed consequently a dangerous identification of the existent with the desirable. " Carlyle is abundantly contemptuous of all who make their intellects bow to their moral timidity by endeavouring to believe Christianity," Mill had written in his diary for February 22, 1854, " but his own creed — that everything is right and good which accords with the laws of the universe — is either the same or a worse perversion. If it is not the resignation of intellect into the hands of fear, it is the subornation of it by a bribe — the bribe of being on the side of Power — irresistible and eternal Power." [63] In *Nature* he explained this creed more charitably as the result of a confusion of thinking. True scientific laws of nature were only " the observed uniformities in the occurrence of phenomena "; descriptions of that which is. But there were laws of another sort, the laws which man makes for the guidance of his own conduct in society, statute laws, international laws, moral laws, which prescribe what ought to be. From a confusion of these two meanings of " law " had arisen the conception of Natural Law, which was both omnipotent and just, and the injunctions in popular literature " to obey the physical laws of the universe, as being obligatory in the same sense and manner as the moral." Fortunately, humanity was condemned neither to acceptance of the existing order of nature as good, nor to impotent moral indignation against it. Though it could do nothing except through laws of nature, it could still use one law to counteract another, and, as Bacon had advised, " obey nature in such a way as to command it." Therefore, Mill concluded hopefully, it was the rational and moral " duty of man to coöperate, not by imitating but by perpetually striving to amend the course of nature — and bringing that part of it over which we can exercise control, more nearly into conformity with a high standard of justice and goodness."

The theme and conclusion of the essay on *Nature* are identical with those of Thomas Huxley's Romanes Lecture on *Evolution and Ethics* (1893), which, attempting " to find out whether there is, or is not, a sanction for morality in the ways of the cosmos," decided that " cosmic nature is no school for virtue, but the headquarters of the enemy of ethical nature." [64] If it had been published during its author's lifetime, it would probably have contained Darwinian concepts and terminology which would have made the similarity even closer.[a] And Mill actually seems nearer to us in his

[a] This was the opinion of Mill's step-daughter, Miss Helen Taylor, expressed in her preface to the first edition of *Three Essays*

freedom from Huxley's ultimate pessimism and in the larger scope which he concedes to intelligent control, the essentially modern contribution to the solution of the eternal problem of Job.

---

on Religion, in which *Nature* finally appeared in 1874. Mill had intended to publish it with a final revision in 1873, having withheld it from publication for fifteen years because he feared that the public was not prepared for its intelligent reception.

Chapter X

OLD FOES WITH NEW FACES.

CARLYLE and Mill were "halves of one dissevered world." That they should have finally regarded one another as opposed rather than complementary was England's loss and their own. Each had more need of the other than was recognized in the days of their friendship. Mill had the ideas which were to mold the future, but endeavored to propagate them by the inefficient methods of eighteenth century rationalism. Carlyle knew the best devices of present-day propaganda, but his ideas lagged in the feudal epoch. He prophesied from the past, and discounted the unprecedented. His ethics were an amalgam of the chivalric and the Protestant. He tried to put democracy and machine industry in a feudal strait-jacket. Mill's championship of industrial democracy, free speech, proportional representation, easy divorce, birth control, and "experiments of living" would range him among the advanced thinkers of to-day. But few thinkers would now be so convinced of the importance of logical proof, or so inclined to leave ideas whose truth they have demonstrated to win their own way in the world. From this point of view Professor Graham Wallas, who has clearly shown the important rôle of suggestion and graphic advertisement in practical politics, is right in saying that Mill invented nothing in the political field.

But Carlyle's essay on *Characteristics,* though written in 1831, is practically contemporary in its emphasis upon the unconscious or subconscious mind.

So sure was Carlyle's understanding of the springs of human action, that Professor Cazamian has justly called him the greatest of Utilitarians. Those who arrogated to themselves the name were utopian idealists who dreamed that men were ready to follow intellectual truth at all costs, and that the railroads, steamships, and trade which were bringing nations into ever closer contact would soon bind them in a league of perpetual peace. They expected the world to resign itself to the iron laws of Ricardian economics, to cast off without a murmur customs and beliefs shown to be irrational, and to accept the findings of a science which proclaimed the universe a soulless and relentless mechanism and man an animal. Carlyle knew that most men would call the truth an enemy when it threatened to belie their most cherished beliefs and check their habitual actions, and would discover in faith and intuition the comforting self-justification which the intellect denied them. Despite his expressed scorn of pleasure, he shrank from saying with Clough,

> It fortifies my soul to know
> That, though I perish, Truth is so.

While the partisans of the greatest happiness principle were offering cold comfort, he strove continually to augment the sources of happiness; faith, hope, admiration, reverence, vigorous activity, colorful imagination, and exuberant health. His writings appealed to what was deepest seated in the British character: moral conservatism, preference of action to thought, practical sagacity, and pride of race. He saw with remarkable clearness the needs of the moment, and advocated the most direct means to satisfy them. He demanded statistics while the economists manipulated *a priori* principles. He disdained tinkering with political machinery, and sought to control political forces.

If Carlyle's firm grasp of actuality could have allied itself with Mill's vision of potentiality, if Mill's liberating ideas could have been clothed in the glamour and vitality of Carlyle's art, which, as Mill said, could make truth " impressive and a living principle of action," England might have answered many of the questions which divide her to-day. Such a union at first seemed possible, for they had good bases of agreement. Both saw that the economic problem underlay the political. They knew that the system of irresponsible private property and free competition, which enslaved the many and materialized the few, was impoverishing the nation physically, morally, and intellectually, and sowing the seeds of class war. Although they therefore sympathized with the demand by the exploited masses for the suffrage as a means of self-protection, they feared its misuse by men so ignorant and debased. They hoped to persuade them to rely upon the judgment of men of conspicuous talent until national education, juster laws and a humaner economic order would give them sufficient leisure and knowledge to participate wisely in the nation's councils. Of this humaner economic order they had much the same vision. They wished to influence industrial and commercial practice by ethical and aesthetic considerations, to unite men by a closer tie than cash payment, and to substitute for the exploitation of man by man the exploitation of the forces of nature by a united humanity. This devotion to the welfare of humanity gave a decidedly practical turn to their thinking. Carlyle's transcendentalism was not a Hegelian " bloodless ballet of categories." It ramified into no elaborate system. It was stripped for action. Mill's *System of Logic* was no exercise of the mind for its own sake, but it was written to supply a foundation for a sound social science. If they sought zealously for knowledge, it was that they might use it for the enhancement and liberation of human life. They never retired to contemplation and let " burly sinners run the world."

In this practical activity they were sustained by a moral passion. The words Duty, Justice, Goodness, and Truth wore for them an awing glory, like the up- lifted Host. Inspired by this vision, they set them- selves to incessant and almost superhuman labors; the favorite maxim of both was, " Work while it is day; the night cometh in which no man can work." They bore the responsibility for the world on their shoulders, and took sides in what they considered moral issues as if in immediate conflict with the Devil. To our self- conscious generation, which permits itself moral vaca- tions, they loom up as perhaps the last men of high seriousness and the grand style. This inflexible earnest- ness made them detest the hypocrisy with which the upper classes concealed the decay of religious ortho-

doxy, and the moral compromises which were so nearly
general among their contemporaries. They wished to
strip away " Hebrew old clothes," and the sophistica-
tions of Pauline theology, and reveal the simple gospel
of Jesus. They saw the astounding incompatibility of
that gospel with the practice of the factory and the
stock exchange. They preferred sincerity in a bad
course to insincere following of a good, and were eager
to clarify issues, and force battle into the open.

These points of agreement form the broad outlines
of an impressive program, much of which has by one
means or another been fulfilled to-day. The advent of
democracy has not left the gentleman and the scientific
expert without honor or political influence. A national
system of elementary education has broadened the outlook of the average voter. The iron laws of the classical political economy have been largely discredited,
and the younger economists, guided by ethical and
aesthetic ideals, are cautiously rebuilding the science on
a firmer foundation of statistics. The condition of the
working classes has been improved by innumerable acts
of protective legislation, and by compulsory industrial
insurance which forms a permanent tie between employer and employee. The inequalities of wealth have
been reduced by taxation of the land of the aristocracy,
death dues, a graduated income tax, and frequent municipal ownership of public utilities. The Englishman
has ceased to worship so devotedly the idol of production, and is prone to smile at the continued devotion of
his American cousin. In the hands of men like Karl
Pearson in England and John Dewey in the United

States, science and philosophy have assumed an increasingly humanistic and pragmatic character. Churches emphasize the social gospel more often than dogma, and professed agnosticism is no longer considered a sign of moral depravity. But achievement of these advances make only the more conspicuous the progress yet to be made toward political wisdom, economic liberty, and moral integrity. A journey from West to East London still reveals an appalling gulf between the rich and the poor. Elementary education suffers from the bickering of religious sects, and higher education from snobbery and traditionalism. Sensational journals and unscrupulous demagogues exercise a dangerous influence upon multitudes of the least intelligent voters. Writers like Galsworthy reveal new aspects of class antagonism, and show the necessity of a more sensitive social compunction. Who knows how much more the coöperation of Carlyle and Mill, the intellectual leaders of the mid-century, might have accomplished?

But the incompatibility of their temperaments was fatal to their design of coöperation. Impatient of Mill's painstaking unraveling, Carlyle tried to cut the knots of their problems with a sword. Fearful of the tyranny of Carlyle's Hero, Mill failed to see that in most men the impulse to obey is stronger than the impulse to assume self-direction. And persistence in these attitudes led to increasing disagreement concerning particular measures.

The lines of their cleavage may be traced in England to-day, for contrasting types like Mill and Carlyle, scientists and artists, positivists and transcendentalists, individualists and authoritarians, constantly recur in the world. Although since the recent death of the veteran Lord Morley, the friend and disciple of Mill, there remains probably no thinker of note who has felt the direct influence of their conflict, the spirit of Carlyle and the spirit of Mill thus continue their strife. Kipling's advocacy of the Carlylian discipline and imperialism provokes attacks from H. G. Wells, who carries on Mill's battle for individual liberty and internationalism. Shaw's searching analysis encounters Chesterton's bland synthesis. The Tory socialism of the Primrose Leagues reflects Carlyle's economic paternalism; the Fabian Socialists, who advocate the confiscation of the unearned increment of land, the abolition of all unearned incomes, and the widest democracy tempered by respect for the expert, owe something to Mill. Modern biology and psychology, in abolishing the abstraction of intellect, will, and emotion as distinct faculties, and in exhibiting the intellect as only one of the organism's instruments of adaptation to environment, has given positivistic justification to Carlyle's exaltation of the " reason " over the " understanding," and to his suspicions of the subjectivity and anthropomorphism of science. Bergson's insistence on the incapacity of the intellect, which cuts up the objects of its knowledge into discrete and lifeless blocks, to know the living and fluid concrete world, William James' defense of the will to believe, and Nietzsche's advocacy of the cultivation of useful illusions, have thus an anticipation in Carlyle. So austere a thinker as Bertrand Russell, in adjudicating

the rival claims of mysticism and logic, admits that
" reason is a harmonizing and controlling force rather
than a creative one. Even in the purely logical realm,
it is insight that first arrives at what is new." But the
intellect has not been bereft of its champions. George
Santayana accuses the Transcendental philosophy from
which Carlyle drank of being " in love with life rather
than with wisdom," and Bertrand Russell commends
the refusal of a truly scientific philosophy " to regard
our own desires, tastes, and interests as affording a key
to the understanding of the world." In politics the
same division is evident. The Labor Party, whose
recent advent to power Mill would have hailed with
delight, contends for control of the nation's policy with
the Unionists whom Carlyle helped to rejuvenate.
Under the stress of the World War, England temporarily put in practice most of the doctrines of the
Latter Day Pamphlets, including a denial of suffrage
and government by all talents, irrespective of their
ability to win seats in Parliament. But during the same
crisis she enacted a fourth Reform Bill which gave
women the suffrage. Carlyle's prophecy of an organized policy of British imperialism has been fulfilled,
and so has been Mill's prophecy that " the vital question
of the future " would be " the nature and limits of the
power which can be legitimately exercised by society
over the individual." Abroad, Mill's influence can be
traced in the Civil Liberties Union in the United
States, and among the Russians who prepared the revolution of 1917; and Carlyle's justification of the seizure
of power by a determined and right-thinking minority

might be invoked to support the present Fascisist government in Italy, although he would undoubtedly reprobate its citation by the present Bolshevist government of Russia.

It seems significant that Carlyle's chief foreign influence has been in Germany, and Mill's in France. If nations, like individuals, have their temperaments, the irreconcilability of France and Germany would seem a bad augury concerning the feasibility of a coöperation of the Carlyles and the Mills of the future. It is probable that their division will be eternal, or at least until the success of Carlyle's jestingly imagined "Heaven and Hell Amalgamation Society." For perhaps the only impassable gulf in the world is that which lies between two temperaments.

APPENDIX A

Notes

Chapter I

1. *Reminiscences*, Thomas Carlyle, ed. J. A. Froude, London, 1881, p. 71.

2. *Carlyle, First Forty Years*, James Anthony Froude, New York, 1910. Vol. II, p. 135.

3. *Letters of Thomas Carlyle* (1826–1836), ed. Charles Eliot Norton, London, 1889. Vol. I, p. 322.

4. *Ibid.*, I, 322.

5. *Carlyle, First Forty Years*, Froude, II, 152.

6. *Charles Kingsley, His Letters and Memories of his Life*, ed. by his wife (Mrs. Fanny C. Kingsley), London, 1878. Vol. II, p. 295.

7. *Conversations with Carlyle*, Sir Charles Gavan Duffy, New York, 1892, p. 167.

8. *Ibid.*, 167.

9. *Carlyle, Life in London*, Froude, New York, 1910. Vol. I, p. 153.

10. *Autobiography*, John Stuart Mill, New York, 1924, p. 172.

11. *Ibid.*, 113, 115.

12. *The Letters of John Stuart Mill*, ed. by Hugh S. R. Elliot, London, 1910. Vol. I, p. 16.

13. *Autobiography*, Mill, 123.

14. *Ibid.*, 76.

15. *Carlyle, First Forty Years*, Froude, II, 179.

16. *Sartor Resartus*, Carlyle, Bk. I, Ch. X.

17. *Ibid.*, Bk. II, Ch. VII.

18. *Carlyle, First Forty Years*, Froude, II, 179.

19. *Letters of J. S. Mill*, I, 15.

20. *Carlyle, First Forty Years*, II, 168.

21. *Ibid.*, II, 213.

22. *Letters of J. S. Mill*, I, 25.

23. *The Letters of Thomas Carlyle to John Stuart Mill, John Sterling, and Robert Browning*, ed. by Alexander Carlyle, New York, 1923, p. 17.

24. *Letters of J. S. Mill*, I, 35, 55.

25. Review of *Remarks on the Use and Abuse of Political Terms* (George Cornewall Lewis), *Tait's Edinburgh Magazine*, Vol. I, 1832.

26. *Carlyle, First Forty Years*, II, 270.

27. Carlyle, *Works*, New York, 1897. Vol. XV, p. 468.

28. J. S. Mill, *Letters*, I, 89.

29. *Ibid.*, I, 47.

30. *Carlyle's Letters to J. S. Mill, Sterling, and Browning*, 55.

31. *Ibid.*, 55.

32. *Ibid.*, 85, 86.

33. *Ibid.*, 85.

34. J. S. Mill, *Letters*, I, 88.

35. *Ibid.*, I, 89.

36. *Ibid.*, 89.

37. *Ibid.*, 92.

38. *Ibid.*, 92.

39. Carlyle's *Letters to J. S. Mill, Sterling, and Browning*, 95.

40. *Ibid.*, 94.

41. J. S. Mill, *Letters*, I, 96.

42. *Carlyle's Letters (1826–1836)*, ed. Norton, London, 1889, I, 205, and *Carlyle, First Forty Years*, II, 35.

43. *Carlyle, First Forty Years*, II, 290.

44. J. S. Mill, *Letters*, I, 84.

45. *Ibid.*, 84–85.

46. *Ibid.*, 85.

47. *Carlyle, First Forty Years*, II, 359 and 360.

48. *Ibid.*, II, 349.

49. Carlyle, *Letters* (1826–1836), II, 200.

50. J. S. Mill, *Letters*, I, 84.

51. *Carlyle, Letters (1826–1836)*, II, 208, and *First Forty Years*, II, 360.

52. *Carlyle, Life in London*, I, 19.

53. *Conversations with Carlyle*, Duffy, 170.

54. *Carlyle, Life in London*, I, 21.

55. *Ibid.*, I, 21.

56. *Carlyle, Letters (1826–1836)*, II, 249.

57. *Ibid.*, II, 240–241.

58. *Carlyle, First Forty Years*, II, 360.

59. Carlyle, *Letters (1826–1836)*, II, 287–288.

60. Carlyle, *Life in London*, I, 64.

61. *Ibid.*, 65.

62. *Carlyle's Letters to Mill, Sterling, and Browning*, 197–198.

63. Carlyle, *Life in London*, I, 72.

64. *Early Essays by John Stuart Mill*, ed. by J. W. M. Gibbs, London, 1907, p. 271.

65. *In Memoriam*, Tennyson, CXXVI.

66. *Memories of Old Friends*, Caroline Fox, Philadelphia, 1882, p. 172.

67. *Ibid.*, 177.

68. *New Letters of Thomas Carlyle*, ed. Alexander Carlyle, New York and London, 1904, p. 133.

69. *Letters of Carlyle to Mill, Sterling, and Browning*, 107.

70. *Carlyle, Life in London*, I, 93.

71. *Ibid.*, I, 148.

72. *Oliver Cromwell's Letters and Speeches*, ed. Thomas Carlyle, London, 1885. Vol. I, p. 406.

73. *The Letters of Charles Eliot Norton*, ed. Sara Norton and M. A. Howe, Boston and New York, 1913. Vol. I, p. 499.

74. *Letters of Carlyle to Mill, Sterling, Browning*, Preface, vii.

75. *Carlyle, Life in London*, I, 366–68.

76. Mill's *Letters*, II, 68.

77. *Carlyle, Life in London*, II, 263.

78. *Ibid.*, II, 280.

79. *Ibid.*, II, 310. Important documents relative to the Eyre case have been collected in *Jamaica Papers*, London, 1866; but these are selected by the committee hostile to Eyre.

80. Mill's *Autobiography*, 209.

81. *Carlyle, Life in London*, II, 263.

82. *Letters of Charles Eliot Norton*, I, 495–500.

83. *Carlyle, Life in London*, II, 358–359.

CHAPTER II

1. *Landmarks in English Industrial History*, George Townsend Warner, 7th ed., London, 1908, pp. 293–4. See also *Industrial Society in England Towards the End of the Eighteenth Century*, Witt Bowden, New York, 1925, pp. 111–113.

2. *Artisans and Machinery*, P. Gaskell, London, 1836, pp. 13 and 18–19.

3. *Ibid.*, 335.

4. *History of the Cotton Manufacture in Great Britain*, Edward Baines, London, 1835, p. 361.

5. *Ibid.*, 361.

6. *The Progress of the Nation*, G. R. Porter, London, 1838, I, 216, 218, and 240.

7. *Ibid.*, I, 254. From 1,475,387 pounds in 1815 to 5,778,457 in 1835.

8. *Ibid.*, I, 198. In 1801, 7,371,774 pounds; in 1834, 46,445,232 pounds.

9. *Ibid.*, revised by F. W. Hirst, London, 1912, p. 295.

10. *Ibid.*, Hirst edition, 295.

11. *History of Cotton Manufacture*, Baines, 489.

12. *The Making of Modern England*, Gilbert Slater, Boston, 1915. Introduction, xxvii.

13. *The Progress of the Nation*, Porter, II, 551.

14. *Ibid.*, II, 553.

15. *Landmarks in English Industrial History*, Warner, 263.

16. *The Making of Modern England*, Slater, Introduction, American edition, xiv–xv.

17. *Ibid.*, Introduction, xxvii.

18. *The Village Laborer*, J. L. Hammond and Barbara Hammond, London and New York, 1913, p. 32.

19. *The English Peasantry and the Enclosure of the Common Fields,* Gilbert Slater, London, 1907, p. 7.

20. *Landmarks in English Industrial History,* Warner, 287.

21. *Ibid.,* 287.

22. *The Village Laborer,* J. L. and Barbara Hammond, 58 *seq.*

23. *Ibid.,* 41.

24. *Progress of the Nation,* Porter (Hirst ed.), 3.

25. *Progress of the Nation,* Porter (Hirst ed.), 35, 38.

26. *Progress of the Nation* (Hirst ed.), 18.

27. *History of Cotton Manufacture,* Baines, 360.

28. *Progress of the Nation,* Porter (1838 ed.), I, 201.

29. *A Tour Thro' Great Britain,* Daniel Defoe, London, 1848, I, 367.

30. *History of Cotton Manufacture,* Baines, 360.

31. *A History of the English People in 1815,* Élie Halévy, tr. by E. I. Watkin and D. A. Barker, New York, 1924, p. 242. Citing Cooke-Taylor, *Handbook . . . of Silk, Cotton and Woolen Manufactures,* London, 1843, p. 156.

32. *A History of England from the Conclusion of the Great War in 1815,* Spencer Walpole, London, 1879, I, 134.

33. *England in 1815,* Halévy, 127.

34. *Ibid.,* 114.

35. *Histoire de L'Angleterre au XIXᵉ Siècle,* Élie Halévy, Paris, 1912–1923, II, 59.

36. *Speeches and Poems,* Lord Macaulay, New York, 1867, I, 48–49.

37. *The Progress of the Nation,* Porter, I, Introduction, p. i.

38. *The Philosophy of Manufactures,* Andrew Ure, London, 1835, p. 18.

39. *History of Cotton Manufacture,* Baines, 531.

CHAPTER III

1. *Discourse on Method,* Réné Descartes. Tr. by John Veitch, Chicago, 1920, pp. 7–8.

2. *The English Utilitarians,* Leslie Stephen, London and New

York, 1900, I, 104. See also *Jeremy Bentham*, Charles Milner Atkinson, London, 1905, pp. 139 ff.

3. *English Utilitarians*, I, 278.

4. Bentham's *Works*, ed. Bowring, Edinburgh, 1843, X, 78; and article " Bentham," *Dictionary of National Biography*, IV, 269.

5. *A Fragment on Government*, Preface. See Bentham's *Works*, ed. Bowring, I, 229.

6. *Early Essays of John Stuart Mill*, ed. Gibbs, 390.

7. *The Life of William Wilberforce*, by his sons, Robert Isaac and Samuel Wilberforce, London, 1888, II, 171–2.

8. Bentham's *Works*, I, 5.

9. *James Mill, a Biography*, Alexander Bain, New York, 1882, p. 96.

10. For an account of the beginnings of the agitation for Parliamentary reform see *The French Revolution in English History*, by Philip Anthony Brown, New York, 1924, chapters III, V–VIII.

11. *Three Tracts Relative to Spanish and Portuguese Affairs*, Bentham's *Works*, VIII, 470.

12. Bentham's *Works*, X, 542. Letter of Bentham to Admiral Mordvinoff.

13. *An Introduction to the Principles of Morals and Legislation*, London, 1907, p. 3.

14. *Ibid.*, 1.

15. *Ibid.*, Preface, xi.

16. *Déontologie, ou Science de la Morale*, Jeremy Bentham, Bruxelles, 1834. Pt. II, Ch. V, Vol. II, p. 272. (The writer's translation.)

17. *Ibid.*, Pt. I, Ch. XI, Vol. I, p. 188.

18. Halévy, *La Formation du Radicalisme Philosophique*, III, 316. " La morale des utilitaires, c'est leur psychologie économique mise à l'imperatif."

19. *An Essay on the Principle of Population*, first edition, London, 1798, Bk. 9, p. 42.

20. Ricardo's *Works*, 2nd ed., London, 1852, p. 378.

21. *The Wealth of Nations*, Adam Smith, Edinburgh, 1806, Bk. IV, Ch. IX, Vol. III, pp. 66–67.

22. *A Modern Symposium*, G. Lowes Dickinson, New York, 1917, p. 67.

23. *La Formation du Radicalisme Philosophique*, Halévy, II, 376 (note 89 to p. 299).

24. Bentham's *Works*, X, 142.

25. *Autobiography*, J. S. Mill, 34.

26. *Ibid.*, 34.

27. *Ibid.*, 34.

28. *La Formation du Radicalisme Philosophique*, Halévy, I, 271, and *note*, p. 48.

29. *Jeremy Bentham*, Atkinson, 209. *English Utilitarians*, Stephen, I, 232. Bentham, on sending his autograph to Lady Ellice, October, 1831.

30. *Autobiography*, J. S. Mill, 34.

31. *The Liberty of the Press*, James Mill, London, no date, p. 22. Published also in the supplement to the fifth edition of the *Encyclopaedia Britannica.*

32. *Westminster Review*, October, 1824. Vol. II, p. 414.

33. *Ibid.*, III, 89, April, 1825.

34. *Ibid.*, XIII, 226, July, 1830.

35. *Ibid.*, XVI, 14, April, 1832.

36. *Ibid.*, II, 410, October, 1824.

37. *Ibid.*, I, 31, January, 1824.

38. *Ibid.*, XIII, 226, July, 1830.

39. *Ibid.*, XIV, 3, January, 1831.

40. *English Utilitarians*, Stephen, II, 34.

41. *Autobiography*, J. S. Mill, 68–69.

42. *Sartor Resartus*, Carlyle, Bk. III, Ch. 5.

Chapter IV

1. *Correspondence avec Gustave d'Eichthal*, Paris, 1898, p. 10.

2. *England in 1815*, Halévy, 333.

3. *The Village Laborer*, J. L. and Barbara Hammond, 185.

4. *The Condition of the Working-Class in England in 1844*,

Frederick Engels, tr. from the German by Florence K. Wischnewetzky, London, 1892.

5. *The Village Laborer*, J. L. and Barbara Hammond, 259.

6. *Ibid.*, 186.

7. For a full account of the agricultural laborers' revolt in 1830–31, see *The Village Laborer*, Ch. XI.

8. *Village Laborer*, 324.

9. Practically, the prohibition of outdoor relief was found unenforceable in periods of great distress, like that of 1841–1842.

10. *Making of Modern England* (1913 edition, London), Gilbert Slater, p. 105.

11. *Histoire de l'Angleterre au XIXe Siècle*, Halévy, III, 271.

12. *Making of Modern England* (1913 ed.), 103.

13. *Village Laborer*, 40.

14. *History of the Factory Movement*, Alfred (Samuel Kydd), London, 1857.   Vol. I, pp. 153–54.

15. *Ibid.*, I, 285–87.

16. *Ibid.*, I, 297–302.

17. *Ibid.*, I, 303.

18. *Ibid.*, I, 284.

19. *Ibid.*, I, 297.

20. *Ibid.*, I, 313–314.

21. For a full account of the movement for factory regulation, see *A History of Factory Legislation*, B. L. Hutchins and A. Harrison, Westminster, 1903.

22. *Letters on the Factory Act*, Nassau W. Senior, London, 1837, p. 27.

23. *History of the Factory Movement*, Alfred (Kydd), II, 254.

24. *Lord Shaftesbury*, J. L. and Barbara Hammond, London, 1923, p. 39.

25. *England in 1815*, Halévy, 399, 397, 382–383.

26. *The Life of William Cobbett*, G. D. H. Cole, New York, 1924, p. 275.

27. *Ibid.*, 203.

28. For an account of the efforts of philanthropy to improve

working conditions in many fields of employment, see *Lord Shaftesbury*, by J. L. and Barbara Hammond.

29. *Industrial Society in England Towards the End of the Eighteenth Century*, Bowden, 261.

30. For evidence as to the character of the early manufacturers, see *England in 1815*, Halévy, p. 243, *The Life of Francis Place*, Wallas, p. 141, *The Town Laborer*, J. L. and Barbara Hammond, p. 8.

31. *The Philosophy of Manufactures*, Ure, 20, 21, and 23.

32. *Ibid*. 489. In 1847, the year of the Ten Hours Act, there were employed in the cotton industry in England, Scotland, and Ireland 85,533 adult males, and 230,794 women, young persons, and children (see *Lord Shaftesbury*, Hammond, note to page 122).

33. *Industrial Society*, Bowden, 282.

34. *A History of Factory Legislation*, Hutchins and Harrison, 28.

35. *The Town Laborer*, J. L. and Barbara Hammond, London and New York, 1917, p. 85.

36. *The Philosophy of Manufactures*, Ure, 423.

37. *Ibid*., 423–24.

38. *Artisans and Machinery*, Gaskell, 294.

39. *The Progress of the Nation*, Porter, 1838 ed., I, 252 and 218.

40. *The Philosophy of Manufactures*, Ure, 336.

41. *Progress of the Nation*, Porter, II, 4, 5.

42. *Letters on the Factory Act*, Senior, 24–25.

43. *England in 1815*, Halévy, 257.

44. *Artisans and Machinery*, Gaskell, 85.

45. *Charles Kingsley, His Letters and Memories of his Life*, I, 216.

46. *Progress of the Nation*, Porter, II, 257.

47. *Ibid*., II, 281.

48. *Education and Social Movements (1700–1850)*, A. E. Dobbs, London, 1919, pp. 157–158.

49. *England and the English*, Lord Lytton (Bulwer), London, 1874, p. 35.

50. *Condition of Working-Class*, Engels, 126–27.

51. *Artisans and Machinery*, Gaskell, 131.

52. *Condition of Working-Class*, Engels, 130–131.

53. *Ibid.*, 131, and *Artisans and Machinery*, 256.

54. *England in 1815*, Halévy, 246.

55. *Condition of Working-Class*, Engels, 107.

56. *Ibid.*, 160.

57. *Industrial Society in England*, Bowden, 288.

58. *Ibid.*, Ch. IV, Sect. 5, pp. 284 ff.

59. *Artisans and Machinery*, Gaskell, 268.

60. *The Skilled Laborer*, J. L. and Barbara Hammond, 128 *seq.*

61. *The History of Trades Unionism*, by Sidney and Beatrice Webb, gives a full account of labor organization in England during the nineteenth century.

62. An excellent *Biography* of Robert Owen has been written by Frank Podmore, London, 1906.

63. See *The Life of Francis Place*, Wallas, New York, 1919, Ch. IX.

64. Cited by William Haller, in his study of *Southey's Later Radicalism* (*Publications of the Modern Language Association*, June, 1922), p. 286.

65. *William Wordsworth, his Life, Works, and Influence*, George MacLean Harper, New York, 1923, I, 417–18.

66. *The Excursion*, William Wordsworth, Book VIII.

67. *A Lay Sermon* (1817), Samuel Taylor Coleridge, The *Complete Works*, ed. W. G. T. Shedd, New York, 1884. Vol. VI, pp. 212–216.

68. *Ibid.*, 224.

69. Coleridge's *Works*, VI, 50.

70. *Ibid.*, VI, 64–65.

71. *Ibid.*, VI, 64.

72. *Ibid.*, VI, 66.

73. *Histoire de l'Angleterre au XIXe Siècle*, Halévy, III, 178, citing *Sir Robert Peel*, by C. S. Parker, I, 371.

74. See *Lord Shaftesbury*, J. L. and Barbara Hammond, Ch. IV, *The Passing of the Ten Hours Bill*.

75. *Principles of Political Economy*, T. R. Malthus, London, 1820, ch. 5, sec. 2, p. 306.

76. *Lord Shaftesbury*, Hammond, 101.

77. *Histoire de l'Angleterre au XIXe Siècle*, Halévy, III, 315–16.

78. *Charles Kingsley, Letters and Life*, II, 295.

79. *Reflections of the Revolution in France, The Works of Edmund Burke*, London, 1792, III, p. 111.

80. *Ibid.*, III, 93.

81. *An Appeal from the New to the Old Whigs, The Works of Edmund Burke*, Boston, 1826. Vol. III, 334.

82. *The Cambridge History of English Literature*, Vol. XI, p. 11.

83. Cit. by John MacCunn, *The Political Philosophy of Burke*, London, 1913, p. 112.

84. *Ibid.*, p. 93, citing Burke's *Speech* of May 7, 1782.

85. *Appeal from the New to the Old Whigs, Works*, III, 432.

86. *Reflections on the Revolution in France, Works* (1792), III, 122–23.

87. Cit. MacCunn, *Political Philosophy of Burke*, 47.

88. *Appeal from New to Old Whigs, Works*, III, 404.

89. Cit. MacCunn, 47.

90. *Appeal from New to Old Whigs, Works*, III, 407.

91. *Ibid.*, III, 334.

92. *Diary and Letters of Frances Burney (Madame d'Arblay)*, Boston, 1911. Entry for June 18, 1792.

93. Coleridge's *Works*, II, 175; *The Friend*.

94. *Ibid.*, II, 302.

95. *Ibid.*, II, 296.

96. *Ibid.*, II, 305.

97. *Ibid.*, II, 208.

98. *Ibid.*, VI, 44.

99. *Ibid.*, VI, 50.

Chapter V

1. *Carlyle Till Marriage*, David Alec Wilson, London and New York, 1923, p. 111.
2. *Reminiscences*, 53, and *Carlyle Till Marriage*, 147–48.
3. *Reminiscences*, 50.
4. *Ibid.*, 78.
5. *Ibid.*, 78.
6. *Sartor Resartus*, Bk. II, Ch. III.
7. *Ibid.*, Bk. II, Ch. VII.
8. *Ibid.*, Bk. II, Ch. VII.
9. *Ibid.*, Bk. II, Ch. VII.
10. *Carlyle, First Forty Years*, Froude, I, 159.
11. *Ibid.*, I, 171.
12. *Ibid.*, I, 181.
13. *Ibid.*, I, 214.
14. *Ibid.*, I, 239.
15. *Ibid.*, I, 200.
16. *Ibid.*, I, 187.
17. *Le nouveau Christianisme, Oeuvres de Saint-Simon*, Paris, 1841, p. 89.
18. The correspondence of Carlyle with the Saint-Simonians has been published in *Carlyle et le Saint-Simonisme*, by Eugene d'Eichthal (*La Revue historique*, t. 82–83, Paris, 1903). An English translation appeared in the *New Quarterly*, London, Vol. II, pp. 277–288, April, 1909. D. A. Wilson has printed excerpts in *Carlyle to " The French Revolution*," 162–64.
19. *Carlyle, First Forty Years*, II, 67.
20. *La Doctrine de Saint-Simon*, Paris, 1830, p. 121.
21. *New Quarterly*, Vol. II, p. 283
22. Ibid., Vol. II, pp. 287, 286.
23. *La Doctrine de Saint-Simon*, 11.
24. *The Characteristics of the Present Age, Fichte's Popular Works*, tr. by William Smith, London, 1847, II, 11.
25. *Carlyle, First Forty Years*, II, 133.
26. *Autobiography*, J. S. Mill, 122.

Chapter VI

1. *James Mill, a Biography*, Alexander Bain, New York, 1882, pp. 119–120.
2. *Autobiography*, J. S. Mill, 25.
3. *Ibid.*, 25.
4. *Ibid.*, 14.
5. *Ibid.*, 16.
6. *Ibid.*, 21.
7. *Ibid.*, 172.
8. *James Mill*, Bain, 100.
9. *Autobiography*, J. S. Mill, 5.
10. *Ibid.*, 39.
11. *Ibid.*, 12.
12. *Ibid.*, 42.
13. *Ibid.*, 40–41.
14. *Ibid.*, 39.
15. *Ibid.*, 47.
16. *Ibid.*, 46–47.
17. *Ibid.*, 93.
18. *Ibid.*, 76.
19. *The Letters of J. S. Mill*, Elliot, I, 88.
20. *Autobiography*, 47.
21. *Ibid.*, 78.
22. Bentham's *Works*, I, 194.
23. *Ibid.*, I, 194.
24. *Ibid.*, I, 194.
25. *Autobiography*, 45.
26. *Ibid.*, 77.
27. *Ibid.*, 76. Some of Mill's early speeches (1823–1829) have been published in the Oxford University Press edition (World's Classics Series) of the *Autobiography*, Appendix, pp. 267 ff.
28. *Autobiography*, 94.
29. *Ibid.*, 94.
30. *Ibid.*, 34.

31. *Ibid.*, 34.

32. *Ibid.*, 99.

33. *Ibid.*, 100.

34. *Ibid.*, 102.

35. *Ibid.*, 103.

36. *Ibid.*, 103.

37. *Ibid.*, 103.

38. *Ibid.*, 104.

39. *Ibid.*, 105.

40. *Ibid.*, 104.

41. *Ibid.*, 107.

42. *Ibid.*, 109.

43. Coleridge's *Works*, II, 197.

44. *Autobiography*, 111.

45. Here, and often elsewhere, Mill interestingly anticipates Matthew Arnold.

46. *Autobiography*, 114.

47. J. S. Mill: *Correspondence avec Gustave d'Eichthal*, Avant-Propos, p. vi. (The writer's translation.)

48. *Two Notebooks of Thomas Carlyle*, privately printed by the Grolier Club, New York, 1898, p. 248. *Journal* for January 21, 1832.

49. *The New Quarterly*, Vol. II, p. 283.

50. *Système de Politique Positive*, Comte, Paris, 1854, IV, 95. Appendice Général, troisième partie; *Plan des travaux scientifiques nécessaires pour réorganizer la société*. (The writer's translation.)

51. *Ibid.*, IV, 97–98.

52. *Ibid.*, IV, 130.

53. *Autobiography*, 116.

54. J. S. Mill: *Correspondence avec d'Eichthal*, 15. (The writer's translation.)

55. *Ibid.*, 18–19.

56. *Ibid.*, 126.

57. *Autobiography*, 117.

58. *Ibid.*, 125.

59. *Ibid.*, 125.

60. J. S. Mill, *Letters*, I, 11.

61. *Ibid.*, 15.

62. *Ibid.*, 16.

CHAPTER VII

1. "The Rationale of Political Representation," *London Review*, July, 1835. Bound in Vol. 30 of *Westminster Review*, p. 348.

2. *Ibid.*, p. 349.

3. *Ibid.*, 348.

4. *Democracy and the Organization of Political Parties*, M. Ostrogorski. Translated from the French by Frederick Clarke. New York and London, 1902, I, 21.

5. *The English Radicals*, Roylance Kent, London, 1899, p. 347. This work contains interesting portraits of Mill's Radical associates.

6. *Life of Place*, Wallas, 352, citing John Stuart Mill, *Notices of his Life and Works*, London, 1875, p. 8 (letter of Mill to Fonblanque).

7. "The Reorganization of the Reform Party," *London and Westminster Review*, April, 1839, Vol. 32, p. 478.

8. "De Tocqueville on Democracy in America," *London Review*, January, 1836. Bound with *London and Westminster Review*, Vol. 31, pp. 85 ff.

9. *London and Westminster Review*, Vol. 31, p. 110.

10. *Sartor Resartus*, Bk. III, Ch. 3.

11. *Correspondence of Thomas Carlyle with Ralph Waldo Emerson*, Boston, 1886, II, 179.

12. Carlyle, *Life in London*, I, 370.

13. Cited by Mill in *On Liberty* (New York, 1874), p. 103, from *The Sphere and Duties of Government*, Wilhelm von Humboldt, 11–13.

14. *Democracy and the Organization of Political Parties*, Ostrogorski, 105.

Chapter VIII

1. *Principles of Political Economy*, Malthus, Introduction, 2, 6, 12.

2. *Political Economy*, Senior, London, 1850 (in *Encyclopaedia Metropolitana series*), 4, 26.

3. *Westminster Review*, October, 1824. Vol. 2, p. 289.

4. *A History of Economic Doctrines*, Charles Gide and Charles Rist. Translated by R. Richards, Boston, 1915, p. 349.

5. *Elements of Political Economy*, James Mill, London, 1826. Preface, 1.

6. *Pelham*, Charles Bulwer, London, 1828. Bk. I, Ch. XXXVI, Vol. I, p. 336. Cited by Halévy, *England in 1815*, 502.

7. *History of Economic Doctrines*, Gide and Rist, 349.

8. Cited by Porter, *Progress of the Nation*, II, 256, from McCulloch's *Principles of Political Economy*, London, 1843.

9. *The Philosophy of Manufactures*, Ure, 279–280.

10. *The Life of William Cobbett*, Cole, 358.

11. *Sixty Years of an Agitator's Life*, John Jacob Holyoake, London, 1892.

12. *Life of Place*, Wallas, 273.

13. *Sybil, or The Two Nations*, Lord Beaconsfield (Disraeli), London, 1916, p. 76.

14. *Carlyle, First Forty Years*, Froude, II, 362.

15. *Ibid.*, I, 187.

16. *Letters of Thomas Carlyle (1826–1836)*, ed. Norton, II, 92–93.

17. *Carlyle on Cromwell and Others*, D. A. Wilson, London and New York, 1925, p. 165.

18. *History of England since 1815*, Walpole, IV, 26.

19. *Ibid.*, IV, 27.

20. *Ibid.*, IV, 22.

21. See *Lord Shaftesbury*, J. L. and Barbara Hammond, Chapter VII; *The Reform of the Mines*.

22. *Carlyle on Cromwell and Others*, Wilson, 165.

23. *Correspondence of Carlyle with Emerson*, II, 10.

24. *Carlyle on Cromwell and Others*, Wilson, 183.

25. *Ibid.*, 187.

26. *Edinburgh Review*, October, 1844, Vol. 81, p. 524.

27. *Selection from the Correspondence of MacVey Napier*, edited by his son, MacVey Napier, London, 1879, p. 480. Letter of N. W. Senior to Napier, December 18, 1844.

28. *Edinburgh Review*, April, 1845. Vol. 81, pp. 499 ff.

29. *Life of Kingsley*, I, 158.

30. *Alton Locke*, Kingsley, London, 1879, p. 336.

31. *Principles of Political Economy*, J. S. Mill. Bk. IV, ch. IV: *Of the Stationary State*.

32. *Alton Locke*, Prefatory Memoir by Thomas Hughes, p. lviii.

33. *Life and Works of Ruskin*, W. G. Collingwood, London, 1893, Vol. I, p. 205.

34. *Principles of Political Economy*, J. S. Mill. Preliminary Remarks, 1.

35. *Munera Pulveris*, Preface, p. xvi. Complete *Works* of John Ruskin, New York, 1894, Vol. XI–XII.

36. *Munera Pulveris*, *Works*, Vol. XI–XII, p. 113. Chapter I, Sec. I.

37. *Letters of John Ruskin to Charles Eliot Norton*, Boston, 1905. Vol. I, 139.

38. *Autobiography*, J. S. Mill, 163.

Chapter IX

1. *An Essay Concerning the Human Understanding*, John Locke, Bk. II, Ch. XX, Sec. 3.

2. *La Formation du Radicalisme Philosophique*, Halévy, I, 282 (note 36 to page 14). Citing letter of Bentham to Dumont, September 6, 1822.

3. Bentham's *Works*, II, 459.

4. *An Enquiry concerning the Principles of Morals*, David Hume, Boston, 1881, p. 154.

5. *Déontologie*, Pt. I, Ch. VII, Vol. I, p. 112. (The author's translation.)

6. *Ibid.*, Pt. I, Ch. VII, Vol. I, p. 116. (The author's translation.)

7. *Westminster Review*, vol. V, pp. 59 ff. (January, 1826).

8. *Introduction to Principles of Morals and Legislation*, Bentham, 313.

9. *Principles of Moral and Political Philosophy*, William Paley, Boston, 1825. Pp. 45, 55, 308. (Bk. I, Ch. VII; Bk. II, Ch. II; Bk. VI, Ch. III.)

10. *The Life of John Sterling*, Thomas Carlyle, Boston, 1852, p. 82.

11. *Carlyle, First Forty Years*, Froude, I, 158.

12. *Ibid.*, I, 282.

13. *A Discourse on the Studies of the University of Cambridge*, Adam Sedgwick, Cambridge, 1850, p. 52.

14. *Ibid.*, 106, 52.

15. *Ibid.*, 59.

16. *Ibid.*, 63.

17. *Ibid.*, 61.

18. *Ibid.*, 76.

19. *Life and Letters of Frederick W. Robertson*, London, no date, p. 195.

20. *In Memoriam*, Tennyson, CXIII.

21. *Dissertations and Discussions*, J. S. Mill, New York, 1874, I, 185.

22. *Early Essays by J. S. Mill*, 400.

23. *Ibid.*, 400.

24. *Ibid.*, 395.

25. *Ibid.*, 393.

26. *Ibid.*, 404.

27. *Ibid.*, 403.

28. *Ibid.*, 405.

29. *Dissertations and Discussions*, J. S. Mill, III, 136.

30. *Ibid.*, I, 185.

31. *Ibid.*, I, 173.

32. *Ibid.*, I, 184.

33. *Ibid.*, I, 185.

34. *Ibid.*, III, 141.

35. *The Elements of Morality, including Polity*, William Whewell, New York, 1845, Bk. I, Ch. IV.

36. *Dissertations and Discussions*, J. S. Mill, III, 190.

37. *Ibid.*, III, 190.

38. *Ibid.*, III, 166; citing Whewell's *Elements of Morality*, 223.

39. *Dissertations and Discussions*, III, 154.

40. *Ibid.*, III, 163 (note).

41. *Ibid.*, I, 371.

42. *Ibid.*, I, 157.

43. *Ibid.*, I, 378.

44. *Ibid.*, I, 376.

45. *Ibid.*, I, 379–380.

46. *Ibid.*, I, 385.

47. *Ibid.*, I, 384.

48. *Ibid.*, I, 412.

49. *Ibid.*, I, 389–390.

50. *Ibid.*, I. 391.

51. *Letters of J. S. Mill*, II, Appendix A, p. 381.

52. *The Life of Thomas Cooper; an Autobiography*, London, 1873, p. 173.

53. *Life of Kingsley*, II, 88.

54. *The Limits of Religious Thought*, Henry Longueville Mansel, London, 1858 (Bampton Lectures, Vol. 77), p. 426, note 15 to page 252.

55. *The Life and Letters of Thomas Huxley*, ed. by Leonard Huxley, London, 1900, II, 321. Letter of Huxley to Lyell, March, 1859.

56. *What is Revelation?*, F. D. Maurice, Cambridge, 1859, p. 214.

57. *An Examination of Sir William Hamilton's Philosophy*, J. S. Mill, New York, 1874, I, 131.

58. *Life and Letters of Frederick W. Robertson*, 223.

59. *Autobiography*, J. S. Mill, 28.

60. *The Characteristics of the Present Age, Fichte's Popular Works*, II, 142.

61. *The Vocation of Man*, Fichte, tr. by William Smith, Chicago, 1916, p. 26.

62. *Carlyle, First Forty Years*, Froude, I, 158.

63. *Letters of J. S. Mill*, Elliot, II, 373.

APPENDIX B

BIBLIOGRAPHY

(Mentions only those books which the writer has found especially useful, and introductory works for the general reader. Other bibliographical references will be found in the Notes (Appendix A). Acquaintance with the works of Thomas Carlyle and John Stuart Mill is assumed.)

GENERAL HISTORY

Halévy (Élie). *Histoire du Peuple Anglais au XIXe Siècle.* 3 volumes (1815–1841), Paris, 1912–1923. Volume I has been translated into English by E. I. Watkin and D. A. Barber (with an Introduction by Graham Wallas) as A History of the English People in 1815, New York, 1924. An English translation of the second volume has been announced for 1926.

A brilliant, clear, and impersonal interpretation of a complex society. Will be complete in seven volumes, covering the period 1815–1895. Invaluable for its present extent.

Walpole (Spencer). A History of England from the Conclusion of the Great War in 1815. 5 volumes (1815–1858), 2nd edition, London, 1879. The History of Twenty-five Years (1856–1880), 4 vols., London and New York, 1908.

Covers the period following 1841 with considerable minuteness.

Slater, (Gilbert). The Making of Modern England, London, 1913, Boston, 1915.

A good short history, especially from the economic standpoint. The Introduction to the American edition, which sketches the social and economic condition of England immediately before the industrial revolution, is illuminating to the general reader.

Cazamian (Louis). *L'Angleterre Moderne*, Paris, 1911. Translated into English by the author with the title, Modern England, London and New York, 1912.

A stimulating short history, especially valuable for the history of thought.

Brown (Philip Anthony). The French Revolution in English History, New York, 1924.

Recreates the atmosphere of the Tory Reaction.

Bulwer (Edward). (Lord Lytton.) England and the English, London, 1833.

An interesting contemporary account of British society immediately after the first Reform Act.

History of Thought

Sorley (William Ritchie). A History of English Philosophy, Cambridge, 1920.

Halévy (Élie). *La Formation du Radicalisme Philosophique*, 3 vols., Paris, 1901–1904.

A brilliant and exhaustive study of the Benthamite School.

Stephen (Leslie). The English Utilitarians, 3 vols., London, 1900.

The best English study of the Benthamite school.

Thorndike (Ashley H.). Literature in a Changing Age, New York, 1920.

An illuminating approach to Victorian literature through social history.

Dobbs (A. E.). Education and Social Movements (1700–1850), London, 1919.

Economics

A. Introductory Works

Tugwell (R. G.), Munro (Thomas), and Stryker (R. E.). American Economic Life, New York, 1925.

> A graphic introduction to economic theory through an inductive study of the contemporary economic order in the United States.

Clay (Henry). Economics; an Introduction for the General Reader, London, 1916. Revised for the American reader by Eugene E. Agger, New York, 1918.

Mitchell (Wesley Clair). The Prospects of Economics. (The leading article in the Trend of Economics, a symposium edited by R. G. Tugwell, New York, 1924.)

> A lucid and succinct account of the origin and development of economic science.

Gide (Charles) and Rist (Charles). A History of Economic Doctrines. Translated from the French by R. Richards, Boston, 1915.

Patten (Simon N.). The Development of English Thought: a Study in the Economic Interpretation of History, New York, 1910.

> Many brilliant insights.

B. Economic History

Hammond (J. L. and Barbara). The Rise of Modern Industry, New York, 1926.

> The story of the industrial revolution told clearly and dramatically for the general reader.

Bowden (Witt). Industrial Society in England Towards the End of the Eighteenth Century, New York, 1925.

> Organizes the results of the best recent scholarship.

George (Dorothy M.). London Life in the Eighteenth Century, London and New York, 1925.

A thorough scholarly investigation. Valuable data concerning sanitary reforms.

Mantoux (P.). *La Revolution Industrielle au XVIIIe Siècle*, Paris, 1905.

A valuable work, but in need of revision.

Hammond (J. L. and Barbara). The Village Laborer (1760–1832), London and New York, 1913. The Town Laborer, London and N. Y., 1917. The Skilled Laborer, London and N. Y., 1919.

These three companion volumes constitute a scholarly and absorbing history of the British working classes, often sharply critical of their superiors.

Porter (G. R.). The Progress of the Nation, 3 vols., London, 1838. Also revised and brought up to date by F. W. Hirst, London, 1912.

Statistical evidence of the amazing material progress of England following the industrial revolution.

Gaskell (P.). Artisans and Machinery, London, 1836.

Industrial problems of the early nineteenth century seen by a liberal-minded but uncritical physician.

Baines (Edward). A History of the Cotton Manufactures in Great Britain, London, 1835.

Hutchins (B. L.) and Harrison (A.). A History of Factory Legislation, Westminster, 1903.

A useful modern work.

Alfred (pseud. for Samuel Kydd). The History of the Factory Movement, 2 vols., London, 1857.

This almost contemporary account makes large excerpts from the Reports of Parliamentary Committees conveniently accessible to the general reader.

Webb (Sydney and Beatrice). The History of Trades Unionism, London, 1894–1920.
A thorough study.

C. The Classical Economists

Smith (Adam). The Wealth of Nations, 1776, etc.
Presents the doctrine of *laissez-faire* before the industrial revolution is well under way.

Malthus (Thomas Robert). An Essay on the Principle of Population, 1798, etc.
This famous essay gave a fundamental principle to both Ricardo and Darwin.

Malthus (Thomas Robert). Principles of Political Economy, London, 1820.
The Preface shows the scientific attitude of the founders of economics toward their subject-matter.

Ricardo (David). Principles of Political Economy, London, 1817, etc.
The orthodox economists and the Marxian socialists both claim descent from Ricardo.

McCulloch (J. R.). Principles of Political Economy, London, 1825.
An optimist, delighted at the material progress of England, and believing in the possible coexistence of high profits and high wages.

Senior (Nassau W.). Political Economy, London, 1836.
Doctrinaire and deductive.

Senior (Nassau W.). Letters on the Factory Act, London, 1837.
Uncompromisingly hostile to the Ten Hours Movement.

Ure (Andrew). The Philosophy of Manufactures, London, 1835.
The progress of the industrial revolution acclaimed by an optimistic contemporary.

D. Opponents of the Classical School

Haller (William). Southey's Later Radicalism (Publications of the Modern Language Association of America, June, 1922).

Southey as a pioneer of Tory Socialism.

Coleridge (Samuel Taylor). A Lay Sermon Addressed to the Higher Classes (1817). In Coleridge's Works, edited by W. G. T. Shedd, Volume VI, New York, 1884.

Precursor of Carlyle's social exhortations.

Owen (Robert). A New View of Society, London, 1814. The Book of the New Moral World, London, 1836.

The philosophic grounds of the Owenite coöperative movement.

Saint-Simon (Comte de). *Le nouveau Christianisme*. In *Oeuvres*, edited by Olinde Roderiguez, Paris, 1841.

The gospel of the religion of humanity.

La Doctrine de Saint-Simon, Paris, 1830.

A keen analysis of the origin and defects of the competitive system.

Engels (Frederick). The Condition of the Working-class in England in 1844, translated from the German by Florence K. Wischnewetzky, London, 1892.

A graphic account of the physical and moral degradation of an exploited proletariat. Revolutionary in sympathies, but generally accurate in facts, which are mainly drawn from Government Reports.

Cazamian (Louis). *Le Roman Social en Angleterre*, Paris, 1904.

A brilliant and thorough account of the development of the novel with a social purpose.

Roe (F. W.). The Social Philosophy of Carlyle and Ruskin, New York, 1921.

A convenient compilation of the social gospels of those allied thinkers.

Hobson (J. A.). John Ruskin, Social Reformer, 3rd edition, London, 1904.

An appraisal of the indebtedness of modern economics to Ruskin.

POLITICS

Lippmann (Walter). A Preface to Politics, New York, 1913.

Accustoms the general reader to the methods of political thinking.

Wallas (Graham). Human Nature in Politics, London, 1909.

A penetrating study of social psychology.

Davidson (W. L.). Political Thought in England from Bentham to J. S. Mill, New York, 1915.

A good manual.

Barker (W. L.). Political Thought in England from Herbert Spencer to the Present Day, New York, 1915.

A good manual.

Ostrogorski (M.). Democracy and the Organization of Political Parties, translated from the French by Frederick Clarke, 2 vols., London, 1902.

A comprehensive and scholarly work.

MacCunn (John). The Political Philosophy of Burke, London, 1913.

A convenient summary.

Mill (James). An Essay of Government, London, no date. Also printed in the Supplement of the fifth edition of the Encyclopaedia Britannica.

The political gospel of the Philosophical Radicals.

Coleridge (Samuel Taylor). On the Constitution of Church and State, London, 1828.

A philosophical plea for increased governmental control of social and economic activities.

Kent (C. R.). The English Radicals, London and New York, 1899.

Contains some interesting portraits of Benthamite members of the early Reformed Parliaments.

Comte (Auguste). *Plan des Travaux Scientifiques nécessaires pour réorganiser la Société (Système de Politique Positive,* Paris, 1854, *Appendice Général, troisième partie).*

A keen critique of the negative character of the principles of the French Revolution.

Fichte (Johann Gottlieb). The Characteristics of the Present Age. See vol. II of Popular Works, translated from the German by William Smith, London, 1847.

An early attempt at a philosophy of history which influenced both Carlyle and Mill.

De Tocqueville (Alexis). Democracy in America, translated from the French by Henry Reeve, New York, 1912.

A vivid portrayal of the vices and virtues of democracy in practice.

ETHICS

Dewey (John) and Tufts (James H.). Ethics, New York, 1908.
An excellent introductory work.

Dewey (John). Human Nature and Conduct, New York, 1922.
Contains a penetrating criticism of both utilitarian and Kantian ethics.

Hume (David). An Enquiry Concerning the Principles of Morals, Boston, 1881.
A pioneer utilitarianism.

Paley (William). Principles of Moral and Political Philosophy, Boston, 1825.
An adaptation of utilitarian ethics to Christianity.

Bentham (Jeremy). An Introduction to the Principles of Morals and Legislation, London, 1907.

> The groundwork of Bentham's ethical system.

Sedgwick (Adam). A Discourse on the Studies of the University of Cambridge, Cambridge, 1850.

> An intemperate attack on Paley and the Utilitarians.

Whewell (William). The Elements of Morality, including Polity, New York, 1845.

> Shows the influence of an unassimilated Kant.

Mansel (Henry Longueville). The Limits of Religious Thought, London, 1858.

> The method of Kant's *Critique of Pure Reason* clears the way for an ethics independent of social utility.

Maurice (Frederick Dennison). What is Revelation? Cambridge, 1859.

> A reply to Mansel by a Broad-Churchman who places social ethics above dogma.

Holyoake (John Jacob). Secularism, London, 1850.

> A pamphlet presenting an ethical system independent of Christianity to the working classes.

BIOGRAPHIES

Bentham, Jeremy. Charles Milner Atkinson, London, 1905.

Carlyle Till Marriage. D. A. Wilson, London and New York, 1923. Carlyle to " the French Revolution," D. A. Wilson, 1924. Carlyle on Cromwell and Others, D. A. Wilson, 1925.

> When completed, this series of volumes will comprise the standard Life of Carlyle. Comprehensive and accurate.

Thomas Carlyle, a History of the First Forty Years of his Life. James Anthony Froude, 2 vols., New York, 1910. Thomas

Carlyle, a History of his Life in London. James Anthony Froude, 2 vols., New York, 1910.

Inaccurate and prejudiced, but intimate and well-written. Contains valuable material not to be found elsewhere.

Letters of Thomas Carlyle (1826–1836). Edited by Charles Eliot Norton, London, 1889. 2 vols.

Letters of Thomas Carlyle to John Stuart Mill, John Sterling, and Robert Browning. Edited by Alexander Carlyle, New York, 1923.

New Letters of Thomas Carlyle. Edited by Alexander Carlyle, New York and London, 1904.

The Correspondence of Thomas Carlyle with Ralph Waldo Emerson. Edited by Charles Eliot Norton, 2 vols., Boston, 1886.

Carlyle, Reminiscences of. Edited by James Anthony Froude, London, 1881.

Carlyle, Conversations with. Sir Charles Gavan Duffy. New York, 1892.

Cobbett, William, Life of. G. D. H. Cole. New York, 1924.

The history of the unavailing efforts of a great, though eccentric popular journalist to defend the rights of the masses against the encroachments of capital. Excellent use of historical background.

Cobden, Richard, Life of. John Morley. Boston, 1890. 2 vols.

A valuable source for the history of the anti-Corn-Law agitation.

Cooper, Thomas, Life of. 4th ed., London, 1873.

The autobiography of a Chartist leader, which was an important source for *Alton Locke*.

Disraeli, Benjamin, Life of. William Flavelle Monypenny and George Earle Buckle. 6 vols., New York, 1910–1920.

A mine of information concerning the political history of Victoria's reign. The account of the Young England group is especially pertinent to this study.

Fox, Caroline. Memories of Old Friends, Philadelphia, 1882.

Intimate glimpses of Carlyle, J. S. Mill, and John Sterling.

Gladstone, William Ewart, Life of. John Morley. 3 vols., London, 1903.

The gradual growth toward liberalism of a typically Victorian mind.

Grote, George, Personal Life of. Mrs. Harriet Grote. London, 1873.

Interesting light upon dissensions among the Benthamite Radicals.

Holyoake, John Jacob, Sixty Years of an Agitator's Life. 2 vols., London, 1892.

An intimate story of efforts to detach the workingman from Christianity, and to educate him politically.

Kingsley, Charles, Letters and Memories of his Life. Edited by his wife (Mrs. Fanny C. Kingsley). 2 vols., 12th edition, London, 1878.

The Christian Socialist movement from the viewpoint of one of its chief originators.

Mill, James, A Biography. Alexander Bain. New York, 1882.

Mill, John Stuart, Autobiography of. The full text, with restoration of excisions made by Miss Helen Taylor, has been edited by John Jacob Coss, Columbia University Press, New York, 1924. The World's Classics edition, Oxford, 1924, contains an excellent Introduction by Harold Laski, and an Appendix with five of Mill's early speeches (1823–1833).

Mill, John Stuart, *Correspondence avec Gustave d'Eichthal. Traduction par* Eugene d'Eichthal, Paris, 1898.

Mill, John Stuart, Letters of.   Edited by Hugh S. R. Elliot, 2 vols.   London, 1910.

Owen, Robert, Life of.   Frank Podmore, London, 1906.

Place, Francis, Life of.   Graham Wallas, New York, 1919.

> A delightfully written and scholarly account of the activities of the best practical politician in the Benthamite group.   Contains an intimate and exciting record of the measures which forced the passage of the first Reform Bill.

Robertson, Frederick W., Life and Letters of.   Edited by Stopford Brooke, London, no date.

Ruskin, John, Life and Work of.   W. G. Collingwood, 2 vols., London, 1893.

Ruskin, John, Life of.   E. T. Cook.   2 vols., London, 1900.

Ruskin, John, Letters of, to Charles Eliot Norton.   2 vols., Boston, 1905.

Shaftesbury, Lord.   J. L. and Barbara Hammond.   London, 1923.

> Valuable for the Parliamentary History of the Factory Regulation Movement.

Wilberforce, William, Life of.   By his sons, Robert Isaac Wilberforce and Samuel Wilberforce.   2 vols., London, 1888.

> Interesting glimpses of the early Evangelicals.

INDEX

COLUMBIA UNIVERSITY PRESS
COLUMBIA UNIVERSITY
NEW YORK
———
FOREIGN AGENTS
HUMPHREY MILFORD
AMEN CORNER, E.C.
LONDON

EDWARD EVANS & SONS, LTD.
30 NORTH SZECHUEN ROAD
SHANGHAI